Religion and War
in
Revolutionary Iran

Library of Modern Middle East Studies

Series ISBN 1 86064 077 X

1 Water in the Middle East: Legal, Political and Commercial Implications
edited by *JA Allan & Chibli Mallat* 1 85043 645 2

2 Yemen and the United States
A Study of a Small Power and Super-State Relationship, 1962–1994
Ahmad Almadhagi 1 85043 772 6

3 Workers and the Working Class in the Ottoman Empire and the Turkish Republic, 1839–1950
edited by *Donald Quataert & Erik J Zürcher* 1 85043 875 7

4 From Land Reform to Revolution
The Political Economy of Agrarian Relations in Iran, 1962–1979
Fatameh E Moghadam 1 86064 006 0

6 Middle Eastern Politics and Ideas: A History from Within
edited by *Ilan Pappé & Moshe Ma'oz* 1 86064 012 5

7 Secret War in the Middle East: The covert struggle for Syria, 1949–1961
Andrew Rathmel 1 85043 992 3

8 Nationalism, Minorities and Diasporas: Identities and Rights in the Middle East
edited by *Kirsten E Schulze, Martin Stokes & Colm Campbell* 1 86064 052 4

9 Water, Peace and the Middle East: Negotiating Resources in the Jordan Basin
JA Allan 1 86064 055 9

10 Islamic Politics in Palestine
Beverley Milton-Edwards 1 86064 475 9

11 'Independent Iraq': The Monarchy and British Influence, 1941–1958
Matthew Elliot 1 85043 729 7

12 The Army and the Creation of the Pahlavi State in Iran
Stephanie Cronin 1 86064 105 9

13 A Clash of Empires
Turkey between Russian Bolshevism and British Imperialism, 1918–1923
Bülent Gökay 1 86064 117 2

14 The Lost Kurds: The Yazidis under British Rule
Nelida Fuccaro 1 86064 170 9

15 A Broken Trust: Sir Herbert Samuel, Zionism and the Palestinians
Sahar Huneidi 1 86064 172 5

16 The Muslim Brothers and the Palestine Question, 1928–1947
Abd al-Fattah Muhammad El-Awaisi 1 86064 214 4

17 Water, Technology and Development: Upgrading Egypt's Irrigation System
Martin Hvidt 1 86064 216 0

18 Religion and War in Revolutionary Iran
Saskia Gieling 1 86064 407 4

Religion and War in Revolutionary Iran

Saskia Gieling

I.B.Tauris *Publishers*
LONDON • NEW YORK

To my mother and the memory of my father

Published in 1999 by I.B.Tauris & Co Ltd
Victoria House, Bloomsbury Square, London WC1B 4DZ
175 Fifth Avenue, New York NY 10010
Website: http://www.ibtauris.com

In the United States and Canada distributed by St. Martin's Press
175 Fifth Avenue, New York NY 10010

ISBN 1 86064 407 4

A full CIP record for this book is available from the British Library
A full CIP record for this book is available from the Library of Congress

Library of Congress catalog card: available

Printed and bound in Great Britain from camera-ready copy supplied by the author by WBC Ltd, Bridgend

CONTENTS

ACKNOWLEDGEMENTS

I am grateful to a number of people and organizations who in different ways helped me to write this book. The Catholic University of Nijmegen gave me a stipendium and enabled me to visit Iran and see how much the memory of the war is still alive in Iran. Nicoline and Herman van Renselaar's hospitality and Prof. Dr. Mansour Nigah's help during my stay in Tehran will not easily be forgotten. The Netherlands Organization of Scientific Research (NWO) gave me a grant for visiting the Dayan Center for Middle Eastern and African Studies at Tel-Aviv University. Yigal Shefi and Haim Gal were very helpful in collecting material there.

I would like to thank Prof. Dr. Kees Versteegh for reading the manuscript and offering helpful comments and Prof. Dr. Johan ter Haar, Dr. Harald Motzki, Prof. Dr. Ruud Peters and Drs. Leon Wecke for their comments. I also thank Marijke Post of the Department of Middle Eastern Studies of the University of Nijmegen for all her assistance. I am indebted to Kamil Banak of the Documentation Centre for Modern Iran, Leiden University, for his help during my numerous visits to the Centre and Mehmet Yıldırım for solving all technical problems which occurred in the production of the text. Without Erik-Jan's patience and support throughout the past years, I could not have written this book.

NOTE ON TRANSLITERATION

The transliteration of Arabic and Persian is based on the system used in the *International Journal of Middle East Studies*.

For the translation of Qur'ânic passages I have used Bell's translation (*The Qur'ân: Translated, with a Critical Re-arrangement of the Surahs* (Edinburgh: Clark, 1953).

ABBREVIATIONS

Dar maktab-i jum'a for *Dar maktab-i jum'a. Majmû'a-yi khuṭbahâ-yi namâz-i jum'a-yi Tehran* Vols. 2-7 (Tehran: Ministry of Islamic Guidance)
Jang wa jihâd for Khumaynî, *Dar justujû-yi râh az kalâm-i imâm: Jang wa jihâd. Az bayânât wa i'lâmiya-hâ-yi imâm Khumaynî az sâl 1341 tâ 1361* Vol.2 (Tehran: Amîr Kabîr, 1363/1984)
Farhang-i jabha for *Farhang-i jabha (tablû-yi niwishtihâ* ed. by Sayyid Mihdî Fahîmî (Tehran: Intishârât-i ḥawza-yi hunarî-yi sâzimân-i tablîghât-i islâmî, 1369/1990)
Jang bâ inqilâb for *Jang bâ inqilâb, barrasî zamînahâ-yi tajâwuz-i rizjîm-i 'Irâq 'alâ Îrân* (Tehran, 1360/1981)

INTRODUCTION

The object of this study

The war with Iraq which started shortly after the establishment of the Islamic Republic has received much attention in Western literature. These studies stress the fact that the Islamic character of the Iranian republic posed a threat to the stability of Iraq and that during the long and difficult period of the war the Iranian government made Islam the focal point of its rhetoric, but the actual religious content of the propaganda has not been analysed yet. By examining in which way and to what extent the Iranian leaders made use of Islamic beliefs, symbols, vocabulary and motifs in defending the war with Iraq, I want to contribute to a better understanding of the way Islam is used for political action in Iran. The main purpose of this study is to examine how the Iranian leaders sacralized the war, or, in other words, gave it a religious dimension. The central questions I ask are firstly: what Islamic beliefs and emotive symbols and imagery were instrumental in the sacralization of the war and secondly: were both beliefs and symbols equally important or was there a difference in importance?

It should not be assumed that the religious dimension of the war was shaped by the doctrinal concept of 'holy war' or *jihâd* - terms which have gained currency even outside the world of Islamic studies. It has been argued that in a society where ideology is dominated by religion and where there is theoretically no difference between religion and politics, war and revolts, regardless of their cause, receive a religious dimension 'in that their aims, their justifications and their appeals for support are expressed in religious terms'.[1] According to Peters, in Islamic history the doctrine of *jihâd* constituted the religious dimension of the war. But Iranian history shows that it was not always the doctrine of *jihâd* which formed the religious dimension of war. In the early Ṣafawid times, at the end of the fifteenth and the beginning of the sixteenth century, the symbol of the martyrdom of Ḥusayn, the third *imâm*, played a major role in the motivation of the warriors for military action. By contrast, during the Qajar period, in the first war which Persia waged against Russia (1810-13), Ḥusayn's martyrdom only played a secondary role, but the Shî'î credenda or beliefs constituted the main instruments for the sacralization of military action. At that time, the Iranian *mujtahids* wrote extensively about the *jihâd* duty, urging the people to fulfil their moral duties and declaring it an individual duty to participate in the *jihâd*.[2]

The study will concentrate on two of the central themes in the war rhetoric of the Iranian leadership: the justification of the war and the mobilization of the Iranian population for the actual warfare. Rhetoric is understood as 'a practical discipline that aims not at producing a work of art but at exerting through speech a persuasive action on an audience'.[3] Mobilization is understood as mass participation in military activity. Justification is defined as a process 'to provide legitimacy or credit for government policy by someone who has decision-making responsibilities', or in other words, 'justifying policy is defending before others what constituted the rationale for action by disclosing the conditions that apply to the policy about the action'. These conditions are divided into substantial, i.e. the material content, and procedural, i.e. the course of action by justifiers when taking political actions. The justifier has a relationship with objective conditions, with laws, norms and standards and a relationship with policy as an object. The justifier is described as one who is engaged in a control function or has decision-making responsibilities.[4]

The purpose both of the process of justification and of mobilization is to increase support for the policies of the regime. Justification is employed with the idea of the regime's stability and legitimacy in mind. Without the consent of the population, the power base of the regime is weakened and the government is susceptible to attack. Justification of the war policies is particularly important because people have to endure the effects of war in all spheres of life. Iranian leaders for instance said that they were convinced that this war was justified: 'This is a war without any doubt or scepticism, it is not a war of which someone asked: Why?' This view was held implicitly in most speeches throughout the war but at the same time the leadership found it necessary to justify Iran's participation in the war with several arguments.

Whereas the consent of the population is passive, mobilization is aimed at gaining the active support of the population for the regime's policies. The regime depends on this active support in the execution of its policies, for instance for its warfare. Justification and mobilization depend on each other: when justification does not succeed in gaining the support of the people, mobilization will fail as well.

As mentioned above, in spite of the interest in the war, and in the phenomenon of the Islamic Republic as such, the attention devoted to the Islamic, that is to say, doctrinal and theological content of the policies of the Islamic Republic, has been scant. The main exceptions are Arjomand, who has written extensively about the innovative role of Khumaynî's thinking in Shî'î Islam and about the fitting of his ideas into traditional Shî'ism, and Ram, who presents a detailed analysis of the Islamic content of political rhetoric in his study of the Iranian Friday sermon. He concentrates on the way the leaders of the Islamic Republic manipulated what he calls key Shî'î myths, narratives of the past or future in dramatic form, in order to legitimize their regime and to keep revolutionary fervour alive.[5]

This work is in the same tradition as that of Arjomand and Ram, but different in two aspects. Firstly, it is written from an islamological perspective and thus gives more emphasis to the theological and doctrinal issues; secondly, it concentrates not on the revolution and the establishment of the Islamic Republic (1977-1980) but on the long war with Iraq.

Sources

This study is based on the speeches of the ruling elite of Iran, those people in society 'who occupy positions which enable them to transmit, with some regularity, opinions about foreign policy issues to unknown persons'.[6] In the Islamic Republic during the period of the war with Iraq, the central figures in this elite were:

- Âyatullâh Rûḥullâh Khumaynî, the most authoritative person in Iran because of his position as *rahbar* (religious and political leader and guide) and as the leading *faqîh*, jurist, of the Islamic Republic of Iran but also because of his role in the success of the revolution and the charisma of his unofficial title of *imâm*. Khumaynî was also Commander-in-chief of all armed forces.
- Ḥujjatulislâm 'Alî Khâmini'î (he became Âyatullâh in 1989 in order to make the position of *rahbar* accessible to him[7]), together with Hâshimî Rafsanjânî, was one of the leading figures in Iran during the war, not only because he and Rafsanjânî occupied several important positions, but also because they were close to Khumaynî. Khâmini'î was Friday prayer leader in Tehran, co-founder and Secretary-general of the Islamic Republican Party (IRP), from October 1981 until 1989 President of the Islamic Republic, and in June 1989 successor to Khumaynî as *rahbar*.
- 'Alî Akbar Hâshimî Rafsanjânî, temporary Friday prayer leader in Tehran, Speaker of the *Majlis*, the Consultative Assembly, Deputy Chairman of the Council of Experts, the *imâm*'s representative in the Supreme Defence Council (after Muṣṭafâ Chamrân, who was killed in June 1981), acting Commander-in-chief of the Defence Forces in the last month of the war, President of the Republic from August 1989 until August 1997.
- Âyatullâh Ḥusayn 'Alî Muntaẓirî, Friday prayer leader in Qum, head of the network of Friday prayer leaders, from 1985 until March 1989 designated successor of Khumaynî as the new leader of Iran.

The Friday prayer leaders in Tehran also belonged to the elite: Khâmini'î, of course, and the temporary prayer leaders: Rafsanjânî (see above),

- Âyatullâh 'Abdul Karîm Mûsawî Ardabîlî, co-founder of the Islamic Republican Party, State Prosecutor-general and President of the Supreme Court from June 1981 onwards.
- Âyatullâh Imâmî Kâshânî, member of the Council of Guardians and member of Parliament.

- Âyatullâh Muḥammad Riżâ Mahdawî Kanî, Minister of the Interior, Prime Minister until October 1981, member of the Council of Guardians, Secretary-general of the Militant Clerics Association, Prosecutor-general.
- Ḥujjatulislâm Muḥammad Yazdî, *Majlis* deputy and head of the Parliamentary Committee for Legal and Political Affairs.

Members of the ruling elite who in their official capacity frequently spoke about the war were:

- Muḥsin Rizâ'î, Commander of the Pâsdârân.
- Mîr Ḥusayn Mûsawî, former Minister of Foreign Affairs, and from October 1981 onwards Prime Minister.

The speeches and interviews held by the Defence Ministers, the commanders of the regular military forces with the exception of 'Alî Sayyid Shîrâzî, commander of the ground forces, who was dismissed in August 1986, in general only concerned the military and strategic side of the war.

Akhavi has identified nine key members of the Iranian political elite who had emerged by late 1986, after a process of consolidation of power. He mentions besides the leaders described above (except Imâmî Kâshânî): Âyatullâh 'Alî Mishkînî, Chairman of the Council of Experts and Friday prayer leader in Qum, Ḥujjatulislâm Mûsawî Khu'înihâ, State Prosecutor-general, and Âyatullâh Muḥammad Riyshahrî, Minister of Information and Intelligence. According to Akhavi, a second echelon of the ruling elite did not take part in the actual daily decision-making but was consulted for advice. To this group belonged the Council of Guardians, officials of the Supreme Judicial Council, Cabinet ministers and the Commander of the Pâsdârân, Muḥsin Rizâ'î. The third echelon was formed by the Friday prayer leaders of the major cities in Iran.[8]

This list differs slightly from mine; Khu'înihâ and Riyshahrî are not on my list since they did not make public statements about the war. My list also includes persons who had belonged to the elite before 1986, such as 'Abdul-Ḥasan Banî Ṣadr, the first President of the Islamic Republic and Commander-in-chief who was dismissed in June 1981; Muḥammad 'Alî Rajâ'î, Prime Minister until he became President in August 1981, member of the Supreme Defence Council, killed in a bomb attack on 30 August 1981.

According to Akhavi, the Iranian clerics who form the political elite in Iran have the same social background, the same education and the same workplace. He asserts that, while one would assume that the uniformity of their background would lead to uniformity in their policies, the ruling elite in fact failed to evolve consistent public policies. In this study I will pay attention to the question whether members of the ruling elite were consistent and uniform in their war rhetoric or not.

Among the speeches and statements of the leadership, the Friday sermon held at the site of the University of Tehran took pride of place. The reason for this is not only because the sermon was consistent and regularly held but also because of the importance given to it by the leaders.

Throughout Islamic history, the function of the Friday sermon has been that of a channel 'for defending certain policies, for stirring public emotions, and/or disseminating sheer propaganda'.[9] After the revolution the sermon became the most important element for legitimizing the policies of the Islamic government and this was the main occasion to mobilize as many people as possible.[10] Thus, a study of the justification of the war cannot do without a study of the Friday sermon. As in the beginning of Islam, attendance at the sermon by the leaders of the Islamic Republic was considered to be a religious as a well as a political act, showing adherence to Islam and to the ruler.[11] The regime stressed the importance of attendance at the sermon, which, after all, was obligatory for all male Muslims. On the one hand the sermons were an instrument for revolutionary mobilization and action. On the other hand they were also used by the regime to reinforce its legitimacy. The connection between religion and politics was made explicit when leading figures of the regime delivered sermons which were then broadcast on television and radio and published in newspapers. The leaders also tried to reinforce the legitimacy of the new republic by imitating former caliphs who had delivered the sermon while leaning on a sword, the symbol of their authority. Instead of a sword the new Iranian leaders held a Kalashnikov.[12] The most important Friday sermon was given in Tehran by leading figures of the regime. It was not given in a mosque but, because of the number of attendants, in the open air in the grounds of the University of Tehran. Even the surrounding streets were sometimes occupied by the audience.

Because the Friday sermon was in fact made up of two separate sermons, the first one dealing with religious subjects, and the second one treating more current political themes, I concentrated on the second sermon. The sermons which were given in Tehran by members of the political and religious elite were partly published by the Ministry of Islamic Guidance. All other sermons were taken from the daily newspaper *Iṭṭilâ'ât*, which published the sermons every week in an abridged version. In 1986 the report on the text of the sermon was somewhat reduced and in 1987 it was reduced again. After important events, however, longer parts of the sermon were published. The speeches which were given before the sermon and which were published in an abridged version in *Iṭṭilâ'ât*, were also used for this study.

Although the Friday sermon was the richest source since it was (and is) delivered each week, it is important to realize that the setting of the sermon was, of course, a religious one, in which Islam played a dominant role. If sermons had been the only source for our study, the religious content of the rhetoric could easily be overestimated. In order to get a more balanced picture of the war rhetoric of the leaders, I have included speeches which were given on other occasions such as days of national remembrance: the anniversary of the foundation of the Islamic Republic or of the revolution, 'War Week', speeches given on the occasion of religious ceremonies or festivities, but also speeches which were not connected to any special occasion. These speeches have been published in Iranian newspapers, or collected and published later.

A second type of source, besides the speeches and sermons, is formed by the statements of Khumaynî, the person who most influenced contemporary history of Iran through his role in the outbreak of the revolution, his founding of the Islamic Republic, and through his position as *rahbar* of the Islamic Republic.

A third type of source is formed by slogans written on billboards. For a large part these slogans were published by the *Sâzimân-i Tablîghât-i Islâmî* (Organization for Islamic Propaganda), a governmental organization. It can therefore be assumed that these slogans reflect the views of the leaders.

It is important to note that this is a study of the statements of the Iranian leaders and not a study of the effect of these statements on the Iranian population. The question of whether the statements of the leadership had any success needs a different kind of study and approach. Although the question is an important one, certainly in the light of the sudden acceptance of Resolution 598 which led to the end of the war, this question is outside the scope this study. Nor have I taken into account the effect which speeches can have on special occasions such as during *'âshûrâ'*, War Week, or the days of remembrance and anniversaries of religious and political persons. Although one can assume that the effect is much larger on some of these occasions, it is my belief that measuring these effects would call for a quantitative fieldwork survey which under the circumstances would not be feasible. However, when I refer to a speech which is given on a special occasion I will mention this.

Theoretical framework

As mentioned earlier, this is in essence an islamological study, but as it deals with propaganda, use has been made (where applicable) of the theoretical framework presented by Rank in *The Pep Talk*.[13] According to Rank, in every form of communication there is a pattern of 'intensifying one's own 'good' (glorification) and intensifying the other's 'bad' (vilification) through repetition, association or composition'. Intensifying through repetition is very effective since people are comfortable with the known and the familiar. Much indoctrination, but education and training as well, is based on repetition to imprint a message on the memory of the receiver. A good example of repetition in the war rhetoric of the Iranian leaders was that of the often heard slogans *jang, jang tâ pîrûzî* (war, war until victory) and *kullu yawm 'âshûrâ', kullu maqâm Karbalâ'* (every day is *'âshûrâ'*, every place is *Karbalâ'*) which had been very popular slogans during the revolution as well. The second form of intensifying, either the good or the bad, is through direct or indirect association, 'intensifying by linking the idea or product with something already loved/desired by - or hated/feared by the intended audience'. An example of direct association was to stress the similarity between the problems and difficulties which the new republic had to face and those of the community of believers in the time of the Prophet. Attacks by enemies and the hardships of war formed part of those problems. The third form is intensifying through composition, pattern or arrangement with design, variations in sequence and in proportion. An effective example of this was the frequent giving of nicknames to Ṣaddâm, such as *Ṣaddâm-i Yazîd* or *Ṣaddâm-i kâfir* (Ṣaddâm, the unbeliever). This is in line with Rank's observation that war propaganda, defined as organized persuasion, commonly intensifies the 'bad' about the enemy. Yet at the same time, it downplays the 'good': war propaganda will not depict enemy soldiers as being humans. War propaganda dehumanizes, depersonalizes through stereotypes and through jargon which downplays the human qualities. At the same time, war propaganda idealizes, romanticizes, glorifies one's own side: intensifies one's own 'good'.

The other part of the pattern is the downplaying of one's own "bad" (exculpation) and the downplaying of the other's 'good' (denigration) through omission, diversion and confusion. Omitting items is common to all forms of communication; however, in relation to downplaying, the omission is made deliberately through, for instance, speaking half-truths, quoting out of context, concealing. One example of omission was the fact that Iran's own part in the War of the Cities was neglected whereas Iraq's part was constantly emphasized. The military defeats at the end of the war which contributed to the acceptance of a cease-fire, were not mentioned either. Downplaying can also take the form of diversion, distracting focus and diverting attention from key issues or important events. The fact that the Islamic Republic said that it was not a warmonger but a peacemaker, but at the same time presented several reasons for not negotiating a settlement, falls into the pattern of downplaying the major issue.

While Rank's categories play a role in most chapters, in chapter five recourse will be had to current insights into the issue of 'authenticity'.

One of the most fruitful approaches has been the discussion of the Islamic revolution in terms of a search for authenticity. Recent Western studies of Muslim politics give much attention to the authenticity debate among Muslims, the idea that parts of Islamic history are as a suitable role model to follow in order to cope with the challenges of modern time. According to Sivan, this does not mean slavish copying of models. Radical Muslims consider the Islamic past a source of inspiration, and they look to this past 'for a set of core values and ground rules for action'.[14] But Piscatori and Eickelman assert that not only radical Muslims but contemporary Muslims in general regard the period of the reign of the Prophet and the first four caliphs, *al-khulafâ' al-râshidûn* (the rightly guided caliphs) as the 'Golden Age' of Islam which serves as the example par excellence in the field of politics, economics, social life and moral behaviour.[15] According to Lapidus, there are Muslims who regard the period of the imperial Islamic age as a model period, because of the existence of separate political and religious elite, and separate state and religious institutions.[16] Arjomand has described the revolution of 1979 as an Islamic cultural revolution in search of cultural authenticity. The revolution showed Khumaynî's rejection of Western cultural dominance and the ensuing efforts to establish an Islamic moral order.[17]

The contents of this study

Chapter one is a chronological overview of the war between Iran and Iraq. In this chapter, the origins of the conflict, Iraqi offensives and Iranian counterattacks, the tanker war, the role of the international community, economic, social and political effects on the internal situation of Iran and the cease-fire negotiations will be treated. The purpose of this survey of the war is to give a chronological reference point, since the chapters on the statements of leaders are all arranged thematically and thus lack a historical context. Chapter 1 is based on secondary sources: the existing literature on the war which can be divided in chronological surveys; studies of the strategic and military aspects of the war; historical outlines and studies of Iranian and Iraqi political decision-making during the war.

The central part of this study then consists of five chapters. In these, I analyse the three types of religious discourse which played a role in the efforts of the Iranian leadership to justify the war and mobilize the Iranian people: the historical exemplary discourse, the theological doctrinal discourse and the discourse of Islamic solidarity and religious nationalism.

In Islam, war between Muslims is forbidden. One would, therefore, assume that this confronted the Iranian leaders with a serious problem, since the war was clearly with another Muslim state. Chapter 2 concentrates on the Islamic theological and doctrinal notions dealing with war and internal strife among Muslims and the way the Iranian leaders used several of these concepts to make clear that the war they fought was in line with Islamic doctrine. The concept of *jihâd* and that of *fitna* play a central role in the justification. The chapter will deal with theological concepts which were used in order to motivate people to go to the front. The most important notion with regard to this was *shahâda* (martyrdom), sacrificing oneself in the cause of Islam in a *jihâd*. In the eyes of the leadership, this was the most noble form of observance of Islam anyone could attain.

Chapter 3 concentrates on the theological and doctrinal issues which played a role in the war rhetoric. They are based primarily on Qur'ânic terms and notions. In the second part of the discussion, the focus is on the elements which characterize the Shî'î world view as interpreted by the Iranian religious and political leadership. In this part, attention will be paid to the theological descriptions used by the Iranian leaders of their enemies, in particular Ṣaddâm Ḥusayn, but also to descriptions of the Islamic Republic. The dichotomy of concepts like *kufr* (unbelief) and *îmân* (belief), *ḥaqq* (truth) and *bâṭil* (falsehood) played a role in this context. These and other notions will be analysed in this chapter.

Chapter 4, on the historical exemplary discourse, concentrates on the sanctioning of the war by way of historical analogies. Part of this chapter is an analysis of the names given to Iranian military operations and slogans. Attention will be given to the line of reasoning built on the historical examples given to the Muslim community by the Prophet Muḥammad and his son-in-law 'Alî in their political and military actions in the first decades of Islam. Next to these two, the symbols of the sacrifice of the third *imâm* Ḥusayn and the twelfth *imâm*, the Lord of the Time, play an important role, but in mobilizing rather than in legitimizing policy. In this context, Ḥusayn is seen as the archetypal revolutionary and the Lord of the Time as a source of strength on the battlefield, rather than in his messianic role. In contrast to these figures who serve as role models for the Iranian people, there are other historical figures like Yazîd and Mu'âwiya, the Umayyad caliphs with whom Ṣaddâm Ḥusayn became identified.

Chapter 5 deals with universalist ideas and the religious-nationalist discourse of the Iranian leaders. According to their line of reasoning, the war was justified primarily because the Iraqi attack endangered the survival of the Islamic Republic and the ideas for which it stood, in particular the universal aspects of the Islamic revolution. The leaders stated that the war had been imposed on the Islamic Republic in order to stop the dissemination of the ideas of the revolution to other Islamic countries in the region; they nevertheless did not hesitate to stress that they regarded the war as an instrument to practise Muslim solidarity, by liberating the holy places in Iraq, Palestine and south Lebanon. The second part of this chapter deals with religious-nationalist ideas emphasizing the leading role of the Islamic Republic in the Islamic world and extolling the special characteristics and virtues of the Iranian nation and its place in Islamic history.

The last chapter deals with the religious arguments which the Iranian leaders used during the war in their opposition to reconciliation and peace but also with the religious arguments which they used after their acceptance of United Nations Security Council Resolution 598, which unofficially ended the war between the two countries.

In order to justify Khumaynî's decision to agree a settlement, the leaders made use of the same line of reasoning they had used during the war. The historical example of Muḥammad, the importance of the revolution and the dichotomy of Islam and *kufr* were again spelt out, but for a different purpose. In chapter seven, finally, I present my conclusions.

Notes

1. Rudolph Peters, *Islam and Colonialism. The Doctrine of Jihad in Modern History* (The Hague: Mouton, 1979) p. 6.

2. Said Amir Arjomand, *The Shadow of God and the Hidden Imam. Religion, Political Order, and Societal Change in Shi'ite Iran from the Beginning to 1890* (Chicago: University of Chicago Press, 1984) pp. 241-242.

3. 'Rhetoric', in: *Encyclopaedia Britannica*[15] Vol.15 p. 893.

4. J.H. Hegeman, *Justifying Policy. A heuristic* (Amsterdam: Free University Press, 1989) pp. 3, 11.

5. Arjomand, Said Amir, *The Turban for the Crown. The Islamic Revolution in Iran* (Oxford: Oxford University Press, 1988) Haggay Ram, *Myth and Mobilization in Revolutionary Iran. The Use of the Friday Congregational Sermon* (Washington: American University Press,1994).

6. James N. Rosenau, *National Leadership and Foreign Policy. A Case Study in the Mobilization of Public Support* (Princeton: Princeton University Press, 1963) p. 6.

7. See my article 'The Institution of Marja'îya in Iran and the Nomination of Khamanei in December 1994', in: *Middle Eastern Studies* 33 (1997) pp. 777-787.

8. Shahrough Akhavi, 'Elite factionalism in the Islamic Republic of Iran', in: *The Middle East Journal* 41 (1987) pp. 181-201, 182-183.

9. Asghar Fathi, 'The Islamic Pulpit as a Medium of Political Communication', in: *Journal for the Scientific Study of Religion* 2 (1981) p. 164.

10. Yann Richard, 'La Fonction parénétique du 'âlem: La Prière du vendredi en Iran depuis la révolution', in: *Die Welt des Islams* 29 (1989) pp. 61-82, p. 76.

11. Richard T. Antoun, *Muslim Preacher in the Modern World. A Jordanian Case Study in Comparative Perspective* (Princeton: Princeton University Press, 1989) p. 186.

12. Haggay Ram, *Myth and Mobilization* p. 30.

13. Hugh Rank, *The Pep Talk. How to Analyze Political Language* (Park Forest, Ill.: The Counter-propaganda Press, 1984).

14. Emmanuel Sivan, *Radical Islam. Medieval Theology and Modern Politics* (New Haven: Yale University Press, 1985) p. 69.

15. Dale F. Eickelman and James Piscatori, *Muslim Politics* (Princeton: Princeton University Press, 1996) p. 33.

16. Ira M. Lapidus, 'The Golden Age: The Political Concepts of Islam', in: *Annals of the American Academy of Political and Social Science* 523 (1992) pp. 13-25, p. 13.

17. Arjomand, *The Turban for the Crown* p. 202.

1 THE WAR: A CHRONOLOGICAL SURVEY

Background to the conflict

On 22 September 1980 the simmering conflict between Iraq and Iran turned into in a full-scale war when Iraq struck at ten Iranian civil and military airports and occupied Iranian territory along the entire border between the two countries. Before the outbreak of the war the relationship between the two countries had already deteriorated since the Islamic revolution in Iran in 1979. This was due not only to a bad relationship between President Ṣaddâm Ḥusayn of Iraq and Âyatullâh Khumaynî, who on 4 October 1978 was expelled from Iraqi territory where he was living in exile, but also to cultural, ideologic and territorial disagreements.

When, on September 28, six days after the Iraqi army had invaded Iran, the UN Security Council called on both countries to refrain immediately from the further use of force, Iraq declared that it was willing to negotiate, but only if and when Iran gave in to Iraqi demands. These demands were made clear by the Iraqi Deputy Prime Minister, Ṭâriq 'Azîz. In short these were: mutual non-interference in the affairs of the two countries; an agreement over good neighbourly relations and an end to all Iranian aggression towards Iraq; Iranian recognition of Iraq's sovereignty over all territories and water it claimed, including the Shaṭṭ al-'Arab (Arwand Rûd in Persian).[1]

Iraq argued that it was obliged to wage a defensive war because it found 'itself obliged to exercise its legitimate right to self-defence of sovereignty and territorial integrity and to recover its territories by force, considering that the Iranian Government had barred the way to all legally recognized ways to resolve the issues emanating from its obligations'.[2] Before its attack, Iraq had accused Iran frequently of acts of aggression against Iraq, such as the attempt on the life of Ṭâriq 'Azîz on 1 April 1980 and of interfering in Iraq's internal affairs, such as the Iranian support of the prohibited *al-Da'wa* (the Call) Party.[3] It is not very clear whether Iran played a role in terrorist actions in Iraq, but it is certain that it fought a fierce war of propaganda.[4] In radio broadcasts in Arabic, Iranian leaders vehemently criticised the Ba'th regime for being against Islam and being a puppet of imperialism. Iraq was also accused of acts of aggression against its neighbour. Iraq publicly supported insurgents in Khûzistân who were striving for autonomy, and promised to help them 'in liberating Arabistân', the Iraqi name for this province. According to the Governor-general of Khûzistân, Madanî, Iraq supplied the rebels with arms. On several occasions, Iraq carried out attacks on border towns, for instance in June 1979 on Kurdish towns in the north, and in the next month on Sâlihâbâd in the south, where several people were killed. During the first half of 1980 more border clashes occurred.[5]

The Iraqi demand for sovereignty over all territories and water it claimed meant that old territorial disagreements which both countries had repeatedly tried to settle, were revived again.[6] Partly, this territorial disagreement was caused by the lack of formal agreements about the division of water resources in the border area. Several rivers arise in the Iranian mountains and flow into Iraq. A comprehensive agreement over the amount of water which both countries can use had never been concluded and this caused serious problems in dry periods.[7]

Three small islands in the Gulf were also part of the territorial dispute. The islands, Abû Mûsâ and Greater and Lesser Tunb, are close to the Strait of Hormuz and have a position of strategic importance. Abû Mûsâ belonged to Shârjah and the two other islands to Ra's al-Khaymah, two of the United Arab Emirates. Iran had seized the islands on 30 November 1971, a few days before the United Arab Emirates were proclaimed. In September 1980, Iraq laid claim to the three islands on behalf of the Arab nation and demanded Iranian recognition of Iraq's legitimate rights over land and water.[8]

But the controversy was mainly about the demarcation of the boundaries in the Shaṭṭ al-'Arab area, sovereignty over the Shaṭṭ al-'Arab and the disputed Iranian province of Khûzistân. Until 1925, this area on the eastern bank of the Shaṭṭ al-'Arab was almost exclusively inhabited by Arabic-speaking tribes.[9] Both the Ottomans and the Persians regarded the Arab population as their subjects. The Ottomans considered the Arab tribes who lived on both sides of the Shaṭṭ al-'Arab as one ethnic and cultural group who fell under Ottoman authority, and therefore claimed the Shaṭṭ al-'Arab and the eastern bank. The Persians considered the Shaṭṭ al-'Arab a natural border. The tribes, however, did not accept any authority, whether Ottoman or Persian. The area was ruled by several tribes, and in 1812 the port of Muḥammara (Khurramshahr) on the eastern bank of the Shaṭṭ al-'Arab became an autonomous state until Riẓâ Shah turned it into an Iranian province.[10] In 1980, many people were still Arabic-speaking. According to the pan-Arab ideology of the Ba'th, Khûzistân or Arabistân was part of the Arab nation and should return to Arab hands.[11]

The most important bone of contention was the Shaṭṭ al-'Arab. It is formed by the confluence of the Tigris, Euphrates and Kârûn rivers and is a waterway of about 130 miles.[12] The last 55 miles form the frontier between Iraq and Iran. The Shaṭṭ al-'Arab has economic and strategic importance for both countries. Basra, the only Iraqi port with an outlet to the Gulf lies 47 miles upstream and large oil installations of both countries are situated near the Shaṭṭ al-'Arab.

As early as the sixteenth century this waterway had been the cause of wars between the Ottoman and Ṣafawid Empires. Negotiations resulted in 1639 in the

Treaty of Zuhâb, which was the first treaty to determine the borders between the two empires. The treaty, however, was imprecise about the status of the Arab nomadic tribes living in the border area and about the boundary in the Shaṭṭ al-'Arab area and this was to cause continuing tensions in the next centuries. The first and second Treaties of Erzurum, confirmed in 1823 and 1847, were attempts to adjust the border in the Shaṭṭ al-'Arab area. The first treaty reaffirmed the principle of non-interference by both countries in each other's affairs as laid down in the Treaty of Zuhâb. In the treaty of 1847, Muḥammara and the island of Khizr ('Abâdân) were allotted to Persia and the western bank to the Ottoman Empire. But the treaty was not precise about the exact course of the border and both sides interpreted the text of the protocol in different ways.[13]

At the beginning of the twentieth century, when the discovery of oil in the Shaṭṭ al-'Arab area made a settlement necessary, a new commission was set up to demarcate the boundary. This time not only Ottoman and Persian interests played a role but also British ones. Britain had large oil concessions in Persia (also in Iraq, but in the north) and was already exploiting oilfields on the eastern bank of the Shaṭṭ al-'Arab.[14] Negotiations resulted in the 1913 Constantinople Protocol which assigned the Shaṭṭ al-'Arab to the Ottoman Empire, with the exception of some islands near 'Abâdân, and drew the boundary at the low-water mark on the eastern bank.[15]

After the dissolution of the Ottoman Empire, when Iraq had become first a British mandate in 1920 and then an independent state in 1932, Iran declared that it did not accept the demarcation line as stated in the Constantinople Protocol. Iran wanted the border to run along the *thalweg*, the deepest point of the navigable channel. Tensions increased because Iran violated agreements about Iraqi control over the Shaṭṭ al-'Arab and because of the resulting boundary clashes. The dispute was brought before the League of Nations in 1934, but no settlement was obtained. Negotiations between the two countries continued, however, and in 1937 Iran and Iraq signed another treaty which established the border on the eastern bank of the river except for a four-mile anchorage zone near 'Abâdân, which was allotted to Iran and where the border was along the *thalweg*. Afterwards, Iraq accused Iran of taking advantage of Iraq's weakened negotiating position during the internal Iraqi turmoil after the military coup of November 1936 by Nûrî al-Sa'îd.[16]

For three decades no important developments in the dispute occurred. But in the 1960s, when Iran had become a strong regional power and Iraq was weakened by several coups, Iran again made use of the weak internal situation in Iraq. First, it sent a delegation to Iraq directly after the Ba'th coup in 1969 and when Iraq refused to start negations over a new treaty, Iran abrogated the treaty of 1937. Then, it weakened Iraq further by supporting Kurdish rebels in the north. Iraq was obliged to give in to Iranian demands concerning the Shaṭṭ al-'Arab, in exchange for an

Iranian promise to end support for Kurdish rebels.[17] This resulted in the Algiers Treaty of 1975 in which the *thalweg* was for the first time recognized as the border along the entire length of the Shatt al-'Arab.[18] But five years later, on 17 September 1980, Iraq suddenly abrogated the Treaty of Algiers. In his speech to the National Assembly, Ṣaddâm Ḥusayn argued that the Islamic Republic refused to abide by the stipulations of the Algiers Treaty and that, therefore, Iraq considered the treaty null and void.[19] Furthermore, Ṣaddâm Ḥusayn declared in the same speech that the Shatt al-'Arab had been Iraqi-Arab throughout history and that Iraqi authority over the Shatt al-'Arab should be restored. Five days later, the Iraqi army crossed the border.

The ideology of the Islamic Republic of Iran, and especially the idea of exporting the Islamic revolution to other Muslim countries, was seen by Iraqi leaders as a threat to the secular ideology of their Ba'th Party and as a danger to the stability of the country. The Iranian propaganda which was intended for the Iraqi population concentrated on the un-Islamic character of the Ba'th ideology and incited the Iraqis to revolt and topple the regime of Ṣaddâm Ḥusayn.[20] Although the Iranian propaganda had a universal message and was meant for all Muslims, it was feared in Iraq that the Shî'îs, who formed the majority of the population but were ruled by Sunnîs, were especially susceptible to Iranian propaganda. To counter this propaganda, the Sunnî Iraqi leaders took measures to lessen the danger of a revolt by the Shî'î population. Firstly, they increased the persecution of people suspected of illegal political activities, such as membership of the clandestine Shî'î party *al-Da'wa* (the Call). The prominent Âyatullâh Bâqir al-Ṣadr was detained and secretly executed in April 1980. Thousands of Shî'îs, most of them of Iranian origin but whose families had been living for generations in the Shî'î religious centers of Karbalâ' and Najaf, were expelled.[21] Secondly, emphasis was laid on the Arab character of Islam, the Arab origin of the prophet Muḥammad, on the Arabic language of the Qur'ân and the location of the holy cities of Islam in Arab countries. By stressing the Arab tradition of Islam, Ṣaddâm Ḥusayn tried to disgrace the Iranian Islamic revolution in the eyes of the Iraqi population. Later, he was to call the war in September 1980 'a second Qâdisîya', after the battle of Qâdisîya in 635/7 where the Sasanian Persians were defeated by the Arabs, in order to emphasize the superiority of the Arabs over the Iranians.[22]

One of the aims Ṣaddâm Ḥusayn had in mind may have been a more important role for Iraq in the Arab world. By fighting a war for the areas that had once been Arab but were now in the hands of the Iranians, Ṣaddâm Ḥusayn made himself the protector and defender of the Arab nation. He may have aspired to a more influential role in the Arab world once he had defeated the Iranians, based on leadership in the Gulf region. Until the Islamic revolution, Iran had been the major power in the region with the support of the United States. Because of its geographical position to the south of the Soviet Union, Iran was of strategic importance to the United States and therefore was supported economically and militarily. After the revolution the relationship between the United States and the Islamic Republic had deteriorated and as a result Iran had lost its position as the major power in the region, because of internal turmoil and because of a cut-off in American supplies during the hostage crisis (4 November 1979 to 20 January 1981). Iraq expected that Iran would accept Iraqi superiority after the invasion and immediately give in to Iraqi demands because of this internal chaos and the weakened situation of the Iranian army and air force.[23] This time, President Ṣaddâm Ḥusayn tried to make use of internal turmoil in Iran to settle things on his terms, as Iran had done in 1936, 1969 and 1975.

Ṣaddâm Ḥusayn may have aspired also to economic and military hegemony in the region. In gaining sovereignty over the Shaṭṭ al-ʻArab, Khûzistân and the three islands in the Gulf, Ṣaddâm Ḥusayn would increase Iraq's income by a considerable amount. Khûzistân contains nearly all of Iran's oil reserves and has large oil facilities and refineries. Moreover, by separating Iran from its most important source of income, Iraq would prevent Iran from emerging again as the most powerful state in the region. Finally, the occupation of Khûzistân would enlarge Iraq's coastline, which was only 40 miles long, and secure Iraq's access to the Gulf. It also seems likely that Iraq claimed the three islands in the Gulf not only to regain a part of the 'Arab nation' but also for economic and strategic reasons, in view of the possibilities for offshore oil installations the islands offered.[24]

The Iraqi war strategy was to fight a limited war and not a general war.[25] This was proven by the fact that only a part of the Iraqi army was engaged in the fighting, which took place in confined areas, and by the fact that it was clearly the intention that the war would be over before winter started and inundation made large parts of the area inaccessible.[26]

Iraq launched its attack at a moment when Iran's political and military position had weakened considerably. One reason was the fact that the Iranian armed forces were neglected and not prepared for a war. This was caused by the arms boycott imposed by the United States during the hostage crisis, which had resulted in a shortage of spare parts for American arms and instruments, and by the fact that the Islamic revolutionaries did not trust the military, who once had been loyal to the shah. The army was seen as a symbol of dependence on the United States and of extravagant expenditure, and it had once been an instrument of oppression.[27] Systematic purges were carried out, first in the senior ranks, afterwards on a larger scale. The Revolutionary Guards (*Sipâh-i Pâsdârân-i Inqilâb-i Islâmî*) were trained as a force to counterbalance and take over functions from the army. The Pâsdârân, headed by Muḥsin Rizâ'î, were closely linked to the radical clerics and in part responsible for the success of the Islamic revolution.[28]

The deterioration of Iran's economy may have been a factor in the Iraqi invasion as well. The whole economy of Iran had been seriously affected by the turmoil during and after the revolution in 1979. For instance, in the oil industry, by far the most important sector of the Iranian economy, production had fallen from 5.7 million barrels per day (MBD) in 1977 to 3.9 MBD in spring 1979 and to 1.4 MBD in summer 1980.[29]

Finally, Ṣaddâm Ḥusayn may have wanted to profit from internal turmoil in Iran. This unrest consisted of revolts by ethnic minorities and of opposition against and from within the leadership. In the northern provinces the Revolutionary Guards and army were engaged in heavy fighting with the Kurds. During the revolution the Kurds had obtained a kind of informal autonomy, which they now wanted to institutionalize. Khumaynî, however, in August 1979, ordered a general mobilization to end all Kurdish resistance. In Khûzistân, the Arab minority was also striving for autonomy. This was wholly unacceptable to Khumaynî, because the Iranian economy depended to a considerable degree on industries, which were situated in this province. Here, heavy clashes occurred between rebels and the Revolutionary Guards.[30]

There was also opposition to the regime from the religious establishment, notably from Âyatullâh Sharî'at-Madârî, the major criticism being that Khumaynî and his followers had appropriated the revolution and were opposed to political and religious power-sharing. Further opposition to the clerical leadership of Khumaynî came from monarchists, liberals such as Bâzargân, the former Prime Minister, and leftist groups such as the Tûda, Mujâhidîn-i Khalq and Fidâ'îyân-i Khalq. Apart from this, there was a power struggle going on between factions among the revolutionary establishment, which also distracted attention from the problems with Iraq.[31]

Why did Iraq invade Iran? There were several factors which separately or taken together may have influenced the Iraqi regime to start the war. These factors can be divided into aims and motives: Iraqi security and the threat of Iranian attacks, the effect of the Islamic revolution on the Iraqi population; Ṣaddâm Ḥusayn's ambitions for political and economic hegemony in the Middle East; securing Iraqi borders; control over the Shaṭṭ al-'Arab and capturing territories which were claimed by Iraq. The situation in Iran may likewise have been seen by Iraqi leaders as an opportunity to start a war. Without a detailed study of Iraqi politics, one can only speculate about the real reasons for the Iraqi decision.

During the initial stage of the war both parties were exhorted to stop warfare and refrain from violence. Resolution 479 of the UN Security Council was accepted by Iraq on condition that Iran gave back territories Iraq claimed. The Iranian leaders in turn were only prepared to negotiate after the Iraqi army had evacuated Iranian territory, and they accused Iraq of aggression. At the UN, both countries defended their part in the war as an act of self-defence. The Iraqi Foreign Secretary, Sa'dûn Ḥammâdî accused Khumaynî during the United Nations session of 15 October 1980 of trying to export the Islamic revolution by inciting religious and sectarian strife. Iran ended its boycott of the United Nations Security Council, which it had started immediately after the revolution in October 1980. Premier Rajâ'î of Iran called the war an imposed war and said that Iran could only accept a truce if and when the aggressor was conquered and punished.[32] Other peace missions were attempted by the Islamic Conference Organization and the Non-Aligned Movement, but neither had any success.[33]

At the onset of the war, the official position of the United States and other Western countries, the Soviet Union and states in the Gulf, was one of neutrality. The Soviet Union, which before the war had been the major supplier of arms to Iraq, told Iraq that arms shipments would be curtailed.[34] The United States' relations with Iran and Iraq were already at a low level. Only King Ḥusayn of Jordan declared open support for Iraq; the states in the Gulf, although their official position was also one of neutrality, supplied Iraq financially. Iran was supported by Syria and Libya.[35]

From the beginning of the war the international community worried about the effect it would have on trade and oils export in the Persian Gulf. Because both countries were important oil producers, another oil crisis was feared, such as had occurred during the Arab-Israeli conflict in 1973 and during the reduction of Iranian oil production in 1978/79. Although Iraq and Iran attacked oil-industry targets from the onset of the war in order to destroy each other's oil-production capacity, oil prices did only go up for a short time and there was no real effect on the world oil market.[36] Different reasons can be given for this. Other oil-producing countries such as Saudi Arabia, Kuwait, the United Arab Emirates and Qatar increased their production and, together with the large amounts of oil stored after the Islamic revolution, there was no shortage of oil on the market. Besides, the worldwide demand for oil had decreased because of the continuing economic recession.[37]

The Iraqi invasion

On 22 September 1980 Iraq started the war with large air raids at ten major Iranian airports and by invading Iran on three points. In the north Qaṣr-i Shîrîn was occupied because of its strategic position. The heights around Qaṣr-i Shîrîn dominate the lowlands and it is near the road to Baghdad. Further south, in Khûzistân, strategic points near Mihrân, and the town of Dizfûl, important because of its military bases and crossroads of oil pipelines, were targeted. The main objective, however, was the Khurramshahr and 'Abâdân region with its large oil refineries. But the position of these two cities on islands, separated from the mainland by rivers and only accessible by two bridges, made them difficult to capture. Heavy fighting between units of the Iraqi army and the Iranian Revolutionary Guards took place during the first weeks.

On 24 October, at the cost of heavy losses, only Khurramshahr was occupied by the Iraqis; 'Abâdân was also besieged but held out. By December only parts of Khûzistân had been occupied by the Iraqi army.[38] After Khurramshahr was captured, the Iraqis changed their war strategy from a limited, dynamic war into a static one with few fights but more shelling and bombing to defend seized territory. With a few exceptions, no ground operations were carried out, and the war consisted of artillery exchanges and air raids from both sides on strategic targets.[39]

Iraq did not succeed in quickly defeating the Iranian armed forces although it had a larger air force and army. One reason was that the Iranians, although surprised by the invasion, had immediately mustered a strong resistance, consisting of a combination of regular army, police, Revolutionary Guards and voluntary units. The main reason, however, was the incompetence of the Iraqi military leadership, which caused strategic and tactical mistakes and failures in assessment.[40] The army was poorly trained and not capable of using and maintaining their advanced major weapons systems. The senior officers in Iraq were promoted not because of their competence but on account of their loyalty to the leadership and on account of their Sunnî or Takrîtî (Ṣaddam Ḥusayn's birthplace) affiliation, which is the most important criterion for promotion in Iraq.[41]

The situation in Iran was not much better. The purges of the military after the revolution had resulted in an overhaul and changes at the top. Key positions were in the hands of officers who had beenpromoted after the revolution and who were loyal to the Islamic principles of the revolution, for instance, the former army captain 'Alî Sayyid Shîrâzî, the commander of the ground forces.[42] The army was, like Iraq's, poorly trained. In October, Khumaynî tried to counter the incompetence of the army and combine the forces of the regular army and the Revolutionary Guards, by appointing the seven-member Supreme Defence Council, which was responsible for the conduct of the war and had to settle military issues.[43] President Banî Ṣadr, who was already Commander-in-chief, was appointed head of the council. The council, however, was ineffective because of the power struggle that was going on at that time between Banî Ṣadr and clerics such as Âyatullâh Muḥammad Bihishtî and Rafsanjanî. The conflict between Banî Ṣadr and Bihishtî was mainly about the political line and the administration.[44] Banî Ṣadr did not accept the involvement in governmental and political affairs of the clerics, who in their turn wanted to reshape the state and society by a process of 'Islamicization'. His opponents used the council and the military leadership as a vehicle to criticize Banî Ṣadr, thus making military decisions dependent on political rivalry.[45] In June 1981 Banî Ṣadr was deprived of the military command and dismissed as President. The struggle between him and Bihishtî was settled in the latter's favour because Khumaynî had stopped protecting Banî Ṣadr. In the first half of 1981, Banî Ṣadr's power had already diminished and he was not consulted over political decisions such as, for instance, the decision to release the

American hostages in January 1981. During the conflict Khumaynî had asked both sides to settle their dispute, but in June he had become afraid of a coup from opposition groups who had began to support Banî Ṣadr. Besides, Khumaynî blamed him for the situation at the front, where the war had changed into a stalemate.[46]

Iranian counterattacks

On 5 January 1981 the Iranians for the first time launched a counterattack. Initially this attack close to Sûsangird, was successful, but the Iraqi forces encircled the Iranian divisions and inflicted heavy losses upon them.[47] Banî Ṣadr had been opposed to this operation, because he considered the time not yet ripe for a large-scale attack, but he had to yield to pressure from Bihishtî and his supporters.[48] In September 1981 the period of stalemate ended when the Iranians started to launch a series of successful offensives. The first one drove the Iraqi army back to the western side of the Kârûn river and thus ended the siege of 'Abâdân which had lasted for almost a year. At the end of 1981 Iran started two minor offensives near Sûsangird on 29 November and in the Qaṣr-i Shîrîn area on 12 December and recaptured some Iranian territory.[49] These offensives were followed by an even more successful attack on 22 March 1982. This operation, in the Shûsh-Dizfûl area, called '*Fatḥ Mubîn*' (A Clear Victory),[50] which involved about 120,000 troops, was the largest offensive since the beginning of the war. It was carried out by the combined forces of the regular army and the Pâsdârân, the Revolutionary Guards, who utilized a war strategy which consisted of a mixture of classical manouvres and revolutionary tactics.[51] Part of these tactics were the human-wave assaults in which Basîj units, the military forces existing of volunteers, attacked Iraqi defence positions with light armor and cleared the way for the Revolutionary Guards. These Basîj-units, officially called *Basîj-i mustaḍ'afîn*, (Mobilization of the Oppressed) loyal to the principles of the Islamic revolution, were formed and trained under the supervision of the Revolutionary Guards.[52] In November 1981, the Ministry of the Revolutionary Guards, headed by Muḥsin Rafîqdûst, was established to coordinate contacts between the government and the rapidly growing forces of the Revolutionary Guards.[53] According to Halliday, the Revolutionary Guards were numerically larger than the regular army, but other sources disagree.[54] Mofid asserts that by 1986 there were some 300,000 volunteers in the ground forces of the Revolutionary Guards (305,000 regular armed forces) but this number did not include the Basîj forces.[55]

The Iranian campaign resulted in an important defeat for Iraq, which lost three divisions and had to withdraw its troops to the border. In spring 1982 the Iranians launched two offensives in which they used the same tactics as in Operation '*Fatḥ mubîn*' to drive the Iraqi army from Khûzistân. The first one, north of Bustân, which started on 22 March, was the largest offensive so far, and some 50 square miles of territory were regained by the Iranians.[56] But the second offensive, which consisted of two separate attacks, was a major turning-point in the war. The first stage, which lasted from 24 April to 12 May, after heavy fighting, drove the Iraqi troops back to Khurramshahr from the Ahwâz-Sûsangird area. In the second stage, on 20 May, the Iranians attacked Khurramshahr, the last stronghold of the Iraqis in the area. Although the Iraqi forces had expected the attack and had fortified the city, they were not able to defend it against the Iranian forces who entered the city on 24/25 May. The majority of the Iraqi troops had already withdrawn when the Iranian army recaptured what was left of Khurramshahr, but about 12,000 troops were taken prisoner and large amounts of military equipment were captured.[57] The Iranian successes of 1981 and 1982 were a result of the use of a combination of conventional and revolutionary tactics which were made possible by better cooperation between the military and the politicians after the dismissal of Banî Ṣadr.[58]

Ṣaddâm Ḥusayn announced on 20 June that all Iraqi troops had started to withdraw from Iranian soil. He was prepared to negotiate about a truce but Iran had gained confidence after its recent successes and increased its conditions for a settlement. Besides the demand for a total withdrawal of Iraqi forces, Iran demanded the overthrow of Ṣaddâm Ḥusayn and the Ba'th regime, $ 150 billion reparations and the repatriation of 100,000 Shî'îs, expelled from Iraq in 1980.[59]

The Invasion of Iraq

In July 1982, Iranian leaders decided to invade Iraq. Before this decision, a fierce debate had been going on within the leadership about whether it was wise to invade Iraq and confront an extensive defence system, erected for the expected Iranian forces, and an Iraqi army that had more than doubled since 1980 from some 200,000 troops to about 475,000 in 1983. The military leadership and religious leaders, such as Premier Mîr Ḥusayn Mûsawî and President 'Alî Khâmini'î, were opposed to an invasion, on the one hand, as the military pointed out, because the Iranian army lacked the capability to invade, on the other hand because it was feared that an invasion would demand considerable human, material and political sacrifices.[60] Those in favour of an invasion believed it was necessary in order to topple the regime of Ṣaddâm Ḥusayn and that it could be successful by further use of revolutionary tactics and by employing zealous fighters, like the Pâsdârân and the Basîj. Moreover, the invasion would be in an area inhabited by Shî'îs and it was expected that they would revolt against the Iraqi regime and support the Iranian forces.[61]

On 13 July, the first day of Ramaḍan, it became clear that the decision had gone against the military, when the Iranian army started an offensive called '*Ramaḍân*' in the direction of Basra, employing around 100,000 men, of whom 50,000 belonged to the regular army. After two weeks of heavy fighting it was clear that the troops had failed to break through the Iraqi defences. This defeat was caused by tactical failures on the Iranian side and by lack of artillery, air support and of well-trained regular forces. Other factors were the Iraqis' superior equipment and their use of chemical weapons.[62] Although Operation '*Ramaḍân*' was a military failure, it was a political success. Because of the heavy fighting it was decided that the seventh summit conference of the Non-Aligned Movement, which was scheduled for September 1982 in Baghdad, would be held in New Delhi instead. This was a great disappointment for Ṣaddâm Ḥusayn, who expected to become President of the Non-Aligned Movement for the next three years. According to *The Economist*, Iraq had spent about $1 billion on facilities for the meeting.[63]

Iranian leaders insisted on launching two more offensives despite growing criticism of the military leadership, who, after the failure of the last offensive, were increasingly critical of the way politicians and the religious leadership interfered in military affairs. These offensives, Operation '*Muslim Ibn 'Aqîl*', from 1 to 10 October near Mandalî, and Operation '*Muḥarram*', from 1 to 11 November near Mûsiyân, were again failures, because mainly the religious leadership did not want to wage conventional warfare or a combination of conventional and revolutionary tactics as in Operation '*Fatḥ mubîn*'. As in the July offensive, the operation was carried out with massive frontal attacks from infantry troops and human-wave assaults without air and artillery support. The bulk of the forces consisted of Pâsdârân and Basîj units, the volunteers being for the most part badly trained, badly dressed and often very young or very old.[64]

The Iranian invasion in July 1982 seemed to be a repetition of the Iraqi invasion in September 1980. From the Iranian invasion onwards, the strategy of both countries had reversed, Iran was engaged in a war with dynamic operations, whereas Iraq fought a war of attrition, with a static defence, in order to exhaust its enemy. For both countries it turned out that it was easier to defend territory than to capture it; the soldiers lost a large part of their motivation once they were not defending their nation any more. It has been argued that Ṣaddâm Ḥusayn expected that the Arab population in Khûzistân would support the Iraqi troops, but that he had misjudged the Arab population, who did not revolt but fled from the area after the invasion.[65] In his turn, Khumaynî hoped that the Iraqis would revolt against Ṣaddâm. In his speeches, Khumaynî stressed the fact that Iran was fighting a war against the Ba'th regime and Ṣaddâm Ḥusayn, not against the people of Iraq, and urged the Iraqis to revolt against Ṣaddâm Ḥusayn and establish an Islamic republic.[66] Iran supported opponents of the Iraqi regime and gave its aid to the formation of the Supreme Council of the Islamic Republic of Iraq, seated in Tehran and headed by Muḥammad Bâqir al-Ḥakîm.[67] Several reasons were given for the fact that the Shî'îs of Iraq did not revolt in 1982. One explanation was that national, Iraqi and Arab identity was more important to the Shî'îs than sectarian, Shî'î identity. This was proven by the fact that the Iraqi ground forces, which were composed mostly of Shî'îs, fought with fervour against the invading Iranians.[68] Another explanation was that the Shî'î community, out of a lack of unity and leadership caused by an Iraqi policy of carrot-and-stick, was not in a position to revolt against the Iraqi government.[69]

Despite high casualty rates during the last operations, Iran continued its attacks.[70] During 1983 three offensives were launched on the central front and two on the northern front. Operation '*Wa-l-fajr*' (6-16 February) on the eve of the fourth annversary of the Islamic revolution was aimed at al-'Amâra and at blocking the road between Basra and Baghdad. The attacks were carried out by units of ill-armed and ill-trained infantry across open ground against well-entrenched Iraqis, who were supported by superior tank, artillery and air power. Operation '*Wa-l-fajr* I' (10-17 April) in the Bustân area and Operation '*Wa-l-fajr* III' (30 July-9 August) near to Mihrân did not yield any result. The northern offensives, Operation '*Wa-l-fajr* II' (22-30 July) in the direction of Kirkûk and Operation '*Wa-l-fajr* IV', directed against Pinjwîn, likewise failed.[71]

In 1984 Iraq threatened to attack Iranian cities if Iran started new offensives. Unimpressed, Iran launched a new offensive. Thereafter Iraq attacked Dizfûl on 11 February with ground-to-ground missiles and air strikes on other cities. Iran retaliated with air strikes on Basra, Mandalî and other border towns and forced Iraq to stop its attacks. This was the first stage of the 'War of the Cities' in which many civilians were killed. Iran nevertheless continued launching offensives. From 15 to 24 February, Operations '*Wa-l-fajr* V' and '*Wa-l-fajr* VI' were carried out on the central front at Mihrân to capture Kût al-'Amâra and cut the road between Basra and Baghdad. On both sides about 500,000 men were engaged. After a week of heavy fighting, the Iranians succeeded only in capturing some strategic heights near the road. On 24 February Operation '*Khaybar*' was launched in the direction of Basra. The Iranian forces, which consisted mainly of Pâsdârân and Basîj units, did not manage to break through the Iraqi defences and their only success was the capture of Majnûn island in the marshes north of Basra. This artificial island is situated above a rich oilfield which had been closed in September 1980. After these operations the war again turned into a stalemate which was only broken by a small offensive in the central border region. Operation '*Wa-l-fajr* VI' aimed at the Miymak Heights, which had been in Iraqi hands from the beginning of the war. Because the mountainous terrain is not suitable for large massed attacks, the attack was carried out by small units of Pâsdârân and Basîj, but they failed to capture the strategic Heights.[72]

On 30 March 1984, after allegations from Iran that Iraq used chemical weapons, the President of the UN Security Council issued a statement to the effect that there was unanimous agreement among UN-appointed experts that chemical weapons had been used in the war. A year later, on 25 April 1985, another statement was issued

by the Security Council which stated that the Council 'was appalled at the use of chemical weapons against Iranian forces during March 1985'.
In these statements Iraq was not mentioned by name.[73]

Extension of the war to the Persian Gulf
Until 1983 the war had taken place on land, but in 1983 it was extended to the Persian Gulf by the Iraqis. By destroying Iranian oil-facilities, Iraq tried to weaken Iran's economy and so to force it to take part in negotiations. In February and March Iraqi aircrafts damaged Iranian offshore installations and caused an oil spill of around 7500 barrels a day which menaced the coast and water-supply installations of Bahrain, Qatar and the Emirates.[74] At the end of the year Iraq warned merchant vessels to stay out of the northern part of the Gulf, declaring it a war zone.[75] The war escalated further when in February 1984 Iraq announced a blockade of Kharg Island, the most important Iranian oil terminal, and started striking at foreign tankers which were loading at Kharg Island. By involving international trade in the conflict, Iraq hoped to provoke the international community into forcing the Iranians to end the war. In September 1983, France and the United States had already become involved, because of the crisis that had broken out after the France's decision to supply Iraq with Five Super Etendard aircraft armed with AM-39 Exocet air-to surface missiles. According to France, it was decided to deliver the planes, which could easily reach Iranian oil installations in the Gulf and Kharg, in order that the military force of Iraq would be able to force Iran to a settlement.[76] It seems, however, more likely that France had an interest in a stronger Iraqi military position: the Iraqi debt to France since the war had started was very large because of arms purchases, and France was afraid that Iraq would not be in a position to pay its debts if it was defeated by Iran.[77] Iran thereupon threatened to close the Strait of Hormuz if Iraq used its Super Etendards against Iran. The United States warned Iran to keep calm and declared that it would keep the Strait open to international shipping. In order to show its determination, it dispatched three warships to the Indian Ocean on 13 October.[78]

On 27 March 1984 Iraq for the first time used the Super Etendards, in an attack on a Greek tanker in the Persian Gulf. Probably because it was almost impossible to close the Strait, which was 12 miles wide, and because this would affect Iran's own oil export, Iran did not attempt to close the Strait of Hormuz after this attack and other attacks on tankers at Kharg. Instead, in May 1984, it followed Iraq's lead in attacking tankers. Iran rarely claimed responsibility for these and subsequent attacks on tankers.[79] During the rest of the year both countries continued their attacks: Iraq carried out 54 attacks and Iran 18.[80] On 1 June the Security Council accepted Resolution 552, in which attacks on ships en route to and from ports of Saudi Arabia and Kuwait were condemned. At the same time, the UN Secretary-general, Pérez de Cuéllar, tried to negotiate with Iran and Iraq about a halt to bombardments of civilian targets, which had resumed. On 11 June he succeeded in formulating a moratorium on shelling and bombing of urban centres, which both sides accepted.[81]

As a result of Iraqi attacks, exports from Kharg Island dropped from around 1.5 to 1.6 million barrels a day to around 600,000 barrels a day in June 1984. Although the actions Iraq had taken to force Iran into a settlement had a serious effect on the economy of Iran, it failed in its primary objective. Iran was not prepared for a truce with Iraq but took measures to meet the financial losses by moving its shipment points further south to Sirrî and Lavan, out of range of Iraqi aircraft.[82]

Iraq, in January 1985, for the first time since its retreat from Iranian soil launched two offensives. During the first one, on 28 January, which was directed at Majnûn, the Iraqis obtained a foothold on the island. The second one on 31 January was in the central zone near Qaṣr-i Shîrîn, where the Iraqi forces regained a few square miles. Iran thereupon launched Operation '*Badr*' on 11 March, north of Basra, again trying to cut the highway between Basra and Baghdad. The Iranians at one point managed to break through the defences of the Iraqis but in the end they were pushed back by the Iraqi forces with the help of chemical weapons. During this operation, the Iranians abandoned the human-wave assaults and returned to conventional war tactics, which were carried out under the leadership of the regular army. Presumably, this decision was taken because the human-wave attacks cost too many lives and resulted in war-weariness among the Iranians, and besides, these tactics had not had any decisive result. During the rest of the year, the ground war again became a stalemate.[83]

In March 1985 Iraq broke the agreement of June 1984 to stop attacking urban centres and resumed its attacks on civilian targets. Iran immediately responded by attacking Iraqi cities, resulting in a new 'War of the Cities'. While Iraq attacked Iranian cities with aeroplanes, Iran used surface-to-surface missiles. On 14 June, Ṣaddâm Ḥusayn proclaimed a 15-day moratorium, which was ignored by Iran. After the moratorium both sides continued their attacks on civilian targets, albeit on a lower level.[84]

In 1985, the war was waged mainly in the Persian Gulf. Iraq increased its attacks on shipping to and from Iranian ports and oil installations, and in the second half of 1985 60 air raids against Kharg and 33 against ships in the Gulf were recorded. Iran answered with attacks against 13 ships and began to inspect ships going through the Strait of Hormuz in order to check whether they carried arms for Iraq. Despite the use by Iraq of modern, advanced weapons systems such as the Super Etendard, a decisive blow to oil installations proved impossible and after two years of attacks on tankers and oil installations it became clear that this part of the war had also produced a stalemate.[85]

More Iranian attacks

On 9 February 1986, Iran launched operation '*Wa-l-fajr* VIII', which would turn out to be the greatest success after the liberation of Khurramshahr. The operation consisted of two attacks, one in the direction of Basra, mainly to divert the Iraqis from the other, main attack in the south in the direction of Fâ'û, a peninsula about 38 miles south of Basra. The main reasons for this attack seems to have been that an Iranian occupation of Fâ'û would cut off Iraq from the Gulf and from the main communication lines of Iraq to Kuwait, giving the Iranian forces the opportunity to attack Basra from the south, and it would disrupt oil production in the south of Iraq.[86] The Iranian forces broke through the Iraqi defence lines without much resistance from the Iraqis, who were surprised by the attack, which was launched during bad weather. While the occupation of Fâ'û was an important victory for Iran, it signified a threat for Saudi Arabia and Kuwait because it brought the Iranian forces to within 40 miles from the border with Kuwait. During another Iranian offensive in the north, '*Wa-l-fajr* IX' on 25 February, the Iranians managed to capture some ground in the neighbourhood of Sulaymânîya. Because of the latest Iranian successes, Iraq was forced to launch an offensive to boost the morale of its troops and population. On 17 May 1986 Ṣaddâm Ḥusayn ordered a major offensive in the central sector. The Iraqi forces succeeded in capturing 60 square miles of Iranian territory near Mihrân. Ṣaddâm Ḥusayn offered to exchange Mihrân for Fâ'û but the Iranians turned down the offer. Instead, they started Operation '*Karbalâ*" on 30 June and recaptured Mihrân in early July.[87]

Despite a worsening economic situation and spiralling inflation, Iran continued its expensive ground war. On 1 and 3 September it launched Operation '*Karbalâ'* II' and '*Karbalâ'* III', two small offensives, the first in the north near Ḥajj 'Umrân, a strategic mountain in Kurdistan and the second in the south near Fâ'û. Both had only limited results. Operation '*Karbalâ'* IV' launched on 23 December was much larger (some 100,000 troops were involved) and was directed against islands in the Shaṭṭ al-'Arab near Basra and Khurramshahr. The attack was mainly carried out by Pâsdârân and Basîj units with only limited support from the regular army. This offensive was a return to the tactics used in 1984: massive infantry assaults without artillery or support from the air force. The outcome of the offensive was a failure and a high casualty rate on both sides.[88] Presumably, this return to human wave assaults, which was supported by the revolutionaries but not by the regular army, was the result of fresh disagreements about tactics of war and the overall war strategy, between the regular army and the revolutionaries, after the capture of Fâ'û was not followed by more successes. As a result, purges at the top of the regular forces were carried out by the Revolutionary Guards, and the commander of the ground forces, Colonel 'Alî Sayyid Shîrâzî, who had been responsible for the successful Fâ'û offensive, was given a position on the Supreme Defence Council where he had no power at all; he was replaced as commander by Colonel Ḥusayn Ḥasanî-Sa'dî.[89]

On 3 November 1986 the Beirut-based magazine *al-Shirâ'* revealed that the United States had extensive secret contacts with Iran and that it had sold arms to Iran despite its assertion that it would not negotiate with terrorists. With what came to be known as the 'Iran-Contra affair', the United States killed two birds with one stone; the proceeds from the secret sale of arms to Iran were transferred to the Contras in Nicaragua, who were secretly supported by the United States. Through the sale of arms the United States tried to get the American hostages in Lebanon released. At the same time, the United States, which saw Iran as a bulwark against the Soviet Union because of its geographic position, saw a chance to strengthen this bulwark and therefore tried to resume contacts.[90] But despite the arms sales only a few hostages were set free and one was even killed after the United States attack on Qadhdhâfî, the President of Libya, on 15 April 1986. The arms were sold to Iran with the help of Israel, which had itself provided Iran with arms. Iran for its part also had an interest in the deal. On the one hand it desired a better relationship with the United States in order to have a stronger position against the Soviet Union; on the other hand, Iran desperately needed arms and spare parts to pursue the war with Iraq.[91]

In 1987 the Islamic Republic had become more and more alienated from the rest of the world as a result of its uncompromising attitude in the Gulf.[92] There was, however, no indication that the Iranian regime was prepared to change its policies and there was a renewed and intensified campaign for mobilization at the end of 1987. Iran continued its ground attacks and the main goal seems to have been to wear Iraq out economically and militarily, and to inflict large numbers of casualties on the Iraqi forces who struggled with shortages of manpower.[93] Iran on 6 January launched Operation '*Karbalâ'* V' near Salâmja. The offensive was mainly carried out by Revolutionary Guards, supported by Basîj units who cleared the way to the defence positions. The Iranians managed to break through and establish a bridgehead on the western side of the Shaṭṭ al-'Arab, about 12 miles from the suburbs of Basra. Iraq responded by launching counterattacks against the Iranian forces and air strikes against cities and oil installations. At the same time Iranian troops launched new infantry assaults against Iraqi defence positions and tried to push forward to Basra. These attacks were accompanied by heavy artillery attacks on Basra, which caused the flight of large parts of the population of Basra. On 18 February both sides agreed to a cease-fire of two weeks in which Iraq stopped its air strikes on Iranian cities and Iran its shelling of Basra. Although they accused each other of violations of the a-greement, the cease-fire held until April. Fighting on the ground went on, however: the Iranians started another offensive on 13 January in the central sector near Sumar to divert the attention of the Iraqis from a new offensive near Basra which had started on 6 January. This limited operation, '*Karbalâ'* VI', was carried out mainly by the regular army, which captured a few miles.[94] On April 4, Iran again launched an offensive aimed at Basra. During this operation, '*Karbalâ'* VIII', Iran made use of human-wave assaults at the cost of a high casualty rate among the Iranians. On 9 April '*Karbalâ'* IX' was launched, north-east of Qaṣr-i Shîrîn, and Operation '*Karbalâ'* VII and X on 3 March and 13 April in the north. Here, the Iranian forces, supported by a coalition of different Kurdish factions, managed to capture strategic heights 60 miles from Kirkûk. During the rest of the year Iran launched limited offensives, '*Naṣr* I-IX' (victory) and '*Fatḥ* I-VII' along the border with well-trained Revolutionary Guards.[95]

Continuation of the war on all fronts

While Iran continued its attacks on land, Iraq answered by increasing its attacks on Iranian oil refineries and shipping installations. Heavy damage was done to the important Tabrîz, Iṣfahân and Tehran oil refineries which lost more than 30 per cent of their capacity. On 12 August the Iraqis caused heavy damage to storage vessels at Sirrî Island, which had become an oil terminal after the Iraqi attacks on Kharg. Through a shuttle service almost all Iran's exports from Kharg were transported to Sirrî and there transshipped. The Iranians, who thought Sirrî out of range of the Iraqi air force, had to move their tanker-loading site to a position closer to their own coastal defences.[96] The Iranian economy, which was already suffering from the fall in oil prices, was damaged further by these attacks. The fall in oil prices, from $27 a barrel at the end of 1985 to $10 in April 1986 was caused by Saudi Arabia and Kuwait, who feared that an Iranian victory had been brought closer by the capture of Fâ'û. By increasing its oil exports from 2 million barrels a day to 4.5 million barrels, Saudi Arabia depressed oil prices in order to make Iranian oil exports unprofitable. Saudi-Arabia and Kuwait could still make a profit on oil produced and exported for less than $10 a barrel, whereas Iran could not go under $10. By inflicting damage on Iran's most important source of income, Saudi Arabia and Kuwait hoped to make it impossible for Iran to continue financing its war. As a result, the decline in oil revenues threatened not only the continuation of the war but also the import of food and other goods because of the lack of foreign exchange earnings, which laid a further burden on the Iranian population.[97]

In the spring of 1987, Iranian and Iraqi attacks on tankers and oil installations brought about a greater involvement of the international community in the war. While only two Kuwaiti tankers had been hit by Iran since 1985, Kuwait had put forward an official request in January 1987 to have its tankers reflagged as American ships, thus securing them American naval support in the Gulf. The United States was reluctant because it was unwilling to get directly involved in the conflict and lose neutrality by giving support to one of Iraq's allies. In the first instance, the United States increased its force in the Indian Ocean to protect oil shipments and ships sailing under the American flag. Britain, France and the Soviet Union also increased their naval activities in the region. The decision to send warships to the region was more easily taken after the installation by Iran of the Chinese-made Silkworm coastal-defence missiles near the Strait of Hormuz. With these powerful missiles the Iranians became capable of sinking tankers and cargo vessels in the Gulf. The decision to place 11 Kuwaiti tankers under the American flag was taken in March when it became clear that Kuwait had also negotiated with the Soviet Union about protection and that the Soviet Union had agreed to lease tankers to Kuwait. In May, excitement about the war in the United States became stronger when the American frigate USS *Stark* was hit by two Exocet missiles fired by an Iraqi aircraft, about 85 miles north-east of Bahrain, killing 37 and injuring 21 of its crew. Ṣaddâm Ḥusayn in a personal message apologized to President Reagan, calling it an accident. Iran responded by describing the attack as an attempt to draw the superpowers into the war.[98] The growing involvement of the United States was seen by the Iranian government as a serious threat to stability in the Gulf and the reflagging of Kuwaiti tankers was presented as a new phase in the conspiracy against the Islamic Republic because the reflagging was seen as a new instrument to destroy the revolution. Rafsanjânî time and again stressed that Iran did not want to endanger stability in the Gulf but that it would retaliate if Iran's oil exports were blocked. According to him, safety for all and not just for one party was the only thing which Iran aspired to in the Gulf.[99]

A new crisis broke out in June after the discovery of mines in the Gulf; it was suspected that Iran had laid them. On 10 August the American-owned supertanker *Texaco Caribbean* was damaged by a mine off the port of Fujaira (UAE) in the Gulf of Oman. Iran admitted that it had laid mines for defence purposes but it denied that it had laid any so far south. On 15 August a supply ship also hit a mine near Fujaira and sank. Iran then started clearing the Gulf outside the coastal waters of the United Arab Emirates, who refused to avail themselves of an Iranian offer to clear their waters of mines. Because the situation in the Gulf had worsened after the discovery of mines in shipping lanes outside the Gulf, the NATO partners went back on their refusal of an American request to send minesweepers to the Gulf. In September minesweepers were sent by Britain, France, Italy, Belgium and the Netherlands.[100] Tensions between the United States and Iran became more severe as the United States increased its naval presence in the Gulf. On 21 September, the US navy attacked the Iranian landing-vessel *Iran Ajr*, killing three people. The US navy alleged that the Iranians were laying mines and had mines aboard. President Khamini'î, addressing the UN General Assembly a day after the incident, declared that the *Iran Ajr* was a merchant ship and called the US account of the incident a 'pack of lies'.[101] Another clash occurred on 8 October when American helicopters destroyed three Iranian gunboats and killed three people. Each side accused the other side of starting the firing. On 16 October the Kuwaiti supertanker *Sea Isle City* which was under the American flag, was damaged in Kuwaiti waters. The Americans retaliated by destroying two Iranian offshore oilrigs, which, according to American officials, were a base for gunboats used by Revolutionary Guards to attack foreign shipping. The Iranians thereupon answered with an attack on a Kuwaiti oil terminal off the port of Aḥmadî. Iraq also attacked in the Gulf: during 1987 it hit 76 ships, while Iran hit 87 ships.[102]

While the war continued on all fronts and other countries became more and more entangled, the United Nations Security Council on 20 July 1987 unanimously accepted Resolution 598. Among the ten articles of the resolution, the most important provided for an immediate cease-fire, an exchange of prisoners of war, the return of both sides' forces behind recognized frontiers and the appointment of a commission to determine responsibility for the war. Iraq accepted the resolution on the condition that Iran would accept also. Iran neither accepted nor rejected but wanted the sequence of articles of the resolution changed. Instead of article 1, which demanded an immediate cease-fire, it wanted the resolution headed by article 6 about the appointment of a commission of inquiry into responsibility for the conflict. By taking this stance instead of refusing, Iran avoided an international embargo which the United Nations wanted to impose on the party that rejected the resolution. Iraq stopped its air strikes on Iranian targets but resumed them when Iran did not react to the request of the Security Council. The peace mission of Pérez de Cuéllar to Iran and Iraq in September to discuss a cease-fire brought no results because Iran reaffirmed that it would only accept a cease-fire if Iraq was identified as the aggressor by the UN.[103]

At the beginning of 1988, there were only limited encounters on land and wider attacks on Gulf shipping and cities. Military, diplomatic and political reasons contributed to the Iranian decision to deviate from former strategies. Shortages of arms, ammunition and military hardware, the fact that there was a lack of volunteers, unsurprising when the government extended conscription from 24 to 28 months, the fear that an international arms embargo would be called off because of a large offensive were some of these reasons. Another, more political reason was the forthcoming Iranian general elections in April, when it would be inopportune to have parts of the population engaged in an offensive with massive assaults on strong Iraqi defence positions, which had always resulted in large numbers of casualties. The Iranians kept up the pressure, however, with offensives in the north along the frontier, which were carried out by Revolutionary Guards. They often succeeded in breaking through Iraqi defensive positions but the gains were not of strategic importance.[104]

The war of attrition which the Iranians thus continued did not fit the plans of Ṣaddâm Ḥusayn. He wanted an immediate cease-fire but, considering the attitude of the Iranians, that seemed a long way off. Therefore the Iraqis decided to force the Iranians into a settlement. In February the 'War of the Cities' was resumed on a larger scale by Iraq and immediately followed by Iran. During the two months of attacks until the truce of 20 April, Iraq carried out about 190 missiles attacks, causing some 2000 deaths.[105] On 16 March the Iraqi air force attacked with poison gas Ḥalabja, an Iraqi town which had been captured by Iranian forces and Kurdish allies the day before. At least 4000 people were killed, most of them civilians.[106]

On 16 April the Iraqi army launched an offensive against Fâ'û. The peninsula was easily captured because of the use of chemical weapons against the defence lines in the north, combined with an attack from the sea behind Iranian lines, and because the Iranians only had a brigade of 5000 men against a overwhelming force of 40,000 Iraqis. The Iranians then had to retreat behind the Shaṭṭ al-'Arab. This offensive was the first of a series of effective Iraqi attacks which pushed the Iranians from their positions in Iraq, for instance the capture of the Iranian border town Mihrân and the recapture of the Majnûn oilfields which had been taken by the Iranians in 1985.[107] The Iranian leaders tried to cope with these losses by changes at the military top. At the beginning of June, President Khamini'î was replaced by Majlis Speaker 'Alî Akbar Hâshimî Rafsanjânî as Commander-in-chief of the armed forces. Khumaynî ordered him to reorganize the armed forces command, to create a general headquarters and to organize the coordination of the armed forces, the Revolutionary Guards and the volunteer forces.[108]

In 1988 the war in the Gulf also continued. Iraq increased its attacks on Iranian targets. On 21 March 50 people were killed during an Iraqi attack on Kharg.[109] Several people were killed in an Iraqi attack on the Lârak island terminal on 14 May, in which five tankers were hit. Confrontations between Iran and the United States also increased. On 18 April the United States destroyed oil platforms near Sirrî island and near Salmân island as retaliation for damage to a navy vessel and two Iranian frigates were damaged by the American navy after these had fired at American aircraft.[110] Fear of Iranian suicide commandos made the Americans very nervous. After the Iraqi attack on the USS *Stark*, in which they had not reacted quickly enough, they did not want to take any risks. This was presumably the reason for the downing of the Iran Air airbus over the Strait of Hormuz on 3 July by a missile of the USS *Vincennes*.[111] The airbus was on a normal flight from Bandar 'Abbâs to Dubai, carrying 290 people. The captain of the *Vincennes* gave orders to fire at the plane after he came to the conclusion that it was an attacking warplane, because it did not identify itself and did not respond to warning signals from the *Vincennes*.

Initially, there was harsh rhetoric on the Iranian side, but no retaliatory action followed; instead Iran called upon the United Nations to have the United States condemned for the incident.[112]

Cease-fire

On 18 July President Khamini'î in a letter to Secretary-General Pérez de Cuéllar announced that Iran had accepted United Nations Security Council Resolution 598, which called for an immediate cease-fire. Khumaynî's speech, in which he said that he had decided to halt the war for the sake of the Islamic Republic and that he personally had endorsed the acceptance of Resolution 598, was made public in the Iranian media.[113] The downing of the Iran Air airbus was not the main reason for Iran's acceptance of Resolution 598 but it certainly accelerated the decision. Furthermore, besides the recent military defeats caused by the shortage of arms and by the superiority of the Iraqi armed forces, the isolation of Iran in the world and the American presence in the Gulf, the war expenses had in 1988 become almost intolerable.[114] Another reason was the deterioration of Iran's economy. Most sectors, except the arms industry, faced serious problems as a result of war damage, shortages of raw materials, spare parts and machinery. According to unofficial estimates, inflation in Iran had reached 40-50 per cent in 1987 and in early 1988. Unemployment was very high (in 1986 28.6 per cent of the labour force), despite the high level of mobilization.[115] A major reason may also have been that the war no longer served the Islamic revolution but on the contrary had become a danger to the existence of the Islamic Republic. This danger came also from within Iran, where criticism of the continuation of a war without victory had increased considerably and was not only coming from opponents of the regime but was supported by larger parts of the population as well. Furthermore, the zeal and enthusiasm of the population for a war against unbelief and despotism had been replaced by loss of morale at home and at the front after the intensive attacks on Iranian cities and the fear that the Iraqis would use chemical weapons against Iranian cities.[116]

Iraq reacted sceptically. It announced that it would continue the war as long as Iran used 'deceptive language' and that it would only accept a truce when Iran agreed with direct negotiations. This hard stance was accompanied by Iraqi attacks on Iranian border towns and the capture of Iranian territory in order to improve Iraq's position before the talks started and to influence the negotiations. On 6 August Ṣaddâm Ḥusayn declared that he agreed to a settlement if Iran agreed to direct talks after the truce. Iran accepted this proposal two days later. Two weeks later, 20 August, the cease-fire between the two countries started formally. The negotiations which started five days later under the auspices of the United Nations in Geneva soon became deadlocked because of the Shaṭṭ al-'Arab issue. Both parties refused to make concessions on this point and other issues such as the occupation of Iranian land by the Iraqi forces. As a result, further rounds of negotiations in September and November 1988 and in the spring of 1989 did not yield any success either.[117]

Two years later, on 15 August 1990, two weeks after the Iraqi invasion of Kuwait, Ṣaddâm Ḥusayn offered a permanent settlement of the war, which technically had not yet ended. He announced that Iraq would accept the Algiers Treaty of 1975, withdraw Iraqi troops from up to 1000 square miles of Iranian territory, which they still occupied, and exchange prisoners of war, who were held by both sides.[118] War reparations and attribution of responsibility for the outbreak of the war were not part of the offer, which in fact never was ratified. Resolution 598 was only implemented to effect a cease-fire and partial separation of forces.[119] Iran called Ṣaddâm's decision 'the greatest victory of the Islamic Republic of Iran' but it also said that it would urge Iraq to a complete acceptance of Resolution 598. Iran was opposed to the Iraqi invasion of Kuwait. In an official reaction, Iran said that it did not tolerate any change in international recognized borders. Apart from this, Iran wanted an Iraqi withdrawal from Kuwait because this presence had resulted in the presence of the United States in Saudi Arabia, which Iran denounced.[120] Although Iranian leaders spoke harsh language and Khâmini'î in September 1990, under pressure from more radical elements, even called for a *jihâd* against the United States' presence in Saudi Arabia, Iran maintained an official position of neutrality throughout the conflict.[121]

Notes

1. Mohsen Massarat, 'Der Gottesstaat auf dem Kriegsschauplatz', in: *Peripherie* 29 (1988) pp. 45-84, p. 55.

2. The Iraqi Minister of Foreign Affairs, Hammadi, in a speech to the United Nations, cited in I.F. Dekker and H. Post, 'The Gulf War from the Point of View of International Law', in: *Netherlands Yearbook of International Law* 17 (1986) pp. 75-105, p. 84. According to these authors, the Iraqi arguments for taking refuge to military action for self-defence and to settle the dispute were very unconvincing, p. 105.

3. *Keesings Historisch Archief* 49 (1980) p. 610.

4. David Menashri, *Iran. A Decade of War and Revolution* (New York: Holmes and Meier, 1990) p. 157.

5. *Keesings Historisch Archief* 49 (1980) p. 609.

6. Ali E. Hillal Dessouki, 'The Iraq-Iran War: An Overview', in: *The Iraq-Iran War. Issues of Conflict and Prospects for Settlement*, ed. by Ali E. Hillal Dessouki (Princeton: Center of International Studies, 1981) pp. 1-5, p. 2.

7. Daniel Pipes, 'A Border Adrift: Origin of the Conflict', in: *The Iran-Iraq War. New Weapons, Old Conflicts*, ed. by Shirin Tahir-Kheli and Shaheen Ayubi (New York: Praeger, 1983) pp. 3-25, p.22.

8. Paul Balta, *Iran-Irak. Une Guerre de 5000 ans* (Paris: Éditions Anthropos, 1987) p. 102.

9. Mustafa al-Najjar and Najdat Fathi Safwat, 'Arab Sovereignty over the Shatt al-Arab During the Ka'bide Period', in: *The Iran-Iraq War. An Historical, Economic and Political Analysis*, ed. by M.S. el-Azhary (London: Croom Helm, 1984) pp. 20-37, p.20.

10. Peter Hünseler, 'The Historical Antecedents of the Shatt al-'Arab Dispute', in: *The Iran-Iraq War. An Historical, Economic and Political Analysis*, ed. by M.S. el-Azhary (London: Croom Helm, 1984) pp. 8-19, p. 10.

11. Pipes, 'A Border Adrift', p. 23.

12. Stephen R. Grummon, *The Iran-Iraq War. Islam Embattled* (New York: Praeger, 1982) p. 3.

13. J.M. Abdulghani, *The Years of Crisis* (Baltimore: Johns Hopkins University Press, 1984) p. 106.

14. Ahmad Mahrad, *Der Iran-Irak Konflikt* (Frankfurt am Main: Peter Lang, 1985) p. 14.

15. Tareq Y. Ismael, *Iraq and Iran: Roots of Conflict* (New York: Syracuse University Press, 1982) p. 10.

16. Abdulghani, *The Years of Crisis* p. 116.

17. Ismail, *Iraq and Iran* p. 20.

18. Hünseler, Peter, 'The Historical Antecedents of the Shatt al-Arab Dispute', in: *The Iran-Iraq War. An Historical, Economic and Political Analysis*, ed. by M.S. el-Azhary (London: Croom Helm, 1984 pp. 8-19, p. 18.

19. *The Iraq-Iran Conflict*, ed. by Nicola Firzli and Nassim Khoury (Paris: Éditions du Monde Arabe, 1981) p. 110; Majid Khadduri, *The Gulf War. The Origins and Implications of the Iraq-Iran Conflict* (New York and Oxford: Oxford University Press, 1988) p. 91. Both works are presented as general studies of the conflict, but they show extreme pro-Iraqi and Ba'th bias. To quote but two examples from Khadduri's study: (p. 84) ' Saddam Husayn, well known for his resolve and bravery' and 'His ability and strength of character had already been acknowledged in the country' and on p. 116 ' One (Iran), claiming to derive its inspiration from religion, stresses doctrines not at all compatible with the modern age. Yet if it is ever to survive, it is bound to make concessions and accommodate to modern conditions of life. The other (Iraq), aspiring to achieve rapid progress and development, has yet to adjust material and technological innovations to the cultural heritage that the people of Iraq, but also in all other Arab countries, still honor'. A work with a more or less pro-Iranian bias is: *The Iran-Iraq War. The Politics of Aggression,* ed. by Farhang Rajaee (Gainesville: University Press of Florida, 1993).

20. Bruce Maddy-Weitzmann, 'Islam and Arabism: The Iran-Iraq War', in: *Washington Quarterly* 5 (1982) pp. 181-185, p. 181.

21. Chibli Mallat, 'Religious Militancy in Contemporary Iraq: Muhammad Baqer as-Sadr and the Sunni-Shia Paradigm', in: *Third World Quarterly* 10 (1988) pp. 699-729, p. 728.

22. Johannes Reissner, *Iran - Irak: Kriegsziele und Kriegsideologien. Zum Problem der Vermittlung* (Ebenhausen: Stiftung Wissenschaft und Politik, 1987) p. 15.

23. Shahram Chubin and Charles Tripp, *Iran and Iraq at War* (London: I.B. Tauris, 1988) pp. 54, 57.

24. Pipes, 'A Border Adrift', p. 22.

25. Efraim Karsh, *The Iran-Iraq War: A Military Analysis* (London: International Institute for Strategic Studies, 1987) p.18.

26. William O. Staudenmaier, 'Military Policy and Strategy in the Gulf War', in: *Parameters* 12 (1982) pp. 25-35, p. 28.

27. Nader Entessar, 'The Military and Politics in the Islamic Republic of Iran', in: *Post-Revolutionary Iran*, ed. by Hooshang Amirahmadi and M. Parvin (Boulder: Westview Press, 1988) pp. 56-73, p. 66; Chubin and Tripp, *Iran and Iraq at War* p. 35.

28. Sepehr Zabih, *The Iranian Military in Revolution and War* (London: Routledge, 1988) p. 136.

29. Eliyahu Kanovsky, 'Economic Implications for the Region and World Oil Market', in: *The Iran-Iraq War: Impact and Implications*, ed. by E. Karsh (London: Macmillan, 1989) pp. 231-251, p. 241.

30. Menashri, *Iran. A Decade of War and Revolution* p. 89.

31. Menashri, *Iran. A Decade of War and Revolution* pp. 127-145.

32. *New York Times*, 18 October 1980.

33. Gary Sick, 'Trial by Error: Reflections On the Iran-Iraq War', in: *Middle East Journal* 43 (1989) pp. 230-245, p. 234.

34. Chubin and Tripp, *Iran and Iraq at War* p. 191.

35. Dilip Hiro, 'Chronicle of the Gulf War', in: *Middle East Report* 126 (1984) pp. 3-14, p. 6.

36. R.K. Ramazani, *Revolutionary Iran. Challenge and Response in the Middle East* (Baltimore: Johns Hopkins University Press, 1986) p. 216.

37. Bijan Mossavar-Rahmani, 'Economic Implications for Iran and Iraq', in: *The Iran-Iraq War. New Weapons, Old Conflicts*, ed. by S. Tahir-Kheli and S. Ayubi (New York: Praeger, 1983) pp. 51-64, p. 61.

38. Edgar O'Ballance, 'The Iraqi-Iranian War: The First Round', in: *Parameters* 11 (1981) pp. 54-59, p. 54.

39. Karsh, *The Iran-Iraq War* p. 21.

40. Anthony H. Cordesman, 'Lessons of the Iran-Iraq War: The First Round', in: *Armed Forces Journal International* 119 (1982) pp. 32-46, p. 47.

41. Karsh, *The Iran-Iraq War* pp. 15-16.

42. Entessar, 'Military and Politics', p. 68.

43. Staudenmaier, 'Military Policy and Strategy in the Gulf War', p. 28.

44. Menashri, *Iran. A Decade of War and Revolution* p. 182.

45. Said Amir Arjomand, *The Turban for the Crown. The Islamic Revolution in Iran* (Oxford: Oxford University Press, 1988) p. 142.

46. Menashri, *Iran. A Decade of War and Revolution* p. 173.

47. William O. Staudenmaier, 'A Strategic Analysis', in: *The Iran-Iraq War. New Weapons, Old Conflicts*, ed. by S. Tahir-Kheli and S. Ayubi (New York: Praeger, 1983) pp. 27-50, p. 39.

48. Menashri, *Iran. A Decade of War and Revolution* p. 173.

49. Edgar O'Ballance, *The Gulf War* (London: Brassey's Defence Publishers, 1988) p. 69.

50. The titles of the Iranian military operations will be discussed in detail in Chapter four.

51. Karsh, *The Iran-Iraq War* p. 24.

52. Kenneth Katzman, *The Warriors of Islam. Iran's Revolutionary Guard* (Boulder: Westview, 1993) p. 67.

53. Menashri, *Iran. A Decade of War and Revolution* p. 219.

54. Fred Halliday, 'Year IV of the Islamic Republic', in: *Middle East Report* 13 (1983) pp. 3-8, p. 4.

55. Kamran Mofid, *The Economic Consequences of the Gulf War* (London: Routledge, 1990) p. 72.

56. O'Ballance, *The Gulf War* p. 79

57. Karsh, *The Iran-Iraq War* p.25.

58. Menashri, *Iran. A Decade of War and Revolution* p. 229.

59. *New York Times*, 21 June 1982.

60. Karsh, *The Iran-Iraq War* p. 25.

61. Shaul Bakhash, *The Reign of the Ayatollahs. Iran and the Revolution* (New York: Basic Books, 1984) p. 127.

62. Karsh, *The Iran-Iraq War* p. 26.

63. *The Economist*, 15 August 1982.

64. Karsh, *The Iran-Iraq War* p. 26.

65. Claudia Wright, 'Religion and Strategy in the Iraq-Iran War', in: *Third World Quarterly* 7 (1985) pp. 839-852, p. 846.

66. *The Imam and the Ommat. The Selected Messages of Imam Khomeini concerning Iraq and the War Iraq Imposed upon Iran* (Tehran: Ministry of Islamic Guidance, 1981) p. 28.

67. Menashri, *Iran. A Decade of War and Revolution* p. 251.

68. Hanna Batatu, 'Shi'i Organizations in Iraq: al-Da'wah al-Islamiyah and al-Mujahidin', in: *Shi'ism and Social Protest*, ed. by Juan R.I. Cole and N.K. Keddie (New Haven: Yale University Press, 1986) p. 200.

69. Chubin and Tripp, *Iran and Iraq at War* p. 102.

70. The *New York Times*, 5 August 1982, gives a total of 80,000 killed, 100,000 wounded and 45,000 prisoners of war for these operations.

71. Karsh, *The Iran-Iraq War* p. 27.

72. Karsh, *The Iran-Iraq War* p. 28.

73. Ralph King, *The Iran-Iraq War. The Political Implications* (London: International Institute for Strategic Studies, 1987) p. 71.

74. *New York Times* 3 April 1983.

75. Karsh, *The Iran-Iraq War* p. 29.

76. King, *The Iran-Iraq War* p. 55.

77. Chubin and Tripp, *Iran and Iraq at War* p. 193.

78. *New York Times*, 19 October 1983.

79. Anthony H. Cordesman, *The Lessons of Modern War. Vol.II The Iran-Iraq War* (Boulder: Westview Press, 1991) pp. 192-194.

80. Dilip Hiro, *The Longest War: The Iran-Iraq Military Conflict* (London: Grafton, 1989) p. 284.

81. Hiro, *The Longest War* p. 130.

82. Ramazani, *Revolutionary Iran* p. 221.

83. Karsh, *The Iran-Iraq War* p. 31.

84. O'Ballance, 'The Iraqi-Iranian War', p. 170.

85. Ramazani, *Revolutionary Iran* p. 223.

86. Cordesman, *The Iran-Iraq War* p. 92.

87. Karsh, *The Iran-Iraq War* p. 33.

88. Cordesman, *The Iran-Iraq War* p. 124.

89. Cordesman, *The Iran-Iraq War* p. 105.

90. Shireen T. Hunter, *Iran and the World. Continuity in a Revolutionary Decade* (Bloomington: Indiana University Press, 1990) p. 65.

91. Menashri, *Iran. A Decade of War and Revolution* p. 378. In the speeches, the leaders kept silent about the fact that the Islamic Republic had shown that it was willing to negotiate with its main enemy but presented the contacts as a disgrace for the United States because of the deals. About the arms supply Rafsanjânî said that as long as Iraq received arms it was not scandalous that Iran received weapons too; in fact, it was not more than fair that Iran should receive the same amount of arms as Iraq. He and other Friday imâms presented these relations with the United States as one of the greatest victories of the Islamic Republic over the superpowers since the revolution. Rafsanjânî in sermon, *Iṭṭilâ'ât* 8/9/65; Khâmini'î, *Iṭṭilâ'ât* 15/8/65; Imâmî Kâshânî, *Iṭṭilâ'ât* 22/9/65.

92. Chubin and Tripp, *Iran and Iraq at War* pp. 219-220.

93. *The Economist*, 2 February 1987.

94. Cordesman, *The Iran-Iraq War* pp. 127-129.

95. *Keesings Historisch Archief* 56 (1987) p. 625.

96. Cordesman, *The Iran-Iraq War* p. 106.

97. R.K. Ramazani, 'The Iran-Iraq War and the Persian Gulf crisis', in: *Current History* 87 (1988) pp. 61-64, and p. 86, p. 62.

98. Joe Stork, 'Reagan Re-flags the Gulf', in: *Middle East Report* 17 (1987) pp. 2-5, p. 4.

99. Rafsanjânî in sermon, *Iṭṭilâ'ât*, 29/1/66; 2/3/66.

100. *Keesings Historisch Archief* 56 (1987) p. 626.

101. *New York Times*, 23 September 1987.

102. Hiro, *The Longest War* p. 287.

103. *Keesings Historisch Archief* 56 (1987) p. 630.

104. Hiro, *The Longest War* p. 199.

105. *Middle East Economic Digest*, 6 May 1988.

106. According to the *Washington Post*, the high casualty rate in Ḥalabja may have been caused by a hydrogen cyanide gas attack fired into the area by the Iranians in order to kill Iraqi soldiers and not by the Iraqi mustard gas attack which preceded the Iranian attack. Cordesman, *The Lessons of Modern War* p. 517.

107. Hiro, *The Longest War* p. 203.

108. *New York Times* 5 June 1988.

109. *New York Times* 22 March 1988.

110. *New York Times* 19 April 1988.

111. An unpublished US military investigation of the downing of the Iran Air airbus revealed that the accident was caused by the psychological stress of the combat situation (*Middle East Journal* 42 (1988) p. 80).

112. *Keesings Historisch Archief* 57 (1988) p. 433.

113. Khumaynî's speech will be discussed at length in Chapter 6.

114. The economic cost of the war for Iran was estimated at $644.3 billion ($452.6 billion for Iraq). In relation to Iran's GNP, on average each year during the war, the cost of the war was for Iran 60 per cent (for Iraq 112 per cent). Kamran Mofid, *The Economic Consequences of the Gulf War* (London: Routledge, 1990) p. 135.

115. Kanovsky, 'Economic Implications', p. 243.

116. Shahram Chubin, 'Iran and the War: From Stalemate to Ceasefire', in: *The Iran-Iraq War: Impact and Implications*, ed. by E. Karsh (London: Macmillan, 1989) pp. 13-25, p. 23.

117. Béatrice Gorawantschy, *Der Golfkrieg zwischen Iran und Irak, 1980-88. Eine konflikttheoretische Analyse* (Berlin: Lang, 1993) p. 156.

118. Gorawantschy, *Der Golfkrieg zwischen Iran und Irak* p. 156.

119. Keith McLachlan, 'Territoriality and the Iran-Iraq War' in: *The Boundaries of Modern Iran*, ed. by K. McLachlan (London: UCL Press, 1994) pp. 57-71, p. 70.

120. Safa Haeri, 'The Missing Prisoners', in: *Middle East International* 388 (1990) p. 13.

121. Said Amir Arjomand, 'A Victory for the Pragmatists: The Islamic Fundamentalist Reaction in Iran', in: *Islamic Fundamentalisms and the Gulf Crisis*, ed. by J. Piscatori (n.p., The American Academy of Arts and Sciences, 1991) pp. 52-69, p. 62.

2 THEOLOGICAL-DOCTRINAL DISCOURSE: ISLAM AND WAR

The war with Iraq confronted the Iranian leaders with a serious problem since according to Islamic law it is forbidden to shed the blood of fellow Muslims; furthermore, in Islam the only lawful war is the *jihâd*.[1] This chapter deals with the way the Iranian leaders made use of Islamic and Shî'î beliefs, in particular the legal concepts of war and theological concepts concerning moral behaviour in order to justify a war in which they fought against other Muslims and to mobilize the Iranian people to fight against these Muslims. Although the leaders only touched upon these concepts briefly and in a very selective way, I will give a brief theoretical background in order to put the statements in perspective.

Classical Islamic conceptions of jihâd

After the outbreak of the war, Khumaynî declared that the Islamic Republic was waging *jihâd* against Iraq.[2] The original meaning of *jihâd* is 'effort' but the term as used in the Qur'ân and in Islamic legal works denotes effort in a strict sense: the armed struggle against unbelievers, more than once stressed with the addition *fî sabîl Allâh* (for the cause of God).[3] Although in Muḥammad's time such a struggle had religious motives, since it was fought against all those who denied and opposed Muḥammad's prophethood and message, according to Western scholarship its purpose was not the extension of the Islamic faith but the protection of the Muslim community against enemies and tributary dependency of the *ahl al-kitâb* (the scriptuaries).[4] The wars fought after Muḥammad's death were intended to expand the Islamic realm politically and geographically rather than to convert those who were attacked. Although the *jihâd* was waged against unbelievers, these unbelievers were also the enemies of the Muslim state; and although the *jihâd* was waged with the motive 'for the cause of God', this cause coincided with the well-being of the state.[5] Thus, on a political level warfare in Islam could have secular reasons, but this was different for those who fought in the *jihâd*. Many people who participated had religious reasons, since fighting in the *jihâd* was a religious duty and a pious deed, and those who died would be rewarded with a place in Paradise.[6]

According to the rules of the *sharî'a*, the *jihâd* can be either a collective duty (*farḍ kifâya*) or an individual one (*farḍ 'ayn*). The first has to be authorized by the leader of the Muslim community and when the duty is fulfilled by a sufficiently large part of the community, others do not have to take part. The *jihâd* is a collective duty when its purpose is offensive.[7] Until the world has submitted to Islam, it is divided in the *dâr al-islâm* (Abode of Islam) and the *dâr al-ḥarb* (Abode of War) or the *dâr al-kufr* (Abode of Unbelief). In theory, this means that the *dâr al-islâm* is in a permanent state of war with the *dâr al-ḥarb*. In practice, however, the state of war was sidestepped by armistices which were concluded with non-Muslims. An armistice could be concluded for a specific period (not longer than ten years) and could be terminated at any moment by the Islamic state. Another kind of treaty with non-Muslims was the *amân* (safe-conduct or quarter), which could be concluded with non-Muslims, allowing them to live in the Islamic state for a time. There were two different kinds of *amân*: during actual warfare quarter can be given to individuals, towns or regions, and in peacetime non-Muslims travellers in the *dâr al-islâm* can obtain a safe-conduct. Treaties can also be concluded with non-Muslims living within the Islamic state in the form of granting a special status, *dhimma*, to the *ahl al-kitâb*, (the People of the Book), i.e. Jews, Christians and Zoroastrians. Those within the Islamic state who were excluded from concluding a *dhimma* had the choice between conversion to Islam and being put to death.[8]

When the Islamic state is attacked and the socio-political order is threatened, it becomes a *farḍ 'ayn* (individual duty) for everyone, (including women and children), to take part in a defensive *jihâd* to protect the state.[9] In this case people do not need the permission of their parents, which is necessary for participation in the offensive *jihâd*. According to Ḥamîdullâh, 'defensive' can be either when the enemy has invaded Muslim territory, or when the enemy has behaved in an unbearable manner.[10] The first form of defence is sanctioned by *al-Baqara* II:190: 'Fight in the way of Allah those who fight you, but do not provoke hostility; verily Allah loveth not those who provoke hostility'; and the second by *al-Ḥajj* XXII:39: 'permission is granted to those who fight because they have suffered wrong; verily to help them Allah is able', which is a reference to the first years of Muḥammad's stay in Medina, when the Muslim community was still harassed by the Meccans.[11] In an offensive *jihâd*, summoning the opponent to submit to Islam is obligatory, but this is not the case in a defensive *jihâd*.[12]

Since Muslim law is based on the principle of the unity of Islam, there are scarcely any regulations about war between Muslim states. According to Ḥamîdullâh, the Qur'ân has one verse which can be applied to the subject of war between two Islamic states: 'If two parties of the believers fight, set things right between them, and if one of the two parties oppresses the other, fight the one which is oppressive until it returns to the affairs of Allah; then if it returns, set things right between them justly, and act fairly; verily Allah loveth those who act fairly' (*al-Ḥujurât* XLIX:9).[13] In practice, Muslim states based their conduct in war with other Muslims states either on the law concerning rebellion (*baghy*) or on that of apostasy (*ridda*), both of them based on the practice of the fourth Caliph, 'Alî, although the first *ridda* took place after the death of Muḥammad.[14]

Shî'î conceptions of jihâd

The rules on *jihâd* developed by Shî'î jurists are to a large extent similar to Sunnî rules, for instance the rules concerning treatment of the enemy, the *farḍ kifâya* and the *farḍ 'ayn*. But the rules differ over a few issues: the people against whom *jihâd* may be declared, the principle of *al-amr bi-l-ma'rûf wa-l-nahy 'an al-munkar* and the role of the *imâm* in proclaiming *jihâd*. According to Shî'î and Sunnî jurists alike, *jihâd* may be waged against polytheists, apostates, rebels and the People of the Book. The classical Twelver Shî'î doctrine differs in two points: firstly, the leadership of the *jihâd* is not in the hands of the *imâm* (caliph) but is limited to one of the twelve divinely appointed *imâms* or someone appointed by the *imâm*. Secondly, Twelver Shî'î doctrine is different in the emphasis laid on the *jihâd* against the *bughât* (rebels), and in its definition of the category of the *bughât*. Unlike Sunnî jurists, who define the *bughât* as those who reject the authority of the ruler,[15] Shî'î jurists define the *bughât* as those who rise against one of the twelve *imâms*. Imâmî jurists considered the *bughât* unbelievers but there are minor differences in the law governing these two groups.[16]

In contrast with Sunnî law, in Shî'î legal texts *al-amr bi-l-ma'rûf wa-l-nahy 'an al-munkar* (commanding the good and forbidding the wrong) is part of the section on the rules of *jihâd*[17] and sometimes the principle is regarded as *jihâd* by the tongue.[18] This is an unconditional duty incumbent on every individual Muslim, who has to do his utmost to correct other Muslims' wrongful behaviour. According to a tradition of 'Alî, in *al-Uṣûl min al-kâfî* on the authority of the fifth *imâm*, al-Bâqir, *jihâd* is one of the pillars of *îmân* (faith) and one of the branches of *jihâd* is *al-amr bi-l-ma'rûf wa-l-nahy 'an al-munkar*.[19] According to Shaykh al-Mufîd, exercising *al-amr bi-l-ma'rûf wa-l-nahy 'an al-munkar* by the tongue is a collective duty; it is the task of the Sultan to lay this duty on the one he appoints for this task, or the one to whom he permits it.[20] Other theologians say that it is an individual duty, provided that the circumstances are favourable; that is, it takes the form of non-violent persuasion and no harm is done to Muslims.[21]

The Shî'î theory of *jihâd* is closely connected with the role of the Shî'î *imâm*. Early Shî'î ideas held that the sole authority to declare *jihâd* was the *imâm* in his capacity as divinely appointed leader of the community. Thus, with the Greater Occultation of the Twelfth *imâm* in 329/941, Shî'î theologians considered the waging of *jihâd* and other functions which were the prerogative of the *imâm* to be in abeyance (*sâqiṭ*).[22] In practice, the abeyance of waging *jihâd*, which signified the prohibition of all forms of warfare, was unattainable and in the following centuries the *jihâd* theory was changed and adapted to political circumstances. Thus, during the reign of the Bûyids (334-945/447-1055), proponents of the Shî'a, the *jihâd* theory was modified by Abû Ja'far al-Ṭûsî (d.460/1067), probably because military pressure from the Sunnî Seljuqs made this necessary.[23] According to al-Ṭûṣî, a defensive *jihâd*, which did not have to be commanded by the *imâm*, was allowed to protect the community. This theory was later developed by al-Muḥaqqiq al-Ḥillî (d.676/1277 and 'Allâma (Ibn al-Muṭahhar) al-Ḥillî (d.726/1325), who declared that people could be summoned to a defensive *jihâd* by the *imâm* or someone appointed by the *imâm*. According to Kohlberg, it can be assumed that this vague formula referred to the *fuqahâ'* (jurists) as the collective representatives of the *imâm*.[24]

The Ṣafawid dynasty (1501-1722) not only claimed descent from the *imâms*, but they believed that they were entitled to their prerogatives as well. According to Kohlberg and Lambton, the authoritative *'ulamâ'* of this period did not support the Ṣafawid claim and their theories of *jihâd* did not alter from earlier theologians.[25] Arjomand, however, states that the political situation of the Ṣafawid state did have consequences for the theory of *jihâd*. In the *Jâmi' 'Abbâsî*, the authoritative legal work of the seventeenth century in Persia, considerable attention was paid to bringing the theory of *jihâd* into line with the political realities of that day. As an example we may mention regulations about the criteria which made People of the Book 'infidels', and thus the Safawid wars against the Georgians legal.[26]

Further efforts to adapt the Shî'a doctrine of *jihâd* to the political realities of the day were made by the theologians during the Perso-Russian wars of 1808-1813 and 1826-1828. Iranian *'ulamâ'* supported the Shah, Fatḥ 'Alî, and declared both wars against Russia defensive *jihâds*. They wrote extensively on the subject of *jihâd*, stressing the fact that the defensive *jihâd* was a duty incumbent on all Muslims and that, furthermore, the *mujtahid* had the right to declare *jihâd*.[27]

In his *Kashf al-asrâr* cited in *Jang wa jihâd*, Khumaynî, in line with earlier Shî'î theologians, distinguished between two lawful wars in Islam. One was *jihâd*, which he understood as the conquest of the world for the spreading of justice and divine law. For this war the presence of the *imâm* is needed and every able-bodied and sane man is obliged to participate, but prisoners and foreigners are excluded. The other form was *difâ'* (defence), not only the traditional concept of defence of Islam and the Muslim community, but in Khumaynî's view also defence and fighting to safeguard the independence of the *kishwar* (country) and defence against [an attack by] foreigners for which the presence of the *imâm* or his representative is not needed and *difâ'* is a duty (*farḍ 'ayn*) for every member of society.[28] When the war with Iraq broke out in 1980, Khumaynî called this a *jihâd* too, albeit a defensive one.[29]

The war against Iraq and jihâd

A major role in the sacralization and the justification of the Iran-Iraq war was played by statements to the effect that Iran was not fighting an ordinary war but was engaged in a *jihâd dar râh-i khudâ* or (as it was frequently called in Arabic) *jihâd fî sabîl Allâh* (*jihâd* for the cause of God), which is, as shown above, the only lawful kind of war for Muslims. Khumaynî even spoke of the *jihâd dar râh-i 'aqîda* (*jihâd* for the cause of conviction).[30] The only motive for fighting was Islam; defence of Islam, the Qur'ân and the honour of the Islamic revolution. Fighting in God's cause was pure, and contrasted sharply with the avaricious wars of imperialists.[31] The justification of the war was in large part based on the idea that the behaviour of the Islamic Republic was completely in line with that of the prophets of God. Khumaynî's remark that defence of Islam, the Islamic country and the *dîn-i ḥaqq* (religion of truth) was the most pious deed for which prophets and saints had also fought, is part of this form of justification.[32] Immediately after the war had started, Iranian leaders declared it to be a *jihâd*,[33] and they kept on repeating this during the whole war. *Jihâd* therefore remained an important instrument for the justification of the war. So in 1983: 'This is a standard Islamic *jihâd*'.[34] The kind of *jihâd* Iran was engaged in, was a defensive *jihâd* and thus obligatory for the whole population: 'Islam has ordered us to defend and wage *jihâd*'.[35] Leaders not only referred to the war as a *jihâd* but used *difâ'-i muqaddas* (holy defence), *jang-i muqaddas*[36] and *jihâd-i muqaddas* as alternatives.[37] Muntaẓirî divided *jihâd* into the *jihâd-i ibtidâ'î* (initiative *jihâd*) and the *jihâd-i difâ'î* (defensive *jihâd*) which he enlarged, as Khumaynî had done earlier. The first type is proclaimed in order to spread Islam in the world of *kufr* (unbelief). There were a number of Shî'î theologians and jurists, however, who considered the permission of the *imâm* a primary condition for this kind of *jihâd*. But, Muntaẓirî said, there was no doubt or controversy about the second form of *jihâd*, which becomes an individual and collective duty for all Muslims in the case of an attack on the religious, national, economic and political interests of Muslims, or if these interests are endangered by the enemy. Nobody needs the *imâm*'s permission for this kind of *jihâd*. Now, Muntaẓirî said, Islam and Muslims are exposed to such an attack. The United States, the Soviet Union and their vassal Ṣaddâm Ḥusayn attacked Muslims and made them *maẓlûm* (oppressed), especially those in Lebanon, in Afghanistan and in occupied Palestine. They have attacked Islamic culture. Muntaẓirî ranged Ṣaddâm Ḥusayn with the non-Muslims against whom *jihâd* is lawful.[38] In this case, the Qur'ân (Muntaẓirî's speech was a reference to *al-Ḥajj* XXII:39, 40) and the *Nahj al-balâgha* (the Path of Eloquence, the collected writings and sayings of 'Alî) say that silence is prohibited and that every Muslim, regardless of his class or tribe, is duty bound to defend the Qur'ân, Islam and the Muslim sanctuaries.[39]

The leaders were clear in that they regarded the religious motive of 'defence of *ḥaqq*' as the primary reason for joining the *jihâd*.[40] In this vein they stated for instance: 'The Islamic government fights for the defence of the honour of Islam and the supremacy of the Qur'ân..., Iran defends the Islamic government and republic against Iraq and it defends the *ḥarîm* of the Qur'ân and the honour of the Islamic Republic'.[41] A second motive was the defence of the divine and moral values,[42] and, by the same token, the defence of Islamic and human values.[43] Another way of formulating this was 'the defence of Islam and the Islamic country';[44] 'this land and this Abode of Islam'.[45] According to Khâmini'î, participation in *jihâd* had its origin in *dîn* (religion), *taqwâ-yi khudâ* (fear of God) and *iṭâ'a* (obedience to God's command).[46] But in almost all speeches, leaders also emphasized that the war was about the defence of the revolution, and that the revolution had been attacked because it had succeeded in reinstalling Islamic values. As was demonstrated above, Khumaynî and Muntaẓirî had added new criteria to the conditions of the defensive *jihâd*, such as defence of country and defence of national and economic interests. By adjusting the traditional *jihâd* theory, the Iranian leaders created a reinterpretation of this theory and thus made *jihâd* applicable to a war waged by a nation-state as well. Khumaynî emphasized that *jihâd* could also be waged for individual reasons, such as the protection of the family.[47] Other leaders distinguished between two kinds of defence, collective defence against *kufr* and individual defence against the aggression of a thief.[48] But both these kinds of defence could be applied to the war against Iraq because Ṣaddâm Ḥusayn had acted like a thief and criminal.

The leaders not only called on men to take part in the war but also paid attention to women and children. The whole population was in fact mobilized and summoned to contribute in one way or another to the *jihâd*. In accordance with the classical rules of *jihâd*, leaders said that the front of *jihâd* was not only on the battlefield but also in hospitals, in the bazaar, in the factory and in workplaces, in universities and in schools.[49] Khumaynî emphasized that people could participate in the *jihâd* behind the front, since the *jihâd* against intruders and hypocrites was as necessary as the *jihâd* on the battlefield.[50] Participating in this *jihâd* was presented as a religious and moral duty. According to Khumaynî, the *jihâd* for the cause of God was the most important order (*ḥukm*) of God, since *jihâd* guarded (Islamic) principles.[51] On the occasion of the *ḥajj* (pilgrimage), Khumaynî said that the obligation to protect *thughûr i islâm* (the borders of Islam) was far more important than the obligation to perform the pilgrimage and the other Islamic obligations. He did not make clear whether this was in the actual situation of the war with Iraq or in a case of aggression.[52]

In a speech addressed to religious leaders and leaders of the Friday sermon, Khumaynî said that Islam was not a religion consisting solely of rules regarding prayer or fasting. He asked them to recite for the people *sûrat al-Barâ'a* (*al-Tawba*) and the verses about fighting.[53] Verses from *al-Tawba* were recited frequently, but also other Qur'ânic verses about fighting.[54] Other leaders illustrated their exhortations to take part in the *jihâd* with Qur'ânic verses and citations from the *Nahj al-balâgha* as well.[55] For instance *Âl 'Imrân* III:169: 'Count not those who have been killed in the way of Allah as dead, nay, alive with their Lord, provided for';[56] *al-Tawba* IX:111: 'Allah hath bought from the believers their persons and their goods at the price of the Garden (in store) for them, fighting in the way of Allah and killing and being killed - a promise binding upon Him in the Torah, the Gospel, and the Qur'ân; and who fulfils his covenant better than Allah?,[57] 'The *jihâd* is one of the gates to Paradise'; 'Death in your life is subjection whereas life in your death is vanquishing';[58] *al-'Ankabût* XXIX:69 'But those who have striven for Us We shall surely guide Our ways'. According to Rafsanjânî, the highest award for a Muslim was the title *mujâhid*, i.e. a participant in *jihâd*. The readiness to sacrifice on this scale which was the result of the revolution could not be found in any other society or revolution.[59] Khumaynî said that the *mujâhidîn*, the youth of Iran, were incomparable with other Muslims from the beginning of history until the present time, even when compared with the period of the Prophet, which was a time of growth of Islam. The Prophet and 'Alî, the Commander of the believers, both suffered for the cause of Islam but many Muslims did not help them. You are now volunteering for martyrdom and death; you are the hope of Islam, Khumaynî said.[60] Fighting in God's path (*mujâhada*) and *îthâr* (altruism) were the guarantees of divine mercy and a place in Paradise, which was a long-term victory, but they were also guarantees of divine help in a more worldly, short-term victory in the war against Iraq, the lesser arrogance and the larger, worldwide arrogance.[61] One of the billboards at the front said: 'The peak of Islam which only excellent Muslims can reach is the *jihâd* for the cause of God'.[62] According to Âyatullâh Ibrâhîm Amînî, it was 'Alî's strong conviction that *jihâd* was the most honourable and best form of *'ibâda* (religious observance).[63] Some leaders compared engagement in *jihâd* with *'ibâda*. 'One hour of *jihâd* is better than 60 years of *'ibâda*';[64] and '*jihâd* is worthier than 700 years of *'ibâda*'.[65] During the Tehran Friday sermon, Mûṣawî Ardabîlî read a few lines from 'Alî's sermon during the battle of Ṣiffîn in which he explained his motive for the *jihâd* against Mu'âwiya. According to 'Alî, even when he had to fight on his own against the whole world he would not be afraid on his chosen path. The *ḍalâl* (straying from the right path or truth) and *kufr* of his enemies and his own *irshâd* and *hidâya* (guidance) gave enough inspiration for this *jihâd*.[66]

Although the war was defensive, the leaders did not consider taking part in the war effort a *farḍ 'ayn*, an individual duty. Khâmini'î told sons to obey their parents and said that there was no question of a *wâjib-i 'aynî* (individual obligation), for which the permission of parents is not necessary. Fighting was still a collective duty, which meant that people were obliged to ask the permission of their parents. But Khâmini'î warned parents not to prevent their sons from going to the battlefield. It was not right to stop someone who wanted to sacrifice himself, because sacrificing oneself in God's cause is the highest virtue a person can achieve: 'The jihâd is one of the gates to Paradise'.[67] In his *fatwâ*, Khumaynî also had made it clear that parents were not allowed to forbid their children to go to the battlefield.[68] In the speeches it was suggested that behind the front line participating in the *jihâd* was an individual duty. Continuously, reference was made to sacrifice and martyrdom as the highest virtues, and to the different forms of *jihâd* a person could join behind the front lines. The war was considered by leaders a defensive *jihâd*, and in Islamic jurisprudence this is generally interpreted as meaning that it has become an individual duty for the whole population to participate: 'persons who are exempt from fighting an offensive *jihâd* (such as women, slaves, the sick, the old and the insane) must participate in a defensive *jihâd*, since such a *jihâd* is tantamount to self-preservation'.[69] But participating in the *jihâd* on the battlefield remained a collective duty, because there was a sufficient number of fighters available.[70] This is in line with Kruse's observation that the duty to take part in a defensive *jihâd* lapses when there is a sufficient number of *murâbiṭûn* (those who guard the borders) to defend the borders of the country.[71]

Although in a defensive *jihâd* the presence of the *imâm* or his representative, who according to Khumaynî's view is the ruling jurist, is not needed, during the war the Iranian leaders constantly emphasized that Khumaynî in his function of leader (*rahbar*) of the Islamic Republic and *imâm-i umma* had endorsed the war. This was made clear in sermons, speeches and statements:

> God almighty has been kind to us by bestowing the leadership of this nation on a great theologian; this has not occurred anywhere else in history except under the rule of prophets. The *imâm* rules the hearts and rules all who live by the word of God and who are armed with 'God is Great'. Therefore, when such a commander issues the order to attack, the battlefields will be filled with popular forces.[72] As far as the war is concerned we follow the views of the leadership. The grand leader has determined that our war policy should be to continue the war until we obtain our rights and victory.[73]

In a few instances, Khumaynî was implicitly compared to the Prophet. According to the newspaper *Jumhûrî-yi islâmî*, during one Friday sermon the audience shouted: 'The Commander-in-chief is our leader, his command is the command of the Prophet; his command is the order of the Messenger of God'.[74] Throughout the war, the slogan '*labbayka yâ imâm*' (at your service, O *imâm*) could be heard. It was the name of a military division, and an official slogan during the War Week of 1986.

Labbayka in general is a reference to God, but in the traditions also to Muḥammad or his helpers. The saying is especially pronounced during the *ḥajj* (pilgrimage).[75] But during the war, *labbayka yâ imâm* referred especially to Khumaynî, leader of the Islamic Republic.

Iranian leaders did not hesitate to stress that women also had an important role. According to Khumaynî, the defence of their home, their country and Islam was also a duty for women. Moreover, women could join the armed struggle for the defence of Islam and the defence of the Islamic country since the participation of women in a defensive *jihâd* was not disputed by the *'ulamâ'*, in contrast with the offensive *jihâd*, which is not obligatory for women. Apart from the fact that women were suited for fighting, their presence on the battlefield had a positive influence on men, since this presence stimulated the fighting spirit of men.[76] Khâmini'î said that every able-bodied woman in Khûzistân had a duty to stay in the place where she lived in order to defend it against the Iraqi enemy.[77] In Sunnî and Shî'î doctrine, women are exempted from the obligation to wage *jihâd*. According to Najm al-Dîn al-Ḥillî, the *jihâd* is obligatory for those who meet eight conditions, of which one is being male.[78] According to Morabia, in contrast with the practice during Muḥammad's time and that of the first caliphs, Muslim jurists in general were of the opinion that women should not participate in fighting. One of the reasons given was the fact that women might excite the opponents. Another was that employing women would be regarded as a weakness of the Muslims.[79] However, these conditions apply to offensive *jihâd*. Concerning the defensive *jihâd*, Morabia says that women and their children were allowed to accompany their husbands to the borders but only when the borders were sufficiently fortified. Other scholars state that women must participate in a defensive *jihâd*.[80]

Other dimensions of jihâd

But there were still other interpretations of the concept of *jihâd* aiming at the total mobilization of the people. The reference to contributions to defence or other ways to perform the *jihâd* was not new. The classical books on *fiqh* distinguish between these different forms.[81] The *risâla-yi jihâdîya*, a collection of *fatwâs* of the Persian *'ulamâ'* sanctioning the second Persian-Russian war of 1826-28 as a defensive *jihâd*, also touched upon financial aid. In contrast with the custom during an offensive *jihâd*, for the defensive *jihâd* personal hardship and financial sacrifice were deemed permissible in order to raise the necessary sums.[82] According to Khâmini'î, the Commander of the Believers, 'Alî, had made it clear that to be engaged in a *jihâd* was a duty for all: 'Allâh Allâh, into the *jihâd* with your possessions, your life and your tongue'. Iran was now engaged in a holy *jihâd*, a holy and blessed war, a *jihâd* and *shahâda* (martyrdom) which, God willing, would bring blessings to the Iranians.[83] The three ways of conducting *jihâd* 'Alî had commanded, Khâmini'î said, could also be waged in this war. Firstly, the *jihâd bi jân* (the *jihâd* with one's life) for which people should be prepared as long as the *imâm* (referring to Khumaynî) did not forbid it. Although Khâmini'î did not explain what he meant by this kind of *jihâd*, it may be understood as partaking in the actual fight on the battlefield and possible sacrifice. The *jihâd bi zabân* (*jihâd* by the tongue), Khâmini'î continued, must be understood as propaganda, which was necessary since the Jewish world conspiracy was spreading lies about Iran. The Ministry of Foreign Affairs, all embassies, and everyone who was abroad should take part in this *jihâd* and propagate the truth about Iran. The third form, Khâmini'î explained, was the *jihâd bâ mâl* (by means of one's possessions) which on the one hand meant austerity, to be abstemious and to economize, and on the other hand to keep production in factories and working-places at a high level. This *jihâd* was necessary in order to lighten the burden of the war expenditure but also to make the Iranian population self-supporting. Iran did not want any foreign support and wanted to stay independent. But this could last only as long as the population took part in this *jihâd* financially:

> Verily the squanderers are the brothers of the devils and Satan is to his Lord unthankful.[84]

Rafsanjânî also distinguished between the *jihâd bâ mâl* and the *jihâd bâ nafs* (the *jihâd* by the soul), but on the basis of *al-Tawba* IX:44: '(Those who believe in Allah and the Last Day do not ask thee for admission that) they may strive with goods and person'. *Jihâd* with one's possessions was rewarded when it was through personal hardship such as the selling of his house by a poor labourer in order to contribute to the war effort. Rafsanjânî and other leaders gave several examples of real financial sacrifice, for instance of women who gave their dowries, or the story of a woman who sold her hair in order to be able to contribute to the *jihâd* financially, but also stories of old people who gave their savings and children who gave their allowances. .[85] Muntaẓirî spoke in the same vein when he said that the *jihâd* of the population of the provinces which were not in the war zone consisted of supporting the economy financially.[86] Rafsanjânî emphasized that the *jihâd bâ nafs* did not necessarily mean that a person should die; this kind of *jihâd* in essence meant exerting oneself physically or spiritually either through strength of body and mind or through (sacrificing) children, families or loved ones.[87] This interpretation of the *jihâd bâ nafs* differs from that of Khumaynî in his *Mubâriza bâ nafs yâ jihâd-i akbar*.[88] In this booklet, *jihâd bâ nafs* (here: *jihâd* against the soul) denotes the spiritual struggle which everyone has to fight with one's sinful inclinations, and which has to precede the *jihâd* with the sword. This form of *jihâd* is called *al-jihâd al-akbar*, the greater *jihâd*, after a saying of the Prophet.[89]

Khâmini'î said that the whole population, men and women, young and old, people with all sorts of occupations, were plunged into *jihâd* since *taqwâ-yi khudâ* (fear of God) required them to do.[90] Rafsanjânî recited *al-Nisâ'* IV:95: 'Those of the believers who sit still - other than those who have some injury - are not on a level with those who strive with goods and persons in the way of Allah, and Allah hath bestowed upon those who strive, in preference to those who sit still, a mighty hire'. Rafsanjânî interpreted the phrase in a broader sense than just those who actually fight or compensate for not fighting with financial aid. He extended the meaning to all people: men, women, children, sick and old people, they are all summoned to support the war in one way or the other, not only on the battlefield, but also behind the front lines.[91] In the Iranian newspapers in the second half of 1987 there appeared an advertisement of the Iranian national bank in which people were asked to participate in a financial *jihâd* (*jihâd-i mâlî*), by which was meant the payment of living expenses, such as food, clothes and transport, of a mobilized soldier for six months. In almost all speeches about the war, examples were given of people who contributed in an astonishing way to one of the forms of *jihâd*.

Another form of *jihâd* promoted by the Iranian government was the *jihâd-i sâzandigî*, the reconstruction *jihâd*. This was the name for an organization, founded in 1979 by a decree of Khumaynî, which consisted of non-clerical militants, mainly technicians and engineers who worked on a voluntary basis. The original purpose of this organization, which in 1982 was turned into a ministry, was the development of rural areas and villages. During the war the organization rebuilt war-damaged areas and coordinated the logistic side of the war, the building of bridges, roads and trenches.[92]

The bughât

The leaders considered the war a *jihâd* not only because it was a defence against the attack on Islam, Muslims and the Islamic Republic by non-Muslims, including Ṣaddâm Ḥusayn, but also because they classified Ṣaddâm Ḥusayn and the Ba'th regime as belonging to the category of the *bughât* (dissenters). Waging war against them was therefore justified on grounds that fighting the *bughât* falls into the category of *jihâd*. According to Shî'î law, a dissenter is someone who rises against one of the twelve legitimate *imâms* and does not accept his authority. He is regarded as an unbeliever, but according to Shî'î law his status is different, and his treatment therefore differs from that of the unbeliever. The rules of warfare are also different.[93] According to Sunnî Islam, too, a dissenter is someone who rejects the leader's authority. He is still regarded as a believer, but fighting him is necessary because he is a danger to the established order.[94] The war practice of 'Alî served as the basis for the Iranian leaders' view on the *bughât*. Imâmî Kâshânî, temporarily Friday prayer leader of Tehran, treated the subject of the *bughât* extensively. He defined the *bughât* as 'those who commit aggression against the *walî* (ruler) of Islam, the ruler of the Muslims and the Islamic community'. He said that although the Ba'th Party was not Islamic, it had to be treated in the same way as the *bughât* because the party had deceived Muslims and had set them up against Iran in order to bring down the system of the Islamic Republic.[95] On another occasion Imâmî Kâshânî recounted a tradition, on the authority of the tenth *imâm*, 'Alî al-Hâdî, from the *Wasâ'il al-shî'a*, one of the four modern shî'î tradition collections. According to this tradition, 'Alî had asked the Prophet who would rise against him after his death. Muḥammad answered that those who received the call for Islam but did not answer were the people who wanted to destroy Islam, and gave 'Alî permission to wage war against them. Imâmi Kâshânî concluded from this statement that the Ba'th Party had acted in the same way as the people mentioned by the Prophet. In order to revive Islam and *ḥaqq*, war against them was permitted.[96]

Khumaynî tried to counter criticism that the Islamic Republic was fighting against Muslims by equating the war with Iraq with the war 'Alî fought against his Muslim opponents. Khumaynî asked his audience: supposing Ṣaddâm is a Muslim, is he a better Muslim than the companions of the Prophet who fought against 'Alî in Nahrawân? 'The moment that the foundation of Islam as a religion depends on war with those who talk of Islam or are true Muslims, then Muslims must draw their swords and fight against them. They wanted [Ali's enemies] to turn Islam to the same things that existed during the Jâhilîya but under the cover of Islam. What was the responsibility of the Commander of the Believers at that time?... When we are in such a situation...it is necessary and an Islamic duty that we defend Islam... This war is not between Iran and Iraq, it is a war between Islam and *kufr*'.[97] On the occasion of 'Alî's birthday Khumaynî said that a Muslim who wants to annihilate the honour of Islam is worse than a non-Muslim and to fight him is more necessary than to fight those who are not Muslims.[98]

As Ḥamîdullâh has stated, Muslim states base their conduct in war with other Muslim states on *al-Ḥujurât* XLIX:9: 'If two parties of the believers fight, set things right between them, and if one of the two parties oppresses (*baghat*) the other, fight the one which is oppressive until it returns to the affair of Allah'.[99] This was also the case in the Islamic Republic. The notion of *bughât* took up a central position in the rhetoric of the leaders with regard to the Islamic countries in the region. The Iranian leaders emphasized, that on the basis of this verse, the Islamic countries in the region had a duty to help Iran.[100] Khumaynî constantly warned the leaders of Middle East countries that they angered God when they did not support Iran. Those who persisted in helping Ṣaddâm Ḥusayn had committed treason against Islam. Iran would therefore carry out against them the prescribed Islamic punishment.[101] Muntazirî said that the Qur'ân and the *Nahj al-balâgha* were very clear about the *jihâd* duty. The Islamic countries therefore had no excuse; they simply had neglected their duty (by not waging a *jihâd* against Iraq).[102]

Khâmini'î devoted a sermon to the question of the attitude of the Islamic countries. According to him, the Shaykh al-Azhar in Cairo had criticized Iran and Iraq for fighting in the sacred month of *muḥarram*, in which fighting is not allowed for Muslims.[103] According to Khâmini'î, fighting in *muḥarram* held a special significance, because this was the month of martyrdom and the month of victory of blood over the sword. He did not deny that *muḥarram* was a sacred month but according to him, fighting was allowed because Iran was defending itself, and this overrode the prohibition of killing. The Shaykh al-Azhar's only reason for condemning the fighting, Khâmini'î told his audience, was that he worked for the United States and Iraq, who regarded a cease-fire as being in the interest of their countries.[104] In their rhetoric, other leaders presented fighting in *muḥarram* as especially valuable and they did not hesitate to refer to Ḥusayn's example of fighting during the first days of *muḥarram*.

Khâmini'î asked the audience why the Sunnî muftîs had stayed silent when Ṣaddâm attacked Iran in the month *dhû-l-qa'da* which was also one of the sacred months.[105] Iran did not violate Islamic law by fighting in a sacred month because it acted in self-defence and had not started a war itself. Khâmini'î said that it was not the Islamic Republic which had neglected its religious duty but the Shaykh al-Azhar and other muftîs in the Sunnî world, by not declaring war on Ṣaddâm Ḥusayn despite the strict orders of the Qur'ân. To make this clear, he recited three Qur'ânic verses about the necessity of fighting the unbelievers: *al-Tawba*, IX:12: 'But if they violate their oaths after they have made a covenant and attack your religion, fight the leaders of unbelief'; *al-Baqara* II:217: 'dissension is more serious than killing',[106] and *al-Ḥujurât*, XLIX:9. Khâmini'î translated verse XLIX:9 with 'when one of them commits aggression (*tajâwuz*) and oppression (*ẓulm*) against the other'.[107] Thus, in refuting criticism that Iran did not obey Islamic rules, Khâmini'î made use of Qur'ânic verses which treated two different subjects: unbelievers and Muslim dissenters. Considering the Shî'î interpretation that a dissenter is equal to an unbeliever, it was understandable that Ṣaddâm could at the same time be called a dissenter and an unbeliever. Azodanloo mentions that Khumaynî on one occasion recited verse *al-Ḥujurât* XLIX:9, but that he omitted the first part about reconciliation ('if two parties of the believers fight, set things right between them') because this was out of the question for him.[108] Khâmini'î, however, recited the complete verse in his sermon. For Khâmini'î, just as for Khumaynî, reconciliation was not an option. But for him Iran's status as aggrieved party seems to have been so evident that he must have regarded the first phrase of this Qur'ân verse as irrelevant to this case.

The injunction Al-amr bi-l-ma'rûf wa-l-nahy 'an al-munkar

Sometimes the leaders tried to mobilize the population by urging them to observe the Qur'ânic injunction of *al-amr bi-l-ma'rûf wa-l-nahy 'an al-munkar* (commanding the good and forbidding the wrong). Interestingly, the aim of this principle is to correct other Muslims for wrongful behaviour.[109] This would imply that the Iranian leaders considered Ṣaddâm Ḥusayn still a Muslim. In his *Taḥrîr al-wasîla*, which appeared in 1964-5, Khumaynî did not explicitly connect *al-amr bi-l-ma'rûf wa-l-nahy 'an al-munkar* with *jihâd*, but he said that theologians, and in their footsteps the whole population, were not allowed to stay silent when tyranny and oppression reigned supreme but had to fight against these two aberrations.[110] Khumaynî repeated his view during the war and linked *al-amr bi-l-ma'rûf wa-l-nahy 'an al-munkar* to the fighting. According to him it was an Islamic duty (*taklîf-i shar'î*) to rise against *ẓulm* (oppression) and *jawr* (violence): 'We cannot accept Ṣaddâm and wait until the earth is filled with injustice and the Mahdi appears. We must act in accordance with Islam and the Qur'ân and fulfil the obligation of *al-amr bi-l-ma'rûf wa-l-nahy 'an al-munkar*. We must pave the way for the appearance of the Lord of the Age'.[111] Muntaẓirî stated that resistance and sacrifice were part of the principle of *al-amr bi-l-ma'rûf wa-l-nahy 'an al-munkar*.[112] According to Âyatullâh Ṣâni'î, State Prosecutor-general, article 31 of the Constitution, which is about *al-amr bi-l-ma'rûf wa-l-nahy 'an al-munkar*, had produced large numbers of volunteers for the battlefield.[113]

Most leaders, however, did not connect this principle with defence or fighting. They regarded it principally as a moral obligation to keep others in society on God's path, and Khâmini'î and Rafsanjanî linked the principle to *taqwâ*.[114] Yazdî said on the basis of *al-Ḥajj* XXII:41: ('Who, if We establish them in the land, will observe the Prayer, and pay the *zakât*, urge to what is reputable and restrain from what is disreputable'), that after the enemies were expelled and a government had been installed on the principle of *al-amr bi-l-ma'rûf wa-l-nahy 'an al-munkar*, the things God wanted would be realized in society and those things God did not want, would be kept far away from society.[115] According to Rabbânî Amlashî, this principle was as important a duty as the pilgrimage and fasting.[116]

Expansion of the Islamic idea

The war rhetoric was sometimes so vigorous that it clashed with the repeated statement that Iran was involved in this war to defend the Islamic revolution. During the war there were several remarks which went much further than mere statements on defence: 'Iraq is the gate to the *futûḥât* (worldwide conquests) of Islam',[117] and 'Our struggle with the superpowers and the branches of colonialism and arrogance will continue until the region is subjected to our vision'.[118] Similarly: 'The militant nation of Muslims noticed that it had to hasten to help the oppressed Muslims of Iraq, i.e. the kind of war of the first situation, the situation of defence of the Islamic Republic, has changed into the second situation, i.e. *mujâhada* (exertion) and *kûshish* (effort) for the protection of the oppressed of Iraq and exertion for the expansion of the Islamic idea. Today, we defend the honour of Islam and Iran and we have the power to work for the collapse of the palace of a puppet who has made millions of people in Iraq his prisoners and slaves. Therefore, this is a *jihâd* in God's cause, a divine war like the *ghazawât* of the messenger of Islam'.[119] Equally not defensive was the statement: 'that time [when Ṣaddâm is deposed] the difficult road of the Islamic conquests becomes easy. The rulers of the world realize this and that is why the unhappy king of Jordan says, "When Ṣaddâm goes, we go too!" He was right in saying this'.[120] In 1988, in his speech on 22 *bahman*, Revolution Day, Khâmini'î said that the holy defence would continue until the dominance of the Islamic system was established.[121] These statements are remarkable since, according to Shî'î Islam, the offensive *jihâd* is in abeyance until the return of the twelfth *imâm*. Furthermore, these statements explicitly refer to armed struggle and therefore were contrary to statements that the Islamic Republic intended to export its ideas by peaceful means. However, these 'aggressive' remarks probably should not be taken literally; they were much more symbolic than realistic and were clearly meant to arouse militant feelings and to mobilize the Iranian population for the war. In the first year Iran was mainly engaged in counterattacks on its own soil and when the Republic launched its first offensive outside Iran in July 1982, the leaders justified this operation as being part of the defence.[122]

War and shahâda

A central place in the rhetoric was reserved for the exaltation of *shahâda* (in this context: martyrdom) in a *jihâd* for the cause of God. The leaders sacralized the war by arguing that death for the cause of Islam was the most noble form of observance to Islam anyone could attain. In the speeches, the function of martyrdom was understood as sacrificing oneself for the cause of Islam and the Islamic country.[123] At the same time this side of things was overshadowed by statements to the effect that martyrdom was the expression of an individual ambition to receive God's reward in the Hereafter. Leaders repeated that martyrdom for the cause of God was the best way to gain *thawâb* (recompense by God given after a pious deed).[124]

The primary meaning of *shahîd/shuhadâ'* is 'witness' and in this meaning the term occurs in the Qur'ân.[125] In Islamic law *shahâda* (testimony) is a statement in court 'based on observation, introduced by the words *ashhadu* ("I testify"), concerning the right of others'.[126] The prevailing Western conception of the subject of martyrdom is that the word *shahîd/shuhadâ'* in the sense of martyrdom was post-Qur'ânic. This contrasts with the view of Muslim scholars, who maintain that the

Qur'ân does refer to martyrs, notably in III:140, IV:69, XXXIX:69 and LVII:19.[127] It is no coincidence that in their war rhetoric the Iranian leaders used the notion of *shahâda* only in the second meaning of martyr. They did not hesitate to cite Qur'ânic verses in connection with martyrdom. 'Say: "Do ye wait for anything in our case but one of the two good?"' (*al-Tawba* IX:52) was cited frequently in this context and leaders explained the meaning of the verse as indicating that Iranians could expect certain victory, either a worldly victory in this war, or an even more honourable victory in the Hereafter by becoming a martyr and receiving God's reward.[128] On one occasion, Muntaẓirî said that the meaning of this verse was that martyrs would become the people of Paradise regardless of whether they killed or were killed.[129] According to Muslim law, martyrdom is reserved for Muslims; the tributary who fights in the Muslim army and is killed does not receive the privileges and prerogatives connected with martyrdom.[130] Rafsanjânî, however, referred in one of his sermons to the large number of Armenians who had been martyred, using the Islamic terminology (see chapter 5).[131]

There is a large body of traditions dealing with martyrdom and many of these were cited in the speeches, notably in the sermons. Many traditions were cited in which God's reward for the martyr was highlighted, for instance the promise of Paradise, forgiveness of smaller and greater sins, the fact that the soul of a martyr is among the souls of the friends of God, the prophets and the martyrs of the dawn of Islam.[132] Nâṭiq Nûrî, the Speaker of the Majlis, cited a few traditions of the Prophet, according to which he had said that the martyr on his arrival in Paradise would sit at the table of Muḥammad and Abraham; that he would live among the angels and that God would keep the *mujâhid* away from Hell. The Prophet furthermore had assured the parents of martyrs that an arrow causing death is more delicious than water in a hot summer.[133] According to another tradition, the martyr in the Hereafter wishes to be born anew in order to become a martyr, not only for a second time but for a third and a fourth time, because the merit (*thawâb*) of martyrdom is so sublime and exalted.[134] Khumaynî referred to a tradition of the Prophet listed in the *Kâfî*, one of the authoritative Shî'î *ḥadîth* collections. According to this tradition, the most important characteristic of a martyr was that he would see God (*ru'yat allâh*) but within the limits of his being. Khumaynî concluded that martyrdom for the cause of God was thus the ultimate perfection a human being could attain.[135]

Leaders reiterated that martyrdom was the surest way to Paradise, to receive God's mercy and the assurance of God's contentment.[136] This tallies with Kohlberg's observation: 'Battlefield martyrdom has captured the imagination of Muslims throughout the ages. A martyr's death in combat is the apogee of the believer's aspirations; it is the noblest way to depart this life and is a guarantee of God's approval and reward'.[137] Throughout the war the benefits of martyrdom were spelt out, especially the fact that martyrdom would lead to eternal life.[138] Khumaynî frequently referred to *al-Baqara* II:157: 'Who when misfortune falls upon them say: "Verily we are Allah's, and to Him do we return', and *Âl 'Imrân* III:169 '... alive with their Lord, provided for', explaining that this world is the lowest form of all worlds and only temporal; everything in this world is transient, in contrast with life after death where martyrs and have God's mercy, and fear or sorrow therefore is not necessary and even out of place.[139] Rafsanjânî asked his audience what better future parents could wish for their children than a fortunate eternal life, a life beside the Messenger of God, where they would guard the actions of Iranians.[140] The martyr would live among all former martyrs of Islam, the martyrs of Karbalâ' and the great saints.[141] He would be God's guest.[142] Khâmini'î gave the Iranian martyrs a place in history: the reason for the victories of Abraham, Moses, all other prophets, of the Prophet of Islam and of the Islamic revolution was that the servants of God were willing to sacrifice themselves for God's cause.[143] Khâmini'î referred to a story connected with the battle of Uḥud according to which a mother did not weep on hearing the news of the death of her son but said that she was happy. The same happens in this war, Khâmini'î said; mothers want to be congratulated instead of receiving condolences.[144] Martyrdom was presented as a blessing for the martyr but also for his family or his neighbourhood. The blood of a martyr would compensate for hardship and be an example for future generations in the form of enthusiasm, inspiration, guidance, and pride.[145] Rafsanjânî stated that war was bitter for Iranians, especially one with a country which was 95 per cent Muslim. But the fact that Iran was engaged in a *jihâd* which brought martyrdom and a place in Paradise meant that this bitterness could be endured. He cited from *al-Nisâ'* 4:19: '... it is possible that ye may dislike a thing in which Allah hath set much good'.[146] In doing so, Rafsanjânî used a verse which is commonly regarded as treating marriage conditions.[147] Khâmini'î referred to a story about a martyr from Muḥammad's time who was washed by angels. This is interesting, because there is agreement among Islamic jurists that the martyr's body should not as a rule be washed.[148] Khumaynî ruled in a *fatwâ* (legal opinion) that it was not an obligation to wash the body of a martyr on the battlefield or wrap it in a shroud, but this applied to other categories of martyrs.[149] *Iṭṭilâ'ât* showed pictures of mobilized men who allegedly shouted that they lived only to die and become martyrs, that they already wore their shrouds and that they washed themselves with their own honourable blood.[150]

In the war rhetoric, *shahâda ṭalabî* (the yearning for martyrdom) was a recurrent theme. Stories were circulated about people from all strata of the population who sought martyrdom. A very revealing connection between the death of Iranian soldiers and Ḥusayn's death at Karbalâ' was made through accounts of those whose heads had been cut off or even stories about potential martyrs who wished that their heads would be cut off from their bodies as had happened with Ḥusayn at Karbalâ'. One account in an Iranian newspaper eight years after the end of the war, gives a good picture of the *shahâda ṭalabî*. According to this story, a boy had wished that his head would be cut off on his death. As he had hoped, this happened. Then, when his family came to bury him, they noticed that the grave which he had dug himself before he went to the front, was only long enough for the body without the head.[151]

Occasionally love or yearning for death in itself was exalted.[152] This raises the question whether the Iranian leaders, with all the stress they laid on *shahâda ṭalabî*, were not urging people simply to kill themselves, which would be strange when one considers the fact that suicide is prohibited by Islam. Khosrokhavar has mentioned that a new kind of martyr had appeared a few years after the beginning of the war, the 'martyropaths', young men who did not sacrifice themselves for a cause but participated in suicidal attacks because they were fascinated by death itself. However, these martyrs formed only a minority of those who volunteered to fight.[153] The existence of a large body of testaments of martyrs, although without question stimulated by the government, made it plain that most martyrs had sacrificed themselves for the cause of Islam, the revolution, Iran or for individual reward in heaven.[154] Furthermore, most of the time leaders were careful to emphasize that martyrdom was not an aim in itself but that its intention, dying in the cause of Islam, the revolution, the nation and the country was what mattered.[155] As they did with the criteria for a defensive *jihâd*, the Iranian leaders enlarged in their war rhetoric the criteria for martyrdom:[156] besides the traditional criteria of dying in a *jihâd fî sabîl Allâh* (for the cause of God), one could now become a martyr in the cause of national aims.

Besides the battlefield martyrs, the Iranian leaders recognized two other categories of martyrs, who had not sacrificed themselves voluntarily but had attained martyrdom accidentally. To the first category belonged the Iranians who had been killed as a result of Iraqi bombardments and missile attacks but also those people who were on the plane which was shot down by the USS *Vincennes* in 1988.[157] In the second category were, surprisingly enough, Iraqi Muslims who were killed as a result of Iranian attacks. Rafsanjânî said that the Iraqi people were martyrs on the basis of the precedent of martyred Muslims at the time of the Prophet. There was a similarity between the Ba'th regime and the way it used the Muslim population of Iraq, and the unbelievers at the time of the Prophet who used Muslims as their shield in one of the wars against the Prophet. According to Rafsanjânî, the Prophet had allowed the killing of these Muslims when this would contribute to the triumph of the Muslim army.[158] Khumaynî emphasized the fact that the killing of a believer was one of the greatest sins, probably the greatest after polytheism. But he assured the Iranians that when believers and Muslims are used as human shields by unbelievers, then, according to Islamic law, consideration of these Muslims is out of the question;

rather, it is a duty to kill them. No duty was more important than the protection of Islam and its boundaries.[159]

The Iranian leaders distinguished between the battlefield martyrs and the two other categories of martyrs. The exaltation of martyrdom and the bliss awaiting martyrs, was solely for the martyrs of the battlefield. Its function must therefore be regarded as a major instrument for the mobilization of soldiers. The second category of martyrs, those who had been killed as a result of the war but had not actively sought death, was used not only to incite feelings of revenge and motivate the population for continuation of the war but also to console the population.[160]

War and fitna

Throughout the war, prayer leaders justified their warfare by representing the war as *fitna*. The phrase '*wa qâtilûhum ḥattâ lâ takûna fitna*' (fight them until there is no dissension [and the religion is entirely Allah's]), as used in *al-Baqara* II:193 and *al-Anfâl* VIII:39, was used as a slogan for the yearly war remembrance week. *Fitna* in the Qur'ân has different meanings: it can mean an ordeal by God; it can denote a danger to the stability of the Muslim community and religion brought about deliberately by unbelievers, or a temptation caused by possessions or children.[161] Post-Qur'ânic meanings of *fitna* are 'disturbance', 'revolt' or 'civil war' which could bring about schism in the Muslim community as had happened after the murder of 'Uthmân and the accession of 'Alî. The battle of Ṣiffîn, the Khawârij and Shî'î schisms were *fitna* par excellence.[162] After the era of the four rightly guided caliphs *fitna* came to be understood as insurrection, communal strife or domestic conflict.[163]

The way *fitna* was used in the war rhetoric, not only at the beginning but during the whole war, suggests that prayer leaders interpreted this notion in the Qur'ânic meaning of chaos brought about deliberately by unbelievers, and not in the post-Qur'ânic meaning of revolt, civil war or domestic conflict.[164] Khâmini'î said that with respect to *fitna*, God had made clear in *al-Anfâl* VIII:39 what the duty of the Iranians was: Fighting until *fitna*, which had been caused by colonialism and arrogance, was eradicated from the entire world. Iran's struggle would continue until this goal was achieved.[165] 'What is *fitna*'? Khâmini'î asked his audience on the occasion of war remembrance week. The *fitna* concerning the Islamic Republic at that moment, he said, was chaos and insecurity, a *fitna* which prevented the Iranian community and nation from living according to their own needs and wishes. In this case, Khâmini'î said, the Qur'ân justified waging war in order to obtain a longlasting peace: *al-Anfâl* VIII:39 and *al-Baqara* II:191 '... dissension is worse than killing..'., one may die or kill in order to eliminate dissension.[166] Khumaynî made a comparison between the Iranian nation, which, thanks to God's mercy, was harmonious and united in its will to defend, and those who caused *fitna* and were warmongers.[167] He asked his audience what *fitna* could be greater than the *fitna* caused by the enemies of Islam in order to destroy the foundation of Islam and to install governments of oppressors.[168] Muntaẓirî referred to *fitna* when he spoke about an Iraqi missile attack which killed several Iranian people. According to him, the brave nation and zealous youth were eager to end this *fitna* and the war caused by Ṣaddâm Ḥusayn.[169] Muntaẓirî justified Iran's invasion of Iraq with the words that Iran was not interested in Iraqi territory but wanted to eliminate *fitna* and the aggression of the bloodthirsty regime and the warmonger Ṣaddâm.[170] In the third year of the war, Rafsanjânî said that Iran fought in order to suppress *fitna* as the Qur'ân has prescribed in *al-Baqara* II:196 and *al-Anfâl* VIII:39: 'fight them until there is no dissension'. But whereas in the first year Khâmini'î had said that Iran's fight would continue until *fitna* was eradicated, Rafsanjânî was more realistic and concrete, saying that Iran took on this duty in only a limited sense, that is, to remove the *fitna* caused by Ṣaddâm Ḥusayn and the Ba'th party.[171] In a speech for the armed forces and civil servants, published the same day in *Iṭṭilâ'ât*, Khumaynî also spoke about *fitna* in this restricted sense. The goal was the removal of the Iraqi regime and 'war, war, until victory'.[172]

The war as God's ordeal

An extra dimension to the sacralization of the war was given by the Iranian leaders with statements which stressed God's role in the war. Throughout the speeches, God's omnipotence was stressed with regard to the war and the war was presented as God's ordeal to test the firmness of belief and moral behaviour of the Iranians.[173] For this aspect they did not use the term *fitna*, but used other terms, such as *imtiḥân* (ordeal), *azmâyish* (experiment) and *tajriba* (test). With this war God tested the belief and moral attitude of the Iranians.[174] The war was not just waged by worldly tyrants and devils but was also ordered by God as an *imtiḥân* (ordeal) and *tajriba* (test) for Muslims.[175] Before the revolution, the ordeal had been manifested in the oppression of the Pahlavi regime. But the greatest ordeal of all was the war that had been imposed on Iran because of the revolution.[176] Until now, the greatest part of the nation had passed the test by showing *rû-sifîdî* (righteousness). From the young men at the front who had given their lives to the disabled who gave their pensions, all people had shown righteousness.[177] This meant that they acted in the right way, i.e. by fighting for *ḥaqq* and supporting the war effort in one way or an other. According to Khâmini'î, the battlefield was a place where people were educated in religious affairs.[178] According to Muntaẓirî, the Qur'ân and the traditions of the Prophet and *imâm*s show that God tests all people, the reason for this being that without this *imtiḥân* people could not be distinguished from each other, such as the believer from the unbeliever.[179] On another occasion Muntaẓirî made a reference to *Muḥammad* XLVII:7 and said: 'We must strive to carry out our duties in order to bear these *imtiḥânât* (tests) with heads high. It is God's promise that he will help those who help him'.[180] But the nation was also tested for *waḥda* (unity) and *ittiḥâd* (unison). This test could be passed by showing *taqwâ-yi khudâ* (piety towards God) in order to guard and preserve the line of the revolution instead of destroying it with selfish motives. *Waḥda* would lead to victory.[181] The Iranians had to work on their duties in order to pass these tests. According to Khumaynî, victory in the war ultimately depended on the creator's *faḍl* (favour) and *luṭf* (benevolence).[182] The use of *luṭf* is striking with regard to the idea that Iranians had to strive to obtain victory, since in Shî'î doctrine this notion refers to something which God will undoubtedly do.[183]

Many statements on God's role in this war were to the effect that the war was preordained by God but that God left the people with a choice to obey or disobey him. The war with Iraq was the most recent in a series of conflicts between *ḥaqq* and *bâṭil* throughout history, which had already been described in the Qur'ân. The war belonged to the catastrophes to which God subjected the world with certain intentions.[184] God had even induced Ṣaddâm Ḥusayn to wage war.[185] In order that the world should not be conquered by falsehood and corruption (*fasâd*), God had chosen some people (*ahl-i ḥaqq*) to defend *ḥaqq* (truth).[186] He made Muslims his standard-bearers and ordered them to fight and shed their blood in His cause.[187]

In spite of God's omnipotence, Iranians were responsible for the outcome of the war themselves.[188] The war was a test and God would help the Iranians only if they helped Him[189] and showed themselves worthy of His favour. Iranians had to keep their promise to God, in the sense that they had to obey the command of God, to serve God only, to trust God, to stay united and not to be tempted by worldly, transient affairs. Otherwise God's blessing (*ni'ma*) would disappear and this would become clear for the Iranians, not through a defeat but at the Day of Resurrection.[190] This promise to God included the protection of Islam, Islamic country and the honour of Islam.[191] In return for the help of the Iranians, God would not allow the Islamic Republic to disappear,[192] and he would render them victorious in this war.[193] Khumaynî stated after the liberation of Khurramshahr that people should remember that victory was in God's hands alone and that taking selfish pride in the liberation of Khurramshahr was a dangerous act and of the same order as being seduced by Satan.[194] God's role was also highlighted by Iranian leaders when they stressed that the war was a blessing, that war was beneficial (*mufîd*) and constructive (*sâzanda*) for people,[195] and that Iranians were grateful to God,[196] and made themselves dependent on Him.[197] God, in fact, had already turned the war into *baraka* (benediction) and a *ni'ma* (blessing) for Iranians in the sense that Iranian society was being reconstructed by the war and had become united, harmonious, and sincere.[198] Furthermore, 'this war has spread the *'aẓama* (exaltedness) and *shukûh* (sublimity) of *îmân* and Islam in the world'.[199]

Stressing the character of the war as an ordeal by an omnipotent God had several reasons. Firstly, it was a response to criticism of the war from certain sections of Iranian society. Iranian leaders wanted to influence the people who might be affected by negative talk about the war and by disappointing results on the battlefield. Khâmini'î assured his listeners that these critics had failed God's test and therefore were not true believers. They endangered the revolution just as much as the United States by disrupting the war effort behind the front lines.[200] Secondly, by emphasizing the fact that God would surely turn this war into a victory for the Islamic Republic if the Iranians were worthy of His blessing, leaders tried to give moral support to those who were afflicted by the war or who were still in doubt about whether the war was justified. Thirdly, they used it to strengthen national unity; by stating that the war was a test which would bring *ni'ma* and *baraka* for the Islamic Republic because 'Iranian society had become united, harmonious and sincere', it was implied that the war had ended the longstanding conflicts between the regime and the ethnic minorities about autonomy; that the minorities had dropped their demands and were now united with the entire nation against Iraq. Rafsanjânî also emphasized the unifying effect of the war (see Chapter 5), saying that even the revolution had not managed to bring unity and that in this respect the war stood above the revolution. This is surprising because the revolution was cherished as almost sacrosanct because of all the benefits it was supposed to have brought to Iran.[201] According to Menashri, the ethnic minorities in Iran comprise almost half of the population and their demand for autonomy constituted a threat to internal stability during the war,[202] something which made the emphasis on the unifying effect of the war understandable.

We have seen in this chapter that the Iranian leaders, immediately after the Iraqi invasion in September 1980, sacralized the war by declaring that Iran was engaged in a *jihâd* because Iraq had initiated not a territorial dispute but chaos (*fitna*) and war in order to destroy Islam, the Islamic revolution and Islamic nation. The whole population had to participate in the *jihâd* in one way or another. The exaltation of martyrdom for the cause of Islam, too, was part of the sacralization but its religious dimension was the expression of an individual ambition to receive God's reward.

Notes

1. Majid Khadduri, 'Harb - The Legal Aspect', in: *Encyclopaedia of Islam*[2] Vol.3 p. 180.

2. Khumaynî, *Ṣaḥîfa-yi nûr. Majmû'a-yi rahnamûdhâ-yi ḥaḍrat-i imâm Khumaynî* (Tehran: Ministry of Culture and Islamic Guidancem 1370/1991) 27/7/59 pp. 570-571.

3. This is also stated by Rafsanjânî in one of his Friday sermons, *Dar maktab-i jum'a* Vol.3, 6/6/60 p. 371.

4. Albrecht Noth, *Heiliger Krieg und heiliger Kampf in Islam und Christentum. Beiträge zur Vorgeschichte und Geschichte der Kreuzzüge* (Bonn: Rörscheid, 1966) pp. 14-15.

5. Noth, *Heiliger Krieg und heiliger Kampf* p. 22. See also: Alfred Morabia, *Le Ğihad dans l'Islam médiéval. Le 'combat sacré' des origines au XIIe siècle* (Paris: Albin Michel, 1993), p. 119.

6. Rudolph Peters, *Islam and Colonialism. The Doctrine of Jihad in Modern History* (The Hague: Mouton, 1979) p. 4

7. Peters, *Islam and Colonialism* pp. 15, 122.

8. Peters, *Islam and Colonialism*, pp. 36-37.

9. Khadduri, 'Ḥarb - The Legal Aspect', p. 180.

10. Muḥammad Ḥamîdullâh, *The Muslim Conduct of State* (Lahore: Muhammad Ashraf, 1953³) p. 164.

11. Ḥamîdullâh, *The Muslim Conduct of State* p. 165.

12. Majid Khadduri, *War and Peace in the Law of Islam* (Baltimore: Johns Hopkins University Press, 1955) pp. 96-98. Etan Kohlberg, 'The Development of the Imâmî Shî'i Doctrine of Jihâd', in: *Zeitschrift der Deutschen Morgenländischen Gesellschaft* 126 (1976) p. 85.

13. Ḥamîdullâh, *The Muslim Conduct of State* p. 175.

14. For instance, during the wars between the Ottoman Empire and Persia when Ottoman *'ulamâ'* declared the Persians to be apostates and rebels in order to justify *jihâd* against them. Hilmar Krüger, *Fetwa und Siyar* (Wiesbaden: Harrassowitz, 1978) pp. 131-134.

15. Joel L. Kraemer, 'Apostates, Rebels and Brigands', in: *Israel Oriental Studies* 10 (1980) pp. 34-73, p. 48.

16. Kohlberg, Etan, 'The Development of the Imâmî Shî'i Doctrine of *Jihâd*', in: *Zeitschrift der Deutschen Morgenländischen Gesellschaft* 126 (1976) pp. 64-86, pp. 77-78.

17. For instance Abû Ja'far al-Ṭûsî, *al-Nihâya fî mujarrad al-faqîh wa-l-fatâwî* (Tehran: Maktabat al-Asad, 1387) Vol.1 p. 199; al-Ḥillî, *al-Mukhtaṣar al-nafî fî fiqh al-imâmîya* (Tehran: Maktabat al-Asad, 1387-1967) p. 139.

18. Peters, *Islam and colonialism* p. 10.

19. Al-Kulaynî, *al-Uṣûl min al-kâfî*, Vol.2 (Beirut: Dâr al-ta'arruf, 1401), p. 51.

20. Al-Mufîd, al-Shaykh, *Awâ'il al-maqâlât fî l-madhâhib al-mukhtârât* (Tabriz, 1371/1952) p. 98.

21. Martin J. McDermott, *The Theology of al-Shaikh al-Mufîd* (Beirut: Dar el-Machreq Éditeurs, 1978) p. 316; Said Amir Arjomand, *The Shadow of God and the Hidden Imam. Religion, Political Order, and Societal Change in Shi'ite Iran from the Beginning to 1890* (Chicago: University of Chicago Press, 1984) p. 175.

22. Kohlberg, 'Development', p. 78.

23. Kohlberg, 'Development', p. 80. According to Lambton, however, because of the Sunnî majority, it was perhaps not fortuitous that there was a tendency among the Shî'a at this period to transfer *jihâd* to the spiritual plane and for it to lapse in the temporal sphere', A.K.S. Lambton, 'A Nineteenth Century View of Jihâd' in: *Studia Islamica* 32 (1970) pp. 181-192, p. 182.

24. Kohlberg, 'Development', p. 80; Lambton, 'Nineteenth', pp. 182-183.

25. Lambton, 'Nineteenth' p. 184; Kohlberg, 'Development', p. 81.

26. Arjomand, *The Shadow of God* p. 175.

27. Kohlberg, 'Development', p. 84; Lambton, 'Nineteenth', p. 187.

28. Khumaynî, as cited in *Jang wa jihâd*, p. 4-5. According to Farhang Rajaee, *Islamic Values and World View. Khomeyni on Man, the State and International Politics* (Lanham, MD: University Press of America, 1983) p. 89, Khumaynî distinguished between *jihâd* which is offensive and *difâ'*.

29. Khumaynî, *Iṭṭilâ'ât*, 10/5/66.

30. Khumaynî, *Iṭṭilâ'ât* 23/11/59.

31. Khâmini'î, *Dar maktab-i jum'a* Vol.2/8/59 p. 356; 16/8/59 p. 377.

32. Khumaynî, *Iṭṭilâ'ât*, 5/9/60-27/11/81.

33. For instance Khâmini'î in the first Tehran Friday sermon after the war had started, *Dar maktab-i jum'a* Vol.2 4/7/59 p. 319. Khumaynî, *Jang wa jihâd* p. 11; *Ṣaḥîfa-yi nûr* 27/7/59 pp. 570-571.

34. Khâmini'î, *Dar maktab-i jum'a*, Vol.6 10/4/62 p. 398; Rafsanjânî, Vol.7 13/8/62 p. 215;. Two weeks before the acceptation of Resolution 598, Rafsanjânî said that Iran was engaged in a *jihâd*, *Iṭṭilâ'ât*, 18/4/67-9/7/88 .

35. Khumaynî, *Jang wa jihâd* p. 11.

36. Banî Ṣadr, *Iṭṭilâ'ât*, 28/8/59, spoke about a *jang-i muqaddas* (holy war) since the war was about Islam and freedom for humanity.

37. Khumaynî, *Iṭṭilâ'ât*, 23/11/59-12/2/81, 5/9/60-27/11/81.
Calling a war 'holy' is an innovation and does not occur in classical Islamic texts. Bernard Lewis, *The Political Language of Islam* (Chicago: University of Chicago Press, 1988) p. 72.

38. As we shall see, Ṣaddâm Ḥusayn was also classified as a *bâghy*.

39. Muntaẓirî, *Jang-i taḥmîlî dar bayânât-i âyatullâh al-'uẓmâ Muntaẓirî* (Tehran: Ministry of Islamic Guidance, 1367/1988) 29/10/63 p. 63.

40. Khumaynî, *Jang wa jihâd* p. 11.

41. Khâmini'î, *Dar maktab-i jum'a*, Vol.2/8/59 pp. 355-356.

42. Khâmini'î, *Dar maktab-i jum'a* Vol.2 16/8/59 p. 376.

43. Khumaynî, *Iṭṭilâ'ât*, 10/5/66.

44. *Jang-i taḥmîlî. Difâ' dar barâbar-i tajâwuz. The Imposed War. Defence versus Aggression. Al Ḥarb al-mafrûdâ. al-Difâ' amâma 'l-'udwân* (Tehran: Supreme Defence Council, 1365/1986) Vol.4 p. 5.

45. Khâmini'î, *Dar maktab-i jum'a* Vol.3 29/12/59 p. 141.

46. Khâmini'î, *Dar maktab-i jum'a* Vol.2 4/7/59 p. 322.

47. Khumaynî, *Iṭṭilâ'ât*, 10/5/66.

48. Prime Minister Muḥammad 'Alî Rajâ'î, *Iṭṭilâ'ât*, 5/8/59.

49. Khâmini'î, *Dar maktab-i jum'a* Vol.3 12/10/59 p. 50 and Mûsawî Ardabîlî, 27/6/60 p. 413. 'I hope that God supplies our nation with this insight, understanding and effort until we respond with 'at your service' to the heavenly call'.

50. Khumaynî, *Iṭṭilâ'ât*, 5/2/62.

51. Khumaynî, *Iṭṭilâ'ât*, 10/5/66.

52. Khumaynî, *Jang wa jihâd* 8/6/61 p. 13; *Kayhân* 19/10/61.

53. Khumaynî, *Iṭṭilâ'ât*, 15/10/63.

54. For instance in *Dar maktab-i jum'a* Vol.3: Khâmini'î, 10/11/59 p. 83: *al-Tawba* IX:39: 'If ye do not march out He will inflict upon you a painful punishment, and will substitute (for you) another people'; Mûsawî Ardabîlî, 27/6/60 p. 411: *al-Tawba* IX:12-15: 'But if they violate their oaths after they have made a covenant and attack your religion, fight the leaders of unbelief; no oath will hold in their case; mayhap they will refrain. Will ye not fight against a people who have violated their oaths, and had it in mind to expel the messenger, and who took the initiative with you the first time? Are ye afraid of them? It is more in order that ye should be afraid of Allah, if ye be believers. Fight them and Allah will punish them at your hands, will humiliate breasts of a people who are believers, and will take away the anger of their hearts; Allah relenth towards whomsoever He willeth; Allah is knowing, wise'; *al-Tawba* IX:73: 'O thou prophet, strive with the unbelievers and the Hypocrites, and be rough with them; their resort is Gehenna -a bad destination'. He also recited *al-Ṣaff* LXI:4: 'Verily Allah loveth those who fight in His way drawn up in ranks, like a building well-compacted', and *Muḥammad* XLVII: 4-6 'So when ye meet those who have disbelieved (let there be) slaughter until when ye have made havoc of them, bind (them) fast; then either freely or by ransom; until war lays down its burdens. That (is the rule); had Allah so willed, He would have vindicated Himself upon them, but (this is) in order that He may try you one by the other; those who fight in the way of Allah - He will not send their works astray. He will guide them and make good their state'.

55. Khâmini'î, *Dar maktab-i jum'a* Vol.2 4/7/59 p. 318.

56. For instance Khumaynî, *Iṭṭilâ'ât*, 3/7/65; Rafsanjânî, *Dar maktab-i jum'a* Vol.3 6/6/60 p. 374.

57. Khâmini'î, *Dar maktab-i jum'a* Vol.3 29/12/59 p. 137.

58. Khâmini'î, *Dar maktab-i jum'a* Vol.2 27 4/7/59 p. 319, *Nahj al-balâgha* sermon 27 and sermon 51. Imâmî Kâshânî, *Dar maktab-i jum'a* Vol.4 10/2/61 p. 389.

59. Rafsanjânî, *Dar maktab-i jum'a* Vol.3 6/6/60 pp. 371-3.

60. Khumaynî, *Jang wa jihâd* 28/9/61 p. 269.

61. Khâmini'î, *Iṭṭilâ'ât*, 4/7/66.

62. *Farhang-i jabha (tablû-yi niwishtihâ*, ed. by Sayyid Mihdî Fahîmî (Tehran: Intishârât-i ḥawza-yi hunarî-yi sâzimân-i tablîghât-i islâmî, 1369/1990) p. 25.

63. Ibrâhîm Amînî, speech before sermon *Iṭṭilâ'ât* 23/6/64. According to Morabia, in contrast with Sunnî theologians, Shî'î theologians did not hesitate to place *jihâd* under *'ibâda*. *Le Ǧihad dans l'Islam médiéval* p. 473, n. 605.

64. Âyatullâh Ḥusayn Nûrî, member of the Assembly of Experts, in speech before sermon, *Iṭṭilâ'ât*, 19/2/66; Sepehr Zabih, *The Iranian Military in Revolution and War* (London: Routledge, 1988) p. 142.

65. Ḥujjatulislam Ḥasan Rûḥânî, chairman of the Defence Commission of the Majlis, in speech before sermon, *Iṭṭilâ'ât*, 26/7/65.

66. Mûsawî Ardabîlî, *Dar maktab-i jum'a* Vol.3 27/6/60 p. 413. This is Ardabîlî's explanation of sermon 42 of the *Nahj al-balâgha*, not the exact citation.

67. Khâmini'î, *Dar maktab-i jum'a* Vol.2 23/8/59 p. 390, *al-Nisâ'*:95, *Nahj al-balagha* sermon 27.

68. Khumaynî, *Jang wa jihâd*, introduction.

69. Kohlberg, 'Development', p. 84; Hans Kruse, *Islamische Völkerrechtslehre* (Bochum: Brockmeyer, 1979[2]) p. 50; Peters, *Islam and Colonialism*, p. 15.

70. Khumaynî, *Jang wa jihâd* 9/6/61 pp. 222-3; 11/11/61 p. 225. Mûsawî Ardabîlî, *Dar maktab-i jum'a* Vol.5 14/8/61 p. 338.

71. Kruse, *Islamische Völkerrechtslehre* p. 51.

72. Khâmini'î, *Iṭṭilâ'ât*, 5/9/63.

73. Rafsanjânî, BBC *Summary of World Broadcasts*, 14 June 1988.

74. *Jumhûrî-yi islâmî*, 26/10/66.

75. A.J. Wensinck, 'Talbiya', in: *Encyclopaedia of Islam*[1] Vol.8 p. 640.

76. Khumaynî, *Iṭṭilâ'ât*, 12/12/64.

77. Khâmini'î, *Dar maktab-i jum'a* Vol.2 25/7/59 p. 353.

78. The other conditions are: *al-bulûgh* (maturity); *'aql* (reason); *al-ḥurriya* (freedom); not being *himm* (old), or *muq'ad* (disabled), or *a'mâ* (blind), or *marîḍ* (ill); al-Ḥillî, *al-Mukhtaṣar al-nâfi' fî fiqh al-imâmîya* p. 133. Al-Ṭûsî gave the same categories in his *al-Nihâya fî mujarrad al-faqîh wa-l-fatâwî* Vol.1 p. 192.

79. Other reasons were that the constitution of women did not allow them to fight; harm could be done to their intimate parts; they were not allowed to take initiatives themselves because they were subservient to their husbands; the Prophet had told his wives that the pilgrimage was their *jihâd*. Morabia, *Le Ǧihad dans l'Islam médiéval*, 218.

80. Kohlberg, 'Development', p. 84; Kruse, *Islamische Völkerrechtslehre* p. 50;Peters, *Islam and Colonialism*, p. 15.

81. Peters, *Islam and Colonialism* p. 10. See pp. 118-121 for modern interpretations.

82. Kohlberg, 'Development', p. 84.

83. Citation from the *Nahj al-balâgha* sermon 47, Khâmini'î, *Dar maktab-i jum'a* Vol.2 4/7/59 p. 319.

84. Khâmini'î, *Dar maktab-i jum'a*, Vol.2 4/7/59 p. 322: *al-Isrâ'* XVII:171.

85. Rafsanjânî, *Dar maktab-i jum'a* Vol.3 6/6/60 p. 373-374; Khâmini'î, 25/7/59 p. 351.

86. Muntaẓirî, Friday sermon *Jang-i taḥmîlî* 23/8/59 p. 105.

87. Rafsanjânî, *Dar maktab-i jum'a* Vol.3 p. 374.

88. I have consulted the Arabic version of this work: *Al-Jihâd al-akbar. qâ'id al-thawra al-islâmiyya fî îrân âyatullâh al-'uẓmâ al-mujtahid al-imâm al-Khumaynî* (Cairo: Manshûrât al-maktabat al-islâmiyya, n.d.).

89. Peters, *Islam and Colonialism* p. 118.

90. Khâmini'î, *Dar maktab-i jum'a* Vol.2 18/7/59 p. 343.

91. Rafsanjânî, *Dar maktab-i jum'a* Vol.7 13/8/62 pp. 211-220. This part of verse IV:95 is also part of the emblem of the *Mujâhidîn-i Khalq*. See Ervand Abrahamian, *Radical Islam. The Iranian Mojahedin* (London: I.B. Tauris, 1989) pp. 102-3. Khâmini'î recited the same verse in his sermon, *Dar maktab-i jum'a*, Vol.2 23/8/59 p. 390.

92. Peter Chelkowski, 'Khomeini's Iran as Seen through Bank Notes', in: *The Iranian Revolution and the Muslim World,* ed. by David Menashri (Boulder: Westview Press, 1990) pp. 85-101, p. 96.

93. Kohlberg, 'Development', p. 69.

94. Kohlberg, 'Development', p. 49; Joel Kraemer, 'Apostates, Rebels and Brigands', in: *Israel Oriental Studies* 10 (1980) pp. 34-73, p. 49.

95. Imâmî Kâshânî, *Dar maktab-i jum'a* Vol.4 10/3/61 p. 389; Vol.5 21/8/61 p. 350.

96. Imâmî Kâshânî in sermon in *Iṭṭilâ'ât*, 23/1/65.

97. Khumaynî, *Iṭṭilâ'ât*, 17/1/64.

98. Khumaynî, *Iṭṭilâ'ât*, 5/1/65.

99. Ḥamîdullâh, *The Muslim Conduct of State* p. 175.

100. Khumaynî, *Jang wa jihâd* pp. 108-9, 111, 135-7; Mahdawî Kanî, *Iṭṭilâ'ât*, 1/7/60.

101. Khumaynî, *Jang wa jihâd* p. 118-9.

102. Muntaẓirî, *Jang-i taḥmîlî* p. 183-184.

103. Even in pre-Islamic times the shedding of blood in one of the sacred months was forbidden as 'the peace of God' prevailed in these months. This was an agreement between the Arabian tribes for safe travel. J. Wellhausen, *Reste arabischen Heidentums* (Berlin: Walter de Gruyter, 1927) p. 96. There is no unanimity in the literature on which months are sacred; there seems to be a consensus that the first month, *muḥarram*, the eleventh, *dhû l-qa'ḍa* and the twelfth, *dhû l-ḥijja*, of the Islamic year are sacred. There is, however, controversy over the fourth sacred month. According to Abû Ja'far Muḥammad b. Jarîr al-Ṭabarî, *Jâmi' al-bayân 'an ta'wîl ây al-qur'ân*, (Cairo: Dâr al-Ma'ârif, 1955-1969) Vol.4 p. 299, the seventh month, *rajab*, is sacred. Also Wellhausen, p. 100, Watt, *Muhammad at Medina*, p. 8; and Th.W. Juynboll, *Handleiding tot de kennis van de Mohammedaansche wet volgens de leer der Sjâfi'itische school* (Leiden: Brill, 1930[4]) p. 302. Majid Khadduri in *War and Peace in Islam*, and A.J. Wensinck give the tenth month, *shawwâl*, as a sacred month, 'Shawwâl' in: *The Encyclopaedia of Islam*[1], Vol.7 p. 343.

104. Khâmini'î, *Dar maktab-i jum'a* Vol.2/8/59 p. 360.

105. War is prohibited in *dhû l-qa'ḍa* because of the pilgrimage. Muntaẓirî, *Jang-i taḥmîlî* p. 36.

106. According to traditional exegesis, *sûra* II:217 was sent down in the month *rajab* 2/624 after a person was killed during an expedition sent by the Prophet against a Meccan caravan at Nakhlah. The whole verse reads: 'They will ask thee about the sacred month, fighting therein: say: "Fighting therein is serious, but debarring (people) from the way of Allah and unbelief in Him, and from the Sacred Mosque and expelling its people from it is in Allah's sight more serious still"; dissension is more serious than killing; nor will they cease to fight you until they turn you from your religion, if they are able; but if any of you turn back from your religion, and die as unbelievers, these (are people) whose works come to nought both in this world and the Hereafter; these are inmates of the Fire, therein abiding'. This verse clearly states that fighting is forbidden in this month, and 'dissension is more serious than killing' means that hindering believers in performing their religious duties is much more serious than the killing of a person. This verse, in fact, was not about allowing Muslims to fight in the sacred month, but about which act was more serious, dissension or the incident in which one person was killed. Ṭabâṭabâ'î, *al-Mîzân*, Vol.3 p. 318.

107. Khâmini'î, *Dar maktab-i jum'a* Vol.2/8/59 p. 360. This is in line with Ṭabâṭabâ'î, who says: *'al-baghy al-ẓulm wa-l-ta'addî bi ghayr ḥaqq'*, Muḥammad Ḥusayn Ṭabâṭabâ'î, *Tafsîr al-mîzân* (Tehran: Muḥammadî, 1363/1984) Vol.18 p. 314.

108. Heidar Ghajar Azodanloo, 'Characteristics of Ayatullah Khomeini's Discourse and the Iraq-Iran War', in: *Orient* 34 (1993) 3, pp. 414-415.

109. Morabia, *Le Ğihâd dans l'Islam médiéval* p. 315.

110. Karl-Heinz Göbel, *Moderne Shiitische Politik und Staatsidee*, (Berlin: Leske & Budrich, 1984), pp. 188-189. Khumaynî's ideas about *al-amr* and *al-munkar* are repeated in *Difâ' wa-l-amr bi-l-ma'rûf wa-l-nahy 'an al-munkar* (Tehran: Mu'âwanîya al-'alâqât al-dawliyya fî munazzama al-'âlam al-islâmiyya, Tehran, 1407/1987) p. 41 and in his *Ḥukûmat-i islâmî. Majmû'a-yi darshâ-yi rahbar-i shî'îyân-i jihân taḥta 'unwân: 'wilâyat-i faqîh'* (n.p., n.p., 1391/1971) p. 162-163.

111. Khumaynî, *Iṭṭilâ'ât*, 15/1/67 and *Iṭṭilâ'ât-i jabha*, 14/1/67. In his *taḥrîr al-wasîla*, which appeared in 1964/65, Khumaynî also referred to the principle of *al-amr* to make clear that the silence of the *'ulamâ'* in the face of tyranny and oppression is prohibited and has to be fought against. Göbel, *Moderne Shiitische Politik und Staatsidee* p. 188.

112. Muntaẓirî, *Jang-i taḥmîlî* 10/2/59, p. 59, 3/8/62 p. 96.

113. Âyatullâh Yûsuf Ṣâni'î, on the occasion of *'ashûrâ'*, *Iṭṭilâ'ât*, 25/6/65. This obligation is stated in Article 8 of the Constitution and not in Article 31: 'In the Islamic Republic of Iran, summoning men to good by enjoining good and forbidding evil is a universal and mutual duty that must be fulfilled by the people with respect to each other, by the government with respect to the people, and by the people with respect to the government. The conditions, limits and nature of this duty will be specified by law. This is in accordance with the Qur'anic verse "The believers, men and women, are the protectors of each other; they enjoin the good and forbid the evil" (9:71)', *Constitution of the Islamic Republic of Iran* (Trans. by Hamid Algar) (Berkeley: Mizan Press, 1980) pp. 30-31.

114. Rafsanjânî, *Dar maktab-i jum'a* Vol.5 4/4/61 p. 49; Vol. 7 29/7/62 p. 177; 2/10/62 p. 317; Khâmini'î, Vol.7 16/10/62 p. 340.

115. Ḥujjatulislâm Muḥammad Yazdî, member of the central committee of the Islamic Republic Party and Majlis deputy, *Dar maktab-i jum'a* Vol.4 17/7/60 p. 31.

116. Âyatullâh Rabbânî Amlashî, member of the Assembly of Experts and temporarily *imâm-i jum'a* of Tehran, *Dar maktab-i jum'a* Vol.4 20/9/60 p. 136, 24/2/61 p. 413.

117. Khâmini'î, *Dar maktab-i jum'a*, Vol.2, 4/7/59 p. 318.

118. Khâmini'î, *Dar maktab-i jum'a* Vol.2 11/7/59 p. 333.

119. Khâmini'î, *Dar maktab-i jum'a* Vol.2/8/59 p. 356.

120. Khâmini'î, *Dar maktab-i jum'a* Vol.2 23/8/59 p. 388.

121. Khâmini'î, *Iṭṭilâ'ât*, 22/11/66.

122. The introduction to the *Constitution of the Islamic Republic* states that the army has to fulfil the ideological mission of *jihâd* in God's path in order to extend the sovereignty of God's law throughout the world. This is contrary to the idea that the *jihâd* cannot be waged as long as the Hidden *imâm* is hiding. But so far, the army has not shown any signs that they take these lines literally.

123. Khumaynî, *Dar justujû-yi râh az kalâm-i imâm: shahîd wa shahâda. Az bayânât wa i'lâmiyahâ-yi imâm Khumaynî az sâl 1341 tâ 1361* Vol.4 (Tehran: Amîr Kabîr, 1370/1991) 15/1/60 p. 18.

124. Muntazirî, *Jang-i tahmîlî* 2/10/60 p. 119; Imâmî Kâshânî, *Dar maktab-i jum'a* Vol. 4 10/2/61 p. 390. Rafsanjânî, *Ittilâ'ât*, 2/3/66.

125. Etan Kohlberg, 'Shahîd', in: *Encyclopaedia of Islam*[2] Vol.9 pp. 203-207, p. 204.

126. R. Peters, 'Shahîd', in: *Encyclopaedia of Islam*[2] Vol.9 p. 207.

127. Kohlberg, 'Shahîd', p. 204.

128. Khumaynî, *Shahîd wa shahâda* 29/2/60 p. 19, 1/4/60 p. 20, 11/12/60 p. 21, 29/1/61 p. 22; Rafsanjânî *Dar maktab-i jum'a* Vol.6 2/2/62 p. 240; Khâmini'î, *Dar maktab-i jum'a* Vol.2 4/7/59 p. 319; Imâmî Kâshânî, Vol.4 13/9/60 p. 127; Muntazirî, *Jang-i tahmîlî* 22/10/59 p. 112.

129. Muntazirî, *Jang-i tahmîlî* 11/7/59 p. 98.

130. Morabia, *Le Ğihâd dans l'Islam médiéval* p. 253.

131. Rafsanjânî, *Dar maktab-i jum'a* Vol.6 22/7/62 p. 169.

132. Khâmini'î, *Dar maktab-i jum'a* Vol.2 25/7/59 p. 352.

133. Speaker of Parliament Hujjatulislâm Nâtiq Nûrî speech before sermon, *Ittilâ'ât*, 4/11/65.

134. Imâmî Kâshânî, *Dar maktab-i jum'a* Vol.4 10/2/61 p. 390.

135. Khumaynî, *shahîd wa shahâda* 21/10/59 p. 26-27. The translation of this speech can be found in *The Imam and the Ommat* p. 143.
The vision of God (*ru'yat allâh*) Khumaynî spoke of should probably not be taken literally. The Twelver Shî'a contest the idea of *tashbîh* (anthropomorphism), God is immaterial and therefore cannot be seen. The vision of God was understood by al-Kulaynî and Ibn Bâbûya as:

> La 'vision' n'est qu'expérience interne, contemplation, dans la coeur de l'homme, de la "lumière de la majesté divine" ou bien connaissance de Dieu à travers les vérités de la foi: si vision matérielle il y a, ce ne peut être que le spectacle des 'signes de Dieu' qui s'offrent au croyant dans le monde créature .

Georges Vajda, 'Le Problème de la vision de Dieu (ru'ya) d'après quelques auteurs šî'ites duodécimains', in: *Le Shî'isme imâmite* (Paris: Presses Universitaires de France, 1970) pp. 31-54, p. 33. See also McDermott, *The Theology of al-Shaikh al-Mufîd* p. 339,367; and J.I. Smith and Y.Y. Haddad, *The Islamic Understanding of Death and Resurrection* (Albany: SUNY Press, 1981) p. 95.
According to Knysh, Khumaynî, by following Ibn 'Arabî's method of reasoning, tried to achieve a reconciliation between a representation of *tanzîh* (denying God any resemblance to anything) and *tashbîh*,. but it falls outside the scope of this study to go much further into this aspect of Khumaynî's thinking. Alexander Knysh, '*Irfan* Revisited: Khomeini and the Legacy of Islamic Mystical Philosophy', in: *Middle East Journal* 46 (1992) pp. 631-653, pp. 641-642.

136. For instance Khâmini'î, *Dar maktab-i jum'a* Vol.2 25/7/59 p. 352; 16/8/59, p. 381.

137. Kohlberg, 'Shahîd', p. 205.

138. Khumaynî, *Shahîd wa shahâda* 15/4/59 p. 17; *Iṭṭilâ'ât* 18/11/65. Munta̤zirî, *Jang-i taḥmîlî* 2/10/60 p. 119.

139. Khumaynî, *Shahîd wa shahâda* 14/2/59 pp. 16-17, 15/1/60, p. 19, 29/2/60 p. 19, 11/4/60 p. 20.

140. Rafsanjânî, *Dar maktab-i jum'a* Vol.6 2/2/62 p. 240.

141. Munta̤zirî, *Jang-i taḥmîlî* 3/2/62 p. 95.

142. Speech before sermon, Âyatullâh Muḥammadî Khîlânî, *Iṭṭilâ'ât,* 25/8/64.

143. Khâmini'î, *Dar maktab-i jum'a* Vol.3 29/12/59 p. 139.

144. Khâmini'î, *Dar maktab-i jum'a* Vol.2 25/7/59 p. 352; 16/8/59 p. 381. Mûsawî Ardabîlî said that parents restrained their tears and showed no emotion but were really happy, *Dar maktab-i jum'a* Vol.3 27/6/60 p. 412-3. According to Mûsawî, parents sent children to the front to replace previously martyred sons, *Dar maktab-i jum'a* Vol.4 20/1/61 p. 346.

145. Khumaynî, *shahîd wa shahâda* 12/8/58 p. 16; Rafsanjânî, *Dar maktab-i jum'a* Vol.6 2/2/62 p. 240.

146. Rafsanjânî in sermon in *Iṭṭilâ'ât*, 16/11/64.

147. See, for instance, Ṭabâṭabâ'î, *Tafsîr al-mîzân* Vol.8 p. 80; Abû Ja'far Muḥammad b. Jarîr al-Ṭabarî *Jâmi' al-bayân 'an tâ'wîl ây al-qur'ân* (Cairo: Dâr al-Ma'ârif, 1955-1969) Vol.4 p. 313; Richard Bell, *The Qur'ân. Translated, with a critical re-arrangement of the Surahs* (Edinburgh: Clark, 1937) Vol.1 p. 70.

148. This is based on the belief that the martyr is purified through his martyrdom and on the basis of Muḥammad's saying at Uḥud: 'wrap them with the blood [of their wounds]', Morabia, *Le Ğihâd dans l'Islam médiéval*, p. 253.

149. Khumaynî, *Jang wa jihâd* n.p.

150. *Iṭṭilâ'ât* 8/8/59.

151. *Tehran Times*, 30 July 1996.

152. For instance Khumaynî, *Jang wa jihâd* 13/10/61 p. 273.

153. Farhad Khosrokhavar, *L'Islamisme et la mort. Le Martyre révolutionnaire en Iran* (Paris: L'Harmattan, 1995) p. 27.

154. Werner Schmucker, 'Iranische Märtyrertestamente', in: *Die Welt des Islams* 27 (1987) pp. 185-249.

155. Khumaynî *shahîd wa shahâda*, for instance, 20/9/60 p. 35; Khâmini'î *Dar maktab-i jum'a* Vol.3 14/9/59 p. 18; 29/12/59 p. 141.

156. Kohlberg, 'Shahîd', p. 204.

157. *Jang-i taḥmîlî. Difâ' dar barâbar-i tajâwuz* Vol.4 p. 135; Rafsanjânî, *Dar maktab-i jum'a* Vol.4 3/7/60 p. 10; Khâmini'î, *Ittilâ'ât*, 28/2/65; Ḥujjatulislâm Muḥammad 'Alî Muwaḥḥad Kirmânî, member of the Assembly of Experts, *Ittilâ'ât*, 25/4/67.

158. Rafsanjânî, *Ittilâ'ât*, 9/3/62.

159. Khumaynî, *Jang wa jihâd* 8/6/61 p. 13; 12/4/60 p. 11.

160. Khâmini'î, *Ittilâ'ât*, 28/2/65.

161. Noth, *Heiliger Krieg und Heiliger Kampf* p. 14. J.C. Vadet, 'Quelques remarques sur la racine FTN dans le Coran et la plus ancienne littérature musulmane', in: *Revue des Études Islamiques* 37 (1969) pp. 87-96, 98-101. See also Ahmed as-Sirri, *Religiös-politische Argumentation im frühen Islam (610-685). Der Begriff Fitna: Bedeutung und Funktion* (Frankfurt/M, 1990), p. 29-35. *Fitna* can sometimes mean test, but mostly it means murder and the collapse and elimination of peace. At the time of the Prophet, the Quraysh oppressed the believers in the Prophet and after the *hijra* to Mecca they agonized and forced them to leave Islam and return to *kufr*, Ṭabâṭabâ'î, *al-Mîzân* Vol.17 p. 120. Cf. al-Ṭabârî, *Jâmi' al-bayân* Vol.13 p. 537:'Fight them until there is no more idolatry *(shirk)* and only God is worshipped without partners, and the test is removed from God's servants from the world, this is *fitna*'.

162. Louis Gardet, 'Fitna' in: *Encyclopaedia of Islam*[2] Vol.2 p. 931.

163. Ami Ayalon, 'From Fitna to Thawra' in: *Studia Islamica* 66 (1987) pp. 145-174, 150-151.

164. Rafsanjânî a few times referred to the ethnical internal opposition in Iran to the Islamic regime as *fitna* but this was not part of the war rhetoric. *Dar maktab-i jum'a* Vol.5 8/4/61 p. 89; 2/7/61 p. 242.

165. Khâmini'î, *Dar maktab-i jum'a* Vol.2 10/7/59 pp. 332-333; This was repeated throughout the war. For instance Nâṭiq Nûrî, speech before sermon: *Ittilâ'ât* 4/11/65.

166. Khumaynî, *Ittilâ'ât*, 31/6/65.

167. Khumaynî, *Ṣaḥîfa-yi nûr* 5/7/59 pp. 549-550.

168. Khumaynî, *Ittilâ'ât* 10/5/66-1/8/87.

169. Muntaẓirî, *Jang-i taḥmîlî* 23/5/62 p. 95.

170. Muntaẓirî, *Jang-i taḥmîlî* 27/11/64 p. 64.

171. Rafsanjânî in sermon, *Ittilâ'ât*, 24/9/63. Cf. Khâmini'î, *Dar maktab-i jum'a* Vol.2 10/7/59, pp. 332-333.

172. Khumaynî, *Ittilâ'ât*, 24/9/63.

173. Rafsanjânî, *Dar maktab-i jum'a* Vol.4 10/7/60 p. 24; Imâmî Kâshânî, *Dar maktab-i jum'a* Vol.5, 21/8/61, p. 351; FBIS, *Daily Report*, Khumaynî, 4 April 1984.

174. Khâmini'î, *Dar maktab-i jum'a*, Vol.3 21/9/59 pp. 19-20; Rafsanjânî Vol.4 10/7/60 p. 24.

175. Khumaynî, *Iṭṭilâ'ât*, for instance: 9/9/60, 11/1/67, 7/3/67; Muntaẓirî, *Jang-i taḥmîlî* 11/7/59 p. 97; Khâmini'î, *Dar maktab-i jum'a* Vol.2 9/8/59 p. 365. Bani Ṣadr, *Iṭṭilâ'ât*, 26/12/59; General Staff Headquarters, *Iṭṭilâ'ât*, 18/4/67: 'great, divine, historical *azmâyish* (test)'.

176. Khâmini'î, *Dar maktab-i jum'a* Vol.3 21/9/59 pp. 19-20: *al-Aḥzâb* XXXIII:22 'When the believers saw the Confederates, they said: "This is what Allah and His messenger promised us"; Allah and this messenger have spoken truth, it only increased them in belief and in (self)-surrender'; *al-'Ankabût* XXIX:2 ' do the people think that they will be left (in the position) that they say: "We have believed", without their being tried?'.

177. Khumaynî, *Jumhûrî-yi islâmî*, 8/10/59; Khâmini'î *Dar maktab-i jum'a*, Vol.3 p. 20.

178. Khâmini'î, *Iṭṭilâ'ât*, 29/10/60.

179. Muntaẓirî, *Jang-i taḥmîlî* 28/11/62 p. 100.

180. Muntaẓirî, *Jang-i taḥmîlî* 2/10/60, p. 120.

181. Khumaynî, *Jang wa jihâd*, Chapter 10; Khâmini'î, *Dar maktab-i jum'a* Vol.3 p. 22, 24.

182. Khumaynî, *Iṭṭilâ'ât*, 31/6/66.

183. J. ter Haar, *Volgelingen van de imam. Een kennismaking met de shi'itische islam* (Amsterdam: Bulaaq, 1995) pp. 46-47.

184. Rafsanjânî, *Dar maktab-i jum'a* Vol.4 10/7/60, p. 23: *al-Ḥadîd* LVII:22 'No misfortune has befallen either the land or yourselves, but it was in a book before We brought it to be; that for Allah is easy'.

185. Khumaynî, *Jang wa jihâd* 11/9/60 p. 50.

186. Rafsanjânî, *Dar maktab-i jum'a* Vol.4 10/7/60 p. 23.

187. Rafsanjânî, *Dar maktab-i jum'a*, Vol.4 3/7/60 p. 10: *al-Baqara* II:216: 'Fighting is prescribed for you, though it is distasteful to you'; Imâmî Kâshânî, Vol.4 13/9/60 p. 125. He referred to the following Qur'ân verses: *al-Ḥajj* XXII:40: 'But for Allah's warding off the people, some by means of others, hermitages and churches and oratories and places of worship in which the name of Allah was had in remembrance would have been destroyed in numbers'; II:251: 'Now if Allah had not beaten off one set of the people by means of others, the land would have gone corrupt'; and *al-Mâ'ida* V:54: 'Allah will produce (another) people whom He loveth and who love Him, humble towards the believers, haughty towards the unbelievers, striving in the cause of Allah, and not fearing the blame of anyone; that is Allah's bounty which He bestoweth upon whomsoever He pleaseth; Allah is unrestricted, knowing'. (verse V:54 will be discussed in detail below); Rafsanjânî, *Dar maktab-i jum'a* Vol.4 3/10/60 p. 158.

188. Rafsanjânî, *Dar maktab-i jum'a* Vol.3 2/5/60 p. 329.

189. Muntaẓirî, *Jang-i taḥmîlî* 2/10/60 p. 120.

190. Khâmini'î, *Dar maktab-i jum'a* Vol.3 12/10/59 p. 45-46; *Yâ'Sîn*:60: '... did I not enjoin you, o ye children of Adam, that ye should not serve Satan'; Mûsawî Ârdabîlî Vol.4 60/8/22, p. 96 and Imâmî Kâshânî Vol.5 21/8/61 p. 351: *Muḥammad* XLVII:7: 'O ye who have believed, if ye help Allah He will help you, and set firm your feet'. Yazdî, *Dar maktab-i jum'a* Vol.4 60/7/17 p. 30.

191. Khumaynî, *Jang wa jihâd* 60/9/11 p. 281.

192. Imâmî Kâshânî, *Dar maktab-i jum'a* Vol.5 61/8/21, p. 351

193. *Iṭṭilâ'ât*, Khâmini'î, 31/6/65; Khumaynî, 7/3/67; Khâmini'î, *Dar maktab-i jum'a* Vol.2 4/7/59 p. 316; Vol.3 14/9/59 p. 13.

194. In introduction to *Khurramshahr az âsâra tâ âzâdî* (Khurramshahr from captivity to liberation) (n.p., Daftar-i nashr-i farhang-i islâmî, 1363/1984).

195. Khumaynî, *Jang wa jihâd* 7/1/60, 11/9/60 pp. 243, *Ṣaḥîfa-yi nûr* 8/7/59 p. 552; Rafsanjânî, *Dar maktab-i jum'a* Vol.4 10/7/60 pp. 22-23.

196. War poster titled: *Namâz-i shakr*, (translated as Thanksgiving Prayer). The picture shows a praying soldier beside a burning tank. *Dah sâl bâ ṭarrâḥân-i grafîk-i inqilâb-i islâmî, 1357-1367*, compiled by Dâwud Ṣâdiq 'Alî (Tehran: Ḥawza-yi hunarî-yi sâzimân-i tablîghât-i islâmî, 1368/1989) Vol.3 p. 189.

197. War poster titled: *Umîd-i man bi khudâ mîpâramat* (trans. as: 'O my hope. I place you in God'). The picture shows a soldier. *Dah sâl bâ ṭarrâḥân-i grafîk-i inqilâb-i islâmî, 1357-1367* Vol.2 p. 165.

198. Khâmini'î, *Chahâr sâl bâ mardum* p. 101.

199. *Farhang-i jabha* p. 26.

200. Khâmini'î, *Dar maktab-i jum'a* Vol.3 59/9/21 pp. 19-21.

201. Rafsanjânî, *Dar maktab-i jum'a* Vol.4 30/11/60 p. 258; Mûsawî Ardabîlî, Prosecutor-general, *Dar maktab-i jum'a* Vol.4 25/10/60 p. 195. On another occasion, Rafsanjânî referred to the internal opposition in Iran to the Islamic regime as *fitna*, *Dar maktab-i jum'a* Vol.5 8/4/61 p. 89; 2/7/61 p. 242.

202. David Menashri, *Iran. A Decade of War and Revolution* (New York: Holmes and Meier, 1990). pp. 13-14, 234-235.

3 THEOLOGICAL AND DOCTRINAL DISCOURSE: THE SHÎ'Î WORLD VIEW

In the speeches, declarations and sermons of the Iranian leadership dealing with the war, the notions *kufr*, *islâm* and *îmân* played a fundamental role. The war was presented as one between *islâm* and *kufr* and sometimes as one between *îmân* and *kufr*. Iranian leaders used these notions in their war rhetoric as metaphors for the Iranian side and the Iraqis and their allies respectively in a manner which bears a certain resemblance to the way the two notions of *kufr* and *îmân* occur in the Qur'ân of the Medinan period, where they refer to 'the military, political and religious polarization between the two actual parties called *mu'minûn* and *kâfirûn*'.[1] In this chapter I shall describe how the Iranian leaders gave a religious dimension to the war by using Qur'ânic and Islamic theological notions such as *îmân*, *islâm*, *kufr*, *ḥaqq*, *bâṭil*, *mustaḍ'afîn* and *mustakbirîn*.

Îmân *and* islâm: *Sunni, Shî'î and Western views*

In Western literature, *îmân* is usually translated as 'faith' or 'belief' and *kufr* as 'unbelief' or 'infidelity'.[2] According to Waldman, it is not correct to translate the Qur'ânic terms *îmân* and *kufr* with 'belief' and 'unbelief', because they are not analogous to belief and unbelief in the Western intellectualized sense of thought-out and reasoned conviction. It is debatable whether it is true that belief in the Western sense is intellectualized and reasoned, but the question falls outside the scope of this study. Waldman's observation is contrary to Ringgren's remark that there is an intellectual element in the Qur'ânic conception of faith.[3] I prefer to use the Arabic original of the terms because in the speeches and sermons both words have several different connotations. The concept of *îmân* has been studied by Islamic scholars and has been the subject of lengthy discussions among Western students of Islam. I will refer briefly to the subject, since it may help our interpretation of the way the Iranian leaders, theologians themselves, explained *îmân*. In the Qur'ân *îmân* sometimes means the act and sometimes the content of faith, or both at the same time. An act of faith consists of three elements: internal conviction (*i'tiqâd* or *taṣdîq bi-l-qalb*), verbal expression (*iqrâr bi-l-lisân* or *qawl*) and performing the prescribed works (*'amal/a'mâl*), which are the pillars of Islam, and the works prescribed in the Qur'ân. The Shî'îs attach special importance to these works, which they regard as an integral part of faith or even as the essence of faith itself.[4] 'Allâmat al-Ḥillî (d.726/1325), one of the important Shî'î scholars, however, explicitly says that *îmân* is assent *(taṣdîq)* and that good works are not a part of it.[5]

The essential beliefs are listed in *al-Baqara* II:285: 'The messenger has believed in what has been sent down on him from his Lord and the believers also; each one has believed in Allah and His angels, and His Books, and His messengers'.[6] In their explanation of what is the content of belief, Wensinck and Watt refer to what Watt calls the 'standard tradition' on *îmân* (Muslim, *Jâmi', al-îmân*, trad. 5). It defines *îmân* as *îmân* in God, His angels, books, meeting, apostles and in the final resurrection, in other words as the contents of faith. The same tradition defines *islâm* as serving God without associating anything with Him, performing the *ṣalât* (prayer ritual), paying *zakât* (alms), and fasting during the month of *ramaḍân*, in other words as the performance of faith.[7] Except for the belief in the imamate and Divine justice (*'adl*), the Shî'î conception of faith does not differ from the Sunnî standpoint: Shî'î commentators on the Qur'ân, too, hold that there is a difference between *islâm* and *îmân*.[8] Like their Sunnî counterparts, Shî'î theologians argue that *îmân* is something hidden in the heart of the believer, while *islâm* consists of his visible actions.[9] In a tradition on the authority of Ja'far al-Ṣâdiq, the sixth *imâm*, both *islâm* and *îmân* contain the *shahâda*, the creed, and the *taṣdîq* (assenting to the word of God and his messenger), but the *mu'minîn* have these qualities established in their hearts and they show this in their works.[10] However, there are also a few traditions in Kulaynî's collection where the difference between *islâm* and *îmân* is more than a distinction between external and internal confession. *Îmân* is loftier than *islâm* (*arfa' min islâm bi-daraja*) because *îmân* implies possessing *islâm* on the surface too, but *islâm* does not automatically imply possession of *îmân* in the innermost heart.[11] Muslims and believers have to perform the *ṣalât*, *zakât*, *ṣawm* (fasting), and *ḥajj* (pilgrimage); they are on the same level in matters of virtues (*faḍâ'il*) and legal punishments (*ḥudûd*), but the believers are superior in their works (*a'mâl*), and the value of their works in the eyes of God is higher.[12]

The difference between *îmân* as the internal and *islâm* as the outward expression of religion led Wensinck to the assumption that *îmân* was regarded as superior to *islâm* by Islamic theologians.[13] This was questioned by Watt, according to whom it is a European distinction not made by early Muslims. He argued that there is no real proof in Islamic theology for this assumption. Since the time of the Kharijites, the discussion about *îmân* and *islâm*, which was carried on by the theologians of the first Islamic centuries, has served to determine who was, and who was not, a member of the Islamic community.[14] This seems to be identical with the ideas of the Twelver Shî'î theologian Shaykh al-Mufîd (d. 413/1022), who argued that the distinction between *islâm* and *îmân* is expressed by the *imâmî* division of the *dâr al-*

îmân, *dâr al-islâm* (and *dâr al-kufr*). According to him, the abode of *islâm* is where the law of Islam prevails, but the abode of the combination of *islâm* and *îmân* is where the law of Islam prevails but people also adhere to the *imâm* from Muhammad's family.[15] On a religious level he also distinguished between *islâm* and *îmân* without, however, explaining the difference between the two:

> The Imamites agree that Islam is other than faith and that every believer is a Muslim, but not every Muslim is a believer. There is a difference between these two ideas in religion as well as language.[16]

Îmân *and* islâm *in Iranian rhetoric*

Throughout the war, the leaders used the notion of *islâm* in a specific, political and religious sense. *Islâm* was presented not only as a religion with practices and beliefs, but also as an ideology, in which politics and religion were inextricably linked with each other. Ideology is used here in the sense of 'a value system or belief system accepted as fact or truth by some group. It is composed of sets of attitudes toward the various institutions and processes of society. An ideology provides the believer with a picture of the world both as it is and as it should be, and, in doing so, organizes the tremendous complexity of the world into something fairly simple and understandable'.[17] *Islâm* as used by Iranian leaders in this sense did not mean the entire Islamic world, neither did it refer to the Sunnî world, as in Shaykh al-Mufîd's thinking. When Iranian leaders spoke of the war as 'one between *islâm* and *kufr*' they in fact referred with the notion *islâm* to the Islamic Republic: the Islamic political system and interpretation of Islam as practised and acknowledged in the Islamic Republic. Immediately after the outbreak of the war Khumaynî sacralized the war by saying that the Iraqi attack was one on *islâm*, on the Qur'ân, and on the Prophet of God.[18] In his early speeches he distinguished between the two sides in the war, *islâm* and *kufr*, thus making clear that the war was a conflict with religious dimensions instead of merely a territorial dispute.[19] In his first sermon after the start of the war, Khâmini'î used *Âl 'Imrân*, III:13 to make this point clear: 'one fighting in the way of Allah, another unbelieving... Allah supporteth with His help whom He willeth'; and *al-Nisâ'*, IV:76: 'those who have believed are fighting in the way of Allah, and those who have disbelieved are fighting in the way of Ṭâghût' as a metaphor for the position of the Islamic Republic and that of Iraq. *Al-Kâfirûn* CIX was also frequently applied to the two sides: '(1) Say: O ye unbelievers, (2) I serve not what ye serve, (3) And ye are not servers of what I serve; (4) I am not a server of what ye have served, (5) Nor are ye servers of what I serve; (6) Ye have your religion, and I have mine'.[20] According to Khâmini'î, one group fought for the Qur'ân and the Islamic Republic, the other one for the United States, Israel, passions (*hawâhâ*), delusions (*hawashâ*), and illusions (*ghurûrhâ*).[21] It was a war against the

Islamic revolution, religion and the Shî'î school of Islam.[22] Iran had been attacked because it was the vanguard of Islam, because it followed the path of the prophets by propagating God's message.[23] The leaders continuously emphasized that it was the people's responsibility to preserve and safeguard Islam.

Iranian leaders regularly referred to *îmân*. In one Friday sermon *îmân* was explained as *îmân bi allâh*, *qiyâma* (resurrection) and 'what God sent down'.[24] This is in accordance with the above cited tradition and the Qur'ânic verses on *îmân*. In the same vein Khâmini'î stated that *îmân* was 'our belief in Islam and in the blessed Islamic revolution'.[25] Their reference to *îmân* had various purposes. Firstly, it was an instrument for mobilizing the Iranian population for the war. Leaders emphasized that *îmân* was expressed through militant activities and that participation in the war for God's sake was a sign of *îmân*.[26] Statements of this kind seem to underline the idea that works (*a'mâl*) are an integral and important part of *îmân*[27] and thus contradict 'Allâmat al-Ḥillî's opinion on the subject.

Secondly, references to *îmân* had the purpose of giving people moral support to endure the afflictions of war and to support those who fought at the battlefront. Pictures of the battlefield often showed soldiers performing the *ṣalât*, for instance, two pictures of a praying soldier with the titles: '*sangar-i 'ishq*' (Trench of love) and '*namâz-i shukr*' (Thanksgiving prayer).[28] Another picture with a praying soldier was entitled '*burâq*' after the horse on which Muḥammad made his night journey to the 'furthest mosque' (*al-Isrâ'* XVII:1).[29] In connection with the war, *al-burâq* must probably be understood as the force supporting martyrs on their journey to heaven. At the same time, and in a more worldly sense, *al-burâq* can be interpreted as coming to the aid of soldiers who are fighting in the war to liberate Jerusalem.

Frequent mention was made of the fact that God would help the believers.[30] By stressing the importance of *îmân*, the population itself was made directly responsible for the outcome of the war. On the one hand, leaders did not hesitate to encourage Iranians to stand firm in their *îmân*. On the other hand, leaders spoke about the exceptional degree of the *îmân* of the Iranian population, who were depicted in the war rhetoric as in every way superior to Muslims from present and previous times and to other nations. When Iranian leaders spoke about the degree of *îmân* in the Islamic Republic, they stressed the fact that it was unparalleled and unsurpassable and that it had even increased during the war.[31] Rafsanjânî stated in reference to the last verses of *Âl 'Imrân* that the Iranian population had a special place in Islamic history. He said that all the fighters in the wars of the prophets, of Muḥammad, and of 'Alî did not have the level of *îmân* and sacrifice that was shown in the war by the Iranian population, whose amount of *îmân* and sacrifice was unprecedented in history. Even at the battles of Badr, Uḥud, the conquest of Mecca, Ṣiffîn, Nahrawân, Baṣra, there had not been this amount of *îmân*.[32]

On the basis of *Yûnus* X:99 ('If thy Lord so willed, all those in the land would believe in a body; wilt thou then put constraint upon the people that they may be believers?), Rafsanjânî said that God had not intended everyone to become Muslim. In Rafsanjânî's eyes, God had given to some people the privilege to become His standard-bearers, to fight, to give blood and to sacrifice themselves so as to receive His benevolence (*lutf*).[33] This interpretation differs from that of Shî'î commentators, whose interpretation seems to be more about God's omnipotence with regards to the *îmân* of mankind than about His preference for one group of people.[34] Âyatullâh Ṣâni'î, leader of the Friday sermon in Qum, did not go as far as Rafsanjânî but said that ever since the revolution of *imâm* Ḥusayn, history had not witnessed a nation such as Iran. The defence of the nation was exceptionally holy (*muqaddas*) because it consisted of *îmân* and sacrifice.[35] *Îmân* was presented as a real and powerful weapon which could resist all kinds of attacks by the enemy.[36] *Îmân* was regarded as a key element in the war effort of the people[37] and gave the Iranians strength.[38]

During the entire war the connection between a victory for the Islamic Republic and *îmân* was repeatedly stressed. Occasionally, *îmân* was presented as a condition for a victory for which the Iranians themselves were responsible. It was said that as long as there was *îmân*, the Iranians would be superior.[39] More often, God's role in making the Iranians victorious was emphasized, but only on the condition that the Iranians were *mu'minîn*.[40] Khâmini'î had already made this clear in the first sermon after the outbreak of the war. Referring again to the Qur'ânic verse *Âl 'Imrân* III:13: 'Allah supporteth with His help whom He willeth' and *Rûm* XXX:47: 'and it lay as a duty upon us to help the believers', he said that God would help the *mu'minîn* and would make them victorious.[41] In another sermon, Khâmini'î, again on the basis of the Qur'ân, said that God would forgive the sins of the Iranians as a reward for *îmân* and *mujâhada*. Furthermore, he distinguished between two kinds of victories.[42] His explanation of this verse was that *îmân* and *mujâhada* would ensure God's forgiveness and ensure a short-term victory, that is, a victory over worldly enemies, and a long-term victory, a place in Paradise. Throughout the war these two options were offered to the Iranian population as the only possible outcome of the war. This was certain because God had promised reward with either a victory or *shahâda*: *al-Tawba* IX:52: 'Say: "Do ye wait for anything in our case but one of the two goods?" while in your case we wait for Allah afflicting you with punishment, either from Himself or at our hands; so wait, we too are with you waiting'.[43] Khumaynî offered the same options in slightly different words when he remarked that, once the enemy was defeated, the Iranians would have freedom (*âzâdî*) or would attain the greatest freedom of all, that is, martyrdom (*shahâda*).[44] The belief that God would come to the rescue of the believers (the Iranians) was expressed by frequent references to *al-Ṣaff* LXI:13: '...help from Allah and a near victory'.[45] This verse, '*naṣr min allâh wa-fatḥ qarîb*', found almost universal use as a slogan during the war.

References to *imân* clearly had the purpose of mobilizing the people and giving them moral support. But it also had the purpose of justifying the war. In his first sermon after the outbreak of the war, Khâmini'î cited a tradition from Muḥammad, dating from the battle of Khandaq: '*qad baraza al-îmân kulluhu ilâ l-kufr kullihi*' (the whole of *îmân* came forth to the whole of *kufr*). According to Khâmini'î, Muḥammad spoke these words when 'Alî appeared on the battlefield.[46] The comparison of the war with one of the wars of the Prophet in which 'Alî represented *îmân* aimed to make clear to the Iranian population that the Islamic Republic had the same role as 'Alî: representing *îmân*.

The Iranians had been attacked because they represented the 'religion of Islam' (*maktab-i islâm*), because of their *îmân* in God, resurrection and the Qur'ân.[47] The fact that the Iranians were *mu'minîn* made it clear that they had to wage this war: *al-Mujâdala* LVIII:22: 'One does not find a people who believe in Allah and the Last Day in friendly relations with any who obstruct Allah and His messenger'.[48] Repeatedly God was said to be on the side of the Iranians in the Islamic Republic because they were the believers to whom *al-Ḥajj* XXII:39-40 referred: '(39) Permission is granted to those who fight because they have suffered wrong. Verily to help them Allah is able. (40) Who have been expelled from their dwellings without justification, except that they say: "Our Lord is Allah"'.[49] The people had shown their support because their *îmân*, which was already unparalleled and unsurpassable, had increased during the war.[50]

Thus, the way in which the concepts *îmân* and *mu'minîn* were used in the war rhetoric shows that the Iranian leaders did not differ in their explanation from Shî'î views, because they stressed the importance of *îmân* as expressed through actions. In a way which brings to mind the distinction used by Shaykh al-Mufîd, they used *îmân* to distinguish the Iranians from the rest of the Muslims, specifically in connection with their behaviour, which was of so much importance for the Iranian war effort.[51] As we saw above the leaders used *islâm* as a specific reference to the Islamic Republic as well.

Just as the Iranian leaders referred to *îmân* to give the people moral support to endure the burdens of the war and to give them support on the battlefield, they also did this in connection with other Qur'ânic concepts, such as *taqwâ* (pious virtue) and *ṣabr* (patience). Real *taqwâ* did not mean indulgence in outward observance of religion such as fasting and praying; on the contrary, it implied caring about political and social issues. *Ṣabr* was presented as perseverance and constancy; it had nothing to do with patient apathy. Moreover, both notions implied active participation in struggle and defence.[52] Leaders frequently referred to these concepts as necessary parts of resistance (*muqâwama*) and struggle. Muntaẓirî said that although *ṣabr* is usually understood as silence and the endurance of *ẓulm* (oppression), this is not its correct meaning. In the Qur'ân and Islamic traditions, *ṣabr* has the meaning of resistance and the endurance of aggression, and, at times, the observance of the duty of *jihâd* and the defence of Islam (as in *al-Anfâl* VIII:45, 66). According to him, the intended meaning of the Qur'ânic verse '... those who endure will be paid their reward in full without reckoning' (*al-Zumar* XXXIX:10) is that the people themselves should take the initiative for resistance and sacrifice and the endurance of hardship.[53] Time and again it was stressed that God would help and make victorious those who were patient and pious and who stood firm.[54] Rafsanjânî referred to *Âl 'Imrân* III:125 to make this clear: 'Ay! if ye endure and act piously, and they come upon you in this very rush of theirs, your Lord will reinforce you with five thousand of the angels, designated'.[55] The leaders also referred to *Muḥammad* XLVII:7: 'O ye who have believed, if ye help Allah He will help you, and set firm your feet'.[56]

Rafsanjânî and Khâmini'î regarded *taqwâ* as another basic requirement for the population to distinguish between *ḥaqq* and *bâṭil*, between truth and falsehood, between God's path and Satan's temptation. They recited *al-Anfâl* VIII:29 to confirm this: 'O ye who have believed, if ye show piety towards Allah (*in tattaqû llâh*), He will appoint for you a *furqân*'.[57]

Throughout the war, Iranian leaders stressed the exceptional mentality (*rûḥîya*) of the Iranians who were fighting at the battlefront and who were willing to sacrifice themselves, and called upon all others to comply with their Islamic duty to defend Islam. Being a true Muslim meant having the mentality of those who were willing to sacrifice themselves, who were militant and active on God's path. This mentality was built upon the above mentioned virtues of patience, trust in God, endurance and piety.[58]

The use of kufr in the Iranian rhetoric

Kufr is the third concept, together with *islâm* and *îmân*, used frequently by the Iranian leaders and, like the other two concepts, often in a very specific sense. As was stated above, the Iranian leadership presented the war as one between *islâm* and *kufr*, where *kufr* was used to denote the enemies of the Islamic Republic, in particular the Iraqi regime and the United States.

Islamic theology distinguishes between different categories of *kufr*. According to the *Lisân al-'arab* there are four categories: *kufr al-inkâr*: neither recognizing nor acknowledging God; *kufr al-juḥûd*: recognizing God, but not acknowledging Him with words, that is, remaining an unbeliever in spite of one's better knowledge; *kufr al-mu'ânada*: recognizing God and acknowledging Him with words but remaining an unbeliever out of hatred or envy; *kufr al-nifâq*: outwardly acknowledging God, but at heart not recognizing Him, and thus remaining an unbeliever, that is, a hypocrite.[59] Kulaynî gives a tradition on the authority of the sixth *imâm*, Ja'far al-Ṣâdiq, in which *kufr* is divided into *kufr al-juḥûd*, neither recognizing nor acknowledging God (this form of *kufr* denies *rubûbîya* (divinity), as in the Qur'ân XLV:23 and II;6); *kufr al-juḥûd 'alâ ma'rifa*, remaining an unbeliever in spite of one's better knowledge (as in XXVII:14 and II:89); *kufr al-ni'am*, ingratitude to God (as in XXVII:40, XIV:7 and II:152); *kufr* in what God has ordered (as in II:84-85); *kufr al-barâ'a* (here probably dissociation as in LX:4, XIV:22 and XXIX:25).[60]

The use of *kufr* for non-Muslim opponents only gained importance after the growth of European influence in Muslim countries. Before that time, *kufr* was used rarely to describe the actions of non-Muslims and only during wars against unbelievers, for instance during the Crusades.[61] It did play a role in political and ideological struggles among Muslims, however. It was not uncommon to accuse other Muslims of unbelief (*takfîr*). This practice was already in use among early Islamic sects, such as the Khârijites. The Wahhâbî and Sudanese Mahdî movements accused their Muslim opponents of unbelief in order to justify war against them.[62] In the wars between the Ottoman Empire and Persia, Turkish *fatwâs* called the Persians *kuffâr*. In the nineteenth century *takfîr* was common practice among the Iranian *'ulamâ'*, who used it as a weapon against their religious rivals.[63] In recent times *takfîr* was used against rulers who were accused of neglecting Islam, for instance for Anwar Sadat, the Egyptian president who was killed for this reason, and the Aḥmadîya movement in Pakistan which had been excluded officially from the Islamic community by the Pakistani parliament in 1974.[64]

Iranian leaders never explained how they understood *kufr*. They never referred to one of the above mentioned categories of *kufr* (*kufr al-nifâq* was used frequently in their speeches and sermons in the derivation *munâfiq*, but this category was not an issue in the war rhetoric). They did not distinguish between *kuffâr* of Muslim origin, such as Ṣaddâm Ḥusayn, and *kuffâr* from other accepted religions. In the war rhetoric there was only one category of *kufr*, to which all *kuffâr* belonged.

The Iranian leaders also referred to *al-Nisâ'* IV:76: 'those who have disbelieved are fighting in the way of Ṭâghût'.[65] *Kufr* was presented as the antithesis of Islam in a political and ethical sense. When leaders spoke of the war in terms of a war between *kufr* and Islam, they did not confine *kufr* to Iraq, but presented *kufr* as the accumulation of all states and ideologies which were not in line with or were opposing the Islamic Republic and its ideology and which, in connection with the war, were seen by the leaders as a threat to the continuation of the Islamic revolution and the well-being of the Islamic Republic.[66] *Kufr* furthermore was an equivalent of *istikbâr* (arrogance) and imperialism, of which the United States, the Soviet Union and their allies (*abar-qudrathâ-yi sharq wa gharb*) were accused, and, in the case of Israel, of Zionism.[67]

The rhetorical use made of *kufr* was a direct continuation of Khumaynî's rhetoric during the time that he opposed the Shah. At that time, the struggle against *kufr* and *ṭawâghît* (see below) was confined to the Shah and his regime, and the United States,[68] but although Khumaynî's political struggle was against the regime of the Shah of Iran, and indirectly against the latter's supporters in the West, it was presented in terms of the liberation of all the oppressed from the hands of the oppressors and tyrants, the removal of illegitimate governments and the installation of Islamic governments.[69] During the first years of the war, attention was shifted to the overthrow of the regime of the *kâfir* and *ṭâghût* Ṣaddâm Ḥusayn and the installation of an Islamic government in Iraq. This was part of the greater struggle against *kufr* and *fitna* (dissension).[70] The purpose of the frequent use of *kufr* by Iranian leaders was to justify the war, to mobilize the people and to give them moral support, so, *kufr* had almost the same function as *îmân*. The justification for fighting a war was primarily found in a number of Qur'ânic verses, which were recited frequently during the sermons. Almost all these verses were about permission to fight the *kuffâr*,[71] or about exhortations to do so.[72] The war was justified on the grounds that hostility to the Islamic Republic amounted to *kufr*.[73] The war had to be fought to protect Islam and the Islamic Republic, whose existence was threatened by the attacks of the *kuffâr* because of these negative characteristics. *Kufr* as the antithesis of *îmân* was associated with cowardice on the part of the Iraqi soldiers. Unlike the Iranians these soldiers were not supported by their *îmân*. References to the cowardice of Iraqi soldiers were probably meant to give the soldiers at the front and those in the war damaged areas moral support.[74]

Kufr was the most important component in the image of Ṣaddâm Ḥusayn and other enemies of the Islamic Republic. The use of *kufr* had the function of drawing boundaries: to distinguish between the Islamic Republic and its enemies, *kufr* was used frequently both for non-Muslims and for Muslims like Ṣaddâm Ḥusayn, *Ṣaddâm-i kâfir* (Ṣaddâm the unbeliever).[75] In the sense in which it was used by Iranian clergy, *kufr* was the antithesis of Islam in the field of ethics and moral behaviour. Whereas Islam was pictured as a world of 'belief, ethics, ideological and revolutionary values, sanctity, honour and resistance', *kufr* was pictured as a 'dirty world of bullying, money, immorality, and debauchery'.[76] One of the characteristics of the *kuffâr* is obstinacy (*qasî-yi qalb*).[77] This presentation of the war is in accordance with the findings of Bakan: 'war is deeply involved with the human sense of morality. In war, the enemy becomes the embodiment of evil, victory over an enemy proves the possibility of a conquest of good over evil'.[78]

Although the war with Iraq was portrayed as one between Islam and *kufr* and Ṣaddâm Ḥusayn was given much attention in his role as a mercenary of the 'world of *kufr*', at times the war was nevertheless considered a diversion from the real struggle of Islam against Zionism and imperialism.[79] During the last years of the war, despite continuing fierce fighting with the Iraqis, the war with Iraq was portrayed as less important and the leaders tended to emphasize this point, referring more and more frequently to the realization of the larger goals of the revolution, the spreading of Islam and Islamic principles, and the installation of Islamic governments, and less to the victory over Ṣaddâm Ḥusayn.[80] This was especially clear after the acceptance of Resolution 598, when Rafsanjânî said that the spreading of Islam and Islamic principles had priority over the war.[81] This shift from specific to more indefinite war aims could be interpreted as an attempt to justify the fact that no real success had been achieved.

The clergy's use of *kufr* and *kâfir* shows that, by considering all its opponents *kuffâr*, Iran again, as was the case with its use of *îmân*, referred to the opponents of the Islamic community of Muḥammad's time and justified the war by making it clear that the Islamic Republic faced the same problems as Muḥammad's community. By calling its opponents *kuffâr*, the Iranian state was to wage war besides being attacked. The frequent quotations of Qur'ânic verses in which Muslims are called to fight the *kuffâr* or which approve of war against them corroborate this.

Some other theological notions

There are a few other Qur'ânic concepts which were used to describe Ṣaddam Ḥusayn, such as *ẓâlim* (wrong doer), *fâsiq* (sinner) *mushrik* (polytheist) and *mulḥid* (heretic, deviator). These concepts are treated here, since in the war rhetoric they were part of the dichotomy of *imân*, *islâm* and *kufr*. When the leaders referred to these notions they neither explained how they understood them nor explained why they used them of Ṣaddâm Ḥusayn.

A *ẓâlim* is someone who transgresses his own bounds or encroaches on the rights of others.[82] According to Ibn Bâbawayhi, *ẓulm* is the placing of a thing at a place which is not its own. Someone who claims the *imâma* without being an *imâm* is a wrong doer.[83] But in the eyes of the Iranian leadership, Ṣaddâm Ḥusayn was a *ẓâlim*, because he was engaged in *situm* (oppression, violence) and had violated the rights of the Iranian people by imposing the war upon them. Of course this description was also applied to the United States and their allies because they were the real instigators of the war.[84] The defence against *ẓulm* was justified, since God had allowed people to go to war with his words: 'permission is granted to those who fight because they have suffered wrong'(*al-Ḥajj* XXII:39), in this case when aggression was committed against someone's land, sanctuaries, religion and *â'în* (doctrines).

On one occasion, Khumaynî said that Ṣaddâm's method was inspired by heresy (*ilḥâd*) and called him a *mulḥid* (heretic, deviator). In the Umayyad era, *ilḥâd* denoted desertion from the community of the faithful and rebellion against legitimate caliphs, and during the 'Abbasid age the concept came to signify rejection of religion, materialist scepticism and atheism. In later times, the Ottomans used *ilḥâd* to describe subversive doctrines among Shî'îs and Ṣûfis.[85] Ṣaddâm was a *mulḥid* because he opposed Islam, the laws of Islam and the Qur'ân.[86] However, one of the speeches in which he said so was also about Michel 'Aflaq and the Ba'th, emphasizing that they were very different from the Iraqi people because of their socialist ideology and the fact that 'Aflaq was a Christian.[87] Ṣaddâm had become a heretic because of his affiliation with the Ba'th ideology and his position in the party. Thus, he used this reference to the concept of *mulḥid* not in the same sense as Muslims in the first centuries of Islam, but according to its connotations in the Ottoman period. Translated to the Iranian situation these subversive doctrines must be seen as the ideologies rejected by Khumaynî, such as Ba'thist socialism.[88] In general, Khumaynî, followed by other leaders, used *ilḥâd* in the meaning of atheism and the rejection of religion, for instance when he said that Iraq fought on the side of *kufr*, *ilḥâd* and worldwide arrogance.[89]

The leaders frequently cited Qur'ânic verses which applied to the negative religious situation of Ṣaddâm Ḥusayn and the Ba'th Party: *al-'Ankabût* XXIX:41: 'Those who choose for themselves patrons short of Allah are to be compared to the spider; it chooseth for itself a house, but verily the frailest of houses is the house of the spider, if they knew', could be applied to the Ba'th Party.[90]

Khumaynî once referred to Ṣaddâm Ḥusayn as a *mushrik* (polytheist, someone who ascribes partners to God), following Iraq's foremost religious leader, Muḥsin al-Ḥakîm, who had declared Ṣaddâm Ḥusayn a *mushrik* because his aim was to revive the era of the Umayyads, who had wanted a return to the Jâhilîya, the era of polytheism.[91] On another occasion, Khumaynî said that Muḥsin al-Ḥakîm had declared Ṣaddâm Ḥusayn and the Ba'th Party *kâfirûn* because the socialist ideology of this party had nothing in common with Islam.[92] Khumaynî stated that someone who was repentant of his deeds could theoretically become a Muslim again. But in Ṣaddâm Ḥusayn's case this was impossible because God had taken care that Ṣaddâm was not capable of being repentant. Ṣaddâm belonged to those whom God had created to be satanical and infernal, who were against humanity, and who pursued their own desires.[93]

Another concept used in the war rhetoric, was that of *munâfiq* (hypocrite). *Munâfiqûn* is applied in the Qur'ân to those upon whose fidelity and enthusiasm Muḥammad could not absolutely rely. *Munâfiq* is usually translated as 'hypocrite', 'doubter' or 'waverer', and this shows that the *munâfiqûn* were not a single party but that they were people who were assigned this name. There were those who lost their belief because of hardship, some who had become only outwardly Muslims, and still others who were Muslims only halfheartedly.[94] Brockett states that, although the translation 'hypocrites' fits the post-Qur'ânic usage of *munâfiqûn*, the term as applied in the Qurân is usually stronger and covers a wide semantic range, such as apostates, liars, arrogants and deviants. The nearest word in English for *munâfiqûn* is 'dissenters'.[95] *Nifâq* as applied in the Qur'ân neither belongs to *kufr* nor to *îmân*. In Izutsu's words: 'the semantic category of *nifâq* is in no way a water-tight compartment situated between *kufr* and *îmân*, but rather an extensive range of meaning with uncertain boundaries. It is, so to speak, a category of a conspicuously dynamic nature, that may extend with elasticity towards either direction to shade off almost imperceptibly into *kufr* or *îmân*'.[96]

Although Ram states that Ṣaddâm Ḥusayn was regularly called a *munâfiq*, this is not, in fact, the case. The term did not play an important role in the war rhetoric.[97] In the speeches and sermons the term was usually applied to the internal enemies of the Islamic Republic like the *Mujâhidîn-i Khalq* (Iranian People's Freedom Fighters), who were called *Munâfiqîn-i Khalq* but also to those who were against the continuation of the war.[98] There were only a few references to Ṣaddâm Ḥusayn as a *munâfiq* by Iranian leaders.[99] According to Khumaynî, Ṣaddâm had said that the Persians were not real Muslims because the Qur'ân was sent down in Arabic and because Muḥammad was an Arab. In reply, Khumaynî cited *al-Tawba* IX:97 'The Arabs (Bedouin) are (even) stronger in unbelief and in hypocrisy and more apt not to know the limits of what Allah has sent down to His Messenger'. Khumaynî scolded Ṣaddâm for not knowing the essence of Islam and the Qur'ân: God sent the Prophet for all humanity, throughout the lands of the East and the West. Other reasons to call Ṣaddâm a *munâfiq* were that he had killed Muslims and damaged the mausoleum of 'Alî. He only pretended to be a Muslim and represented the kind of Arab God spoke about in this verse.[100] A further sign that Ṣaddâm only pretended to be a Muslim was that he, like Muḥammad Rizâ Shah, visited mosques, but did not perform his *ṣalât* correctly, because he left out the *rukû'*.[101] (I shall deal in more detail with Arab-Iranian antagonism in Chapter 5).

The 'hypocrisy' of the Iraqi regime was never used formally as a reason for waging war on Iraq or, as Ram implies, as a justification for *jihâd*.[102] By calling Ṣaddâm a *munâfiq* the leadership apparently did not intend to justify a *jihâd*, although it could have had this effect. The fact that the concept was not used formally for justifying a *jihâd* seems to be in accordance with the interpretation by Ṭabâṭabâ'î and by Ṭabarsî (d.573/1178) of the verses in which Muslims are called upon to wage *jihâd* against the *munâfiqûn*. According to Ṭabâṭabâ'î, *jihâd* as mentioned in *al-Tawba*, IX:73, and *al-Taḥrîm* LXVI:9: 'O thou Prophet, strive with the unbelievers and the hypocrites, and be rough with them; their resort is Gehenna - a bad destination', is meant for the *kuffâr* and not for the *munâfiqûn*. They argue in favour of a different reading of the Qur'ânic verses: not '*wa-l-munâfiqûn*' (and the hypocrites) but '*bi-l-munâfiqîn*' (by means of the *munâfiqîn*).[103] Although the *munâfiqûn* are in reality *kuffâr*, though much more dangerous than the *kuffâr* because of their intrigues and deceptions, the *jihâd* verse does not include them because they do not openly commit *kufr* and hostility; they even appear better Muslims than the rest of the Muslims. The verse does not imply that the *munâfiqûn* themselves should be fought, but only their intrigues and deceptions.[104] According to Ṭabarsî, the *jihâd* against the *munâfiqûn* differs from the *jihâd* against the *kuffâr* in the sense that the *jihâd* against the *munâfiqûn* could not be carried out with the sword or by killing them but had to be carried out with the tongue, by admonition, by scaring and the implementation of punishments. Because they never showed *kufr* it was not allowed to fight them. Only God knew about their *kufr*.[105] Indeed, the Prophet never fought the *munâfiqûn*.[106]

A concept of Qur'ânic origin which is often used by Iranian leaders in combination with *kufr* is *ṭâghût*,[107] but the way they use it suggests that their concept of *ṭâghût* differs from its Qur'ânic meaning of 'idol'.[108] It is presented as the driving force of the Iraqi regime and as the evil force which imposes oppression.[109] This is in accordance with one of the interpretations of *ṭâghût* given by Ṭabâṭabâ'î. According to him, *ṭâghût* means rebellion (*ṭughyân*) and transgression (*tajâwuz az ḥaddhâ*). It is used for the agents and causes of rebellion and transgression like deities other than God, devils, jinn, deviated leaders belonging to the human race and all leaders who have not been appointed by God.[110] Algar described *ṭâghût* as 'one who surpasses all bounds in his despotism and tyranny and claims the prerogatives of divinity for himself'.[111]

Khumaynî used *ṭâghût* for all governments whom he described as 'illicit forms of power that have revolted against divine government in order to establish monarchy or some other form of rule'.[112] Before the revolution Khumaynî identified the government of the Shah with the *ṭâghût*:

> In the Qur'an, God almighty has forbidden men to obey the *taghut* illegitimate regimes - and encouraged them to rise up against kings, just as He commanded Moses to rebel.[113]

> The existence of a non-Islamic political order necessarily results in the non-implementation of the Islamic political order. Then, all non-Islamic systems of government are the system of *kufr*, since the ruler in each case is an instance of *taghut*, and it is our duty to remove from the life of Muslim society all traces of *kufr* and destroy them.[114]

During the war, Ṣaddâm Ḥusayn was referred to a few times as the *ṭâghût* of the time,[115] but in general *ṭâghût* was used for the superpowers and especially the United States.

Ṭâghût and *ṭâghûtî* were used in combination with other religious categories carrying an extremely negative connotation: *ẓulm* and *fashâr* (oppression), *zûr* (violence), *tajâwuz* (transgressing); most of the time these referred to governments which did not rule on the basis of what God had sent down by means of his prophets. This is a reference to *al-Mâ'ida* V:48: 'Whoever does not judge by what Allah hath sent down - they are the unbelievers'. These governments were opposed by those which were based on *taqwâ*, *îmân*, *faḍîla* (virtue), *sharâfa* (nobility), which acted according to *ḥaqq* and whose people cared for *khudâ-parastî* (divine worship) and *'adâla*.[116] During the revolution, the Shah's government had been considered the *ṭâghûtî* government par excellence,[117] and after the revolution the term continued to be used to illustrate the difference between the government of the Islamic Republic and hostile governments.[118] The reason why *ṭâghût* was used in the war rhetoric was twofold: on the one hand to dehumanize the opponent, thus justifying both the righteousness of the Islamic Republic and its policies with regard to the war, on the other hand as an extra stimulus to motivate Iranians to participate in the war effort. This was supported by Qur'ânic verses[119] and Islamic traditions.[120] As has been mentioned earlier, Iranian leaders justified the war by presenting Islam in their speeches as the political and religious ideology which had to be defended against the enemies who were symbolized by references to *kufr* and *ṭâghût*.[121]

Iranian leaders regularly referred to the fact that Satan was the instigator of conflicts. He was behind this war through the 'Big and Smaller Satan' (United States and Ṣaddâm Ḥusayn). In some of these statements these devils had willingly worked for Satan,[122] in other statements they were unconscious of the fact that Satan had used them to do his dirty work.[123] The war was presented as something *sharr* (evil), brought about by *fâsid* (perverse) people and devils. Although war was created by Satan, human devils and *jinns*, God was all-powerful and would therefore make an end to war and conflict the moment it pleased Him.[124]

Ṣaddâm Ḥusayn was described as just as *fâsiq* (sinful) as the Shah.[125] In Islamic theology a *fâsiq* (sinner) is someone who has committed great sins. He can be either a Muslim or a *kâfir*.[126] However, in the Qur'ân, *fâsiq* did not yet have the technical meaning of someone committing a great sin. Here, the notion frequently was equated with *kufr*, as for instance in *al-Baqara* II:93: 'Verily we have sent down upon thee signs, tokens manifest, and none will disbelieve therein - save the *fâsiqûn*'.[127] In one of the traditions in Kulaynî's collection, *fisq*, defined as the committing of great sins, is regarded as one of the pillars of *kufr*.[128] Khumaynî also considered Ṣaddâm to be a *kâfir* because he was a *fâsiq*.[129] He was called a *mufsid* and his regime *fâsid* (immoral).[130] The reason most frequently given for considering Ṣaddâm Ḥusayn a *kâfir* was his opposition to the Islamic Republic and hence to Islam. The Islamic Republic was the representative of the age of Islam and the successor of Muḥammad and 'Alî as leader of the Islamic community. Waging a war against Islam and the Republic made Ṣaddâm Ḥusayn a *kâfir*.[131] But his cooperation with the United States, too, made him a *kâfir*. For this reason Khâmini'î referred to him as 'one of those who lose both this world and the Hereafter'.[132] This is a reference to *al-Ḥajj* Xxll:11: 'And amongst the people are those who serve Allah shiftily; if good comes to them they are content therewith, but if trial comes upon them, they turn a somersault; they lose both this world and the Hereafter; that is the manifest loss'.

The leaders tried to degrade Ṣaddâm by referring to him as 'Ṣaddâm 'Aflaqî'. This was meant to degrade him in the eyes of the Iranians because Michel 'Aflaq, a Christian, had founded the Ba'th Party based on secular principles.[133] Ṣaddâm in his guise of mercenary (*mazdûr*) of the United States belonged to the army of unbelief; he therefore was considered to be a *kâfir*.[134]

Unlike Ṣaddâm, the Iraqi people did not belong to the abode of either *îmân* or *kufr* but were placed in a position in between. During the first years of the war the fact that the majority of the Iraqi population was Muslim was often discussed. The Sunnî and Shî'î Iraqis were considered brothers in religion, and this applied both to the Iraqi civilians and to those who were fighting in Ṣaddâm's army who had been forced to fight against Iran.[135] But as Muslims they were asked whether they were prepared to fight for the reign of God, of the Qur'ân, of Islam and of the Prophet of Islam.[136] They were warned that the Ba'th and Ṣaddâm, for whom they were fighting, were turning Iraq into a land of moral decay.[137] It was unclear, however, what was, in the eyes of the Iranian leaders, their future if they remained loyal to the Iraqi regime and did not revolt. The Iraqi soldiers were warned that fighting against Islam is one of the greatest sins, which God does not forgive.[138]

During the first three years of the war, the Iranian leaders constantly emphasized Iran's humane way of waging war, that Iran was not at war with the Iraqi population, and that Iran took great care not to involve the Iraqi population in the warfare.[139] The Friday *imâms* time and again told their audience that the war was imposed on the Iranian and the Iraqi populations and that both nations were in this together. When they spoke about the suffering of the Iraqi population it even seemed as if Iranian leaders had more compassion for the Iraqi population than for their own people. However, as a result of the use of chemical weapons by Iraq and the continued Iraqi bombardments of Iranian cities, in 1363/1984 a change in the rhetoric of the sermons could be detected. At that time the prayer leaders began to speak about *qaṣâṣ* (retaliation) as an Islamic duty (In contrast to Christ, who turned the other cheek, Rafsanjânî said). With *al-Baqara* II:179 'In retaliation is life for you,

O ye of insight', as a point of departure, the Friday speakers justified their attacks on Iraqi cities, but it probably served more as an instrument to give heart to the Iranian population, whose hardship as a result of the Iraqi attacks could not be denied any longer. With the exception of the four holy cities, all Iraqi cities would be attacked as revenge for the Iranian victims.[140] However, the leaders alternated these remarks about the destruction of all Iraqi cities and all of Iraq,[141] with remarks which still showed consideration with the Iraqi population.[142]

Mustakbirûn *and* mustaḍ'afûn

Other distinctions in the way the war was portrayed by Iranian leaders were also expressed in Qur'ânic terms and were all related to *islâm* and *kufr*. These terms were again used to dehumanize the image of Ṣaddâm Ḥusayn and other enemies. Islam was the champion of the oppressed (*maẓlûmûn*), the disinherited (*mustaḍ'afûn*), while the *kâfirûn* were the oppressors (*ẓâlimûn*) and the arrogant (*mustakbirûn*).

In the Qur'ân, the *mustakbirûn* are those, like Iblîs and Pharaoh, who are too haughty to accept revelation, God and the Prophet. They are considered unbelievers. The Qur'ân commentators do not mention specific people as *mustakbirûn* in the time of the Prophet.[143] For the Iranian leaders, *istikbâr* (arrogance) was also an expression of *kufr*. Before and during the revolution, for Khumaynî, the *mustakbirûn* were those who supported the regime of the Shah. After the revolution, *mustakbirûn* was used a in broader sense to describe also external enemies of the Islamic Republic.[144] *Istikbâr* was used by Khumaynî in a negative sense for the industrialized world, with the United States as its major representative. In this sense, *istikbâr* was synonymous with other concepts with a negative connotation like colonialism and imperialism.[145] In the war rhetoric, the *mustakbirûn* were those who were opposed to the Islamic revolution because it endangered their interests. They had waged this war to prevent the major goal of the Islamic revolution: the dissemination of the divine message, which constituted the real threat to their interests.[146] More than once, Ṣaddâm Ḥusayn was presented as the agent of worldwide arrogance.[147] In the view of the clergy, the Islamic Republic was credited with the same task of the Prophet, whereas the *mustakbirûn* not only were too haughty to accept God's signs but actually opposed the divine message. The way Khumaynî and other leaders used *istikbâr* in this sense is identical to the Qur'ânic use.

In the Qur'ân, the *mustakbirûn* are in an opposite position to Muslims and *mu'minûn*. In their war rhetoric, the Iranian leadership presented the same picture of Muslims, *mustakbirûn* and *mu'minûn*. But they put the *mustakbirûn* also in an opposite position to the *mustaḍ'afûn*, for which there is no Qur'ânic basis. In the Qur'ân, the *mustaḍ'afûn* are minors, and those who are under guardianship. According to Ṭabâṭabâ'î's Qur'ân commentary, *mustaḍ'afûn* are those who are not capable of removing obstacles or do not have access to the physical, mental or financial power to acknowledge religion or *ḥaqq*, or to move to the *dâr al-Islâm*.[148] In his *Kashf al-Asrâr*, Khumaynî gave a more directly social explanation than Ṭabâṭabâ'î: those who do not have the strength to support themselves and of whom the state should take care.[149] In his later thought, he gave a different meaning to the concept of *mustaḍ'afûn*; following 'Alî Sharî'atî he used *mustaḍ'afûn* to denote the 'disinherited' and 'oppressed masses'. Sharî'atî had introduced this interpretation in the early sixties with his translation of *Les Damnés de la terre* by Fanon as *Mustaḍ'afîn-i zamîn*.[150]

Before and during the revolution Khumaynî turned the terms *mustakbirûn* and *mustaḍ'afûn* into a central theme in his rhetoric.[151] Central in his understanding of the *mustaḍ'afûn* are two themes. Firstly, the *mustaḍ'afûn* had been deprived, oppressed and exploited during history and, secondly, improvement of their situation had always been a priority of Islam.[152] The *mustakbirûn* represented all those who plundered and oppressed. They were the powerful who misused their position to enrich themselves at the expense of the *mustaḍ'afûn*.[153] A novelty in his thinking was that he ascribed to the *mustaḍ'afûn* revolutionary power to change their situation. During and after the revolution, the *mustaḍ'afûn*, in the words of Khumaynî, were the ones who really brought about the Islamic revolution.[154]

Closer study of Khumaynî's use of this concept shows that he used it for different goals before and during the revolution, after the revolution and during the war. In his revolutionary language Khumaynî stressed the active role of the *mustaḍ'afûn* in order to mobilize them against the regime of the Shah. According to Khumaynî, during the whole history of the prophets, the *mustaḍ'afûn* had stood up and fought with the *mustakbirûn* and defeated them.[155] A clear example is the *mustaḍ'afûn*, the poor, in the days of Muḥammad who revolted against the oppressors.[156] Khumaynî did not explicitly say that he regarded *mustaḍ'afûn* as Muslims. He did, however, say that God always was with the *mustaḍ'afûn*, that Islam wanted to help them until they could take care for themselves. 'It is this strength of Islam, of *îmân*... which made the *mustaḍ'afûn* stand up against the *mustakbirûn*... Our oppressed (*mustaḍ'af*) nation is obedient to the teachings of Islam and the Qur'ân and accepts the Islamic call'.[157] Khumaynî stressed the responsibility of Islam for the *mustaḍ'afûn* by referring to the examples of Moses, Muḥammad and 'Alî who fought against the *mustakbirûn*, the *ṭawâghît* of their time, that is: Pharaoh, Abû Sufyân and now the Shah, the *ṭâghût* of this time.[158] This goal was elaborated upon during the first years of the Islamic Republic by stressing the responsibility of the Iranian leaders for the *rafâh* (well-being) of the *mustaḍ'afûn*.[159]

However, after the revolution the aims changed: now popular discontent could no longer be exploited; instead, support for the Islamic Republic had to be increased and its legitimacy defended. Here, again, the concept of the 'downtrodden' played an important part. Not only was the Islamic Republic the heir of the Prophet in taking responsibility for the cause of the *mustaḍ'afûn*, but by its very existence it had realized God's promise in *al-Qaṣaṣ*, XXVIII:5 : 'But we wished to bestow favour upon those who had been weakened in the land, and to make them leaders, and to make them the inheritors'.[160] Khumaynî referred to the twelfth of *fawardîn*, the day when the foundation of the Islamic Republic of Iran is commemorated, as the day the government of the *mustaḍ'afûn* over the *mustakbirûn* became official; the promise of the *ḥaqq-i ta'âlâ* (God) was fulfilled, and God's benevolence (*minnat-i khudâ*) was shown, the day that the *mustaḍ'afûn* triumphed over the *mustakbirûn*.[161]

In a booklet which summarizes the official line of the Islamic Republic with regard to several subjects, the *mustaḍ'afûn* are also treated.[162] The official line with regard to them is protection and this is a crystallization of God's promise as laid down in *al-Qaṣaṣ* XXVIII:5/6: (5) 'But we wished to bestow favour upon those who had been weakened in the land, and to make them leaders, and to make them the inheritors (6) to give them position in the land, and to let Pharaoh, Hâmân and their hosts see from them the very thing they were on their guard against'.[163] Here, the superpowers from the West and the East who fear the Islamic government and Islamic community were presented as the Pharaohs and Hâmâns of the present time. Through Muḥammad, the *mustaḍ'afûn* once obtained government and *imâma* and they will obtain this again with the help of the *imâm-i zamân* as promised in *al-Isrâ'* XVII:81: 'the truth has come and the false has vanished; verily the false is apt to vanish'.[164] Hence, one of the characteristics of the line of the *imâm* is the protection of the *mustaḍ'afûn* until the *imâm-i zamân* (Lord of the Age) appears and God's wish that they will become the leaders and inheritors is realized. This can only be realized by abiding by the laws of Islam which God has made for the benefit of the *mustaḍ'afûn*. Abiding by these laws is also the wish of the *imâm-i zamân*. Thus, the implementation of the laws of Islam, to which the laws of the *walî-yi faqîh* (leading jurist) also belong, is protecting the *mustaḍ'afûn*. The author of the booklet, Âyatullâh Âzarî Qumî, also says that the *mustaḍ'afûn* are the oppressed, exploited and slaves who have the right and ability to take upon themselves the leadership of the community. According to him, Ḥusayn, the sixth *imâm* Ṣâdiq and the *imâm-i zamân* are considered to be among the *mustaḍ'afûn*.[165]

In the first years of the republic, the active and revolutionary role of the *mustaḍ'afûn*, which was stressed during the revolution, was transferred to the 'oppressed' outside Iran, who were exhorted to revolt against their oppressors.[166] Although Khumaynî continued to refer to the fact that the *mustaḍ'afûn* were the active supporters and instigators of the revolution and would always differ from the powerful,[167] within Iran their revolutionary role was reduced to that of victim of political and economical problems, caused by opponents of the Islamic Republic who, with their terrorist activities against the state, made the *mustaḍ'afûn* their only victims. Usurers, profiteers and speculators were the cause of economic problems which mainly affected the *mustaḍ'afûn*.[168]

In the war rhetoric, the term *mustaḍ'afûn* was used, but far less prominently than had been the case during the revolution. *Mustaḍ'afûn* was used to describe the victims of war, those who had lost their husbands, war refugees and those who had fallen victim to the Iraqi bombardments.[169] The difference between the use of the term during the revolution and during the war was that between the revolutionary *mustaḍ'afûn* who had the strength to revolt and the weak *mustaḍ'afûn* who had to be supported. This last role comes close to the traditional interpretation of *mustaḍ'afûn*, as described above. In the speeches of Khumaynî this aspect is emphasized when he calls for the mobilization of all Iranians who have the strength to fight for the *mustaḍ'afûn*, on the front or in the *jihâd-i sâzandigî* (the reconstruction *jihâd*).[170]

Ḥaqq *and* bâṭil

Two other Qur'ânic concepts which were used by Iranian leaders in their speeches in a way very similar to the opposition between *kufr* and *îmân* were *ḥaqq* and *bâṭil*.[171] Although Iranian leaders did not explain what they meant by either *ḥaqq* or *bâṭil*, both concepts were used, like *islâm*, *kufr* and *îmân*, in a very specific sense. In this war Iran was defending, and fighting, for *ḥaqq* and *islâm*, against *bâṭil* and *kufr*.

The concept of *ḥaqq* takes up a central position in the thinking of the Iranian leaders. They base themselves on two Qur'ânic verses: *al-Anfâl* VIII:8: 'In order that He might verify the truth and falsify the false, even though the sinners were averse' and *al-Isrâ'* XVII:81: 'And say: "The truth has come and the false has vanished; verily the false is apt to vanish"'. Two leading Shî'î theologians who discussed the concept in the context of their commentaries on the Qur'ân, are Ṭabarsî and Ṭabâṭabâ'î. Ṭabarsî equates *ḥaqq* with *islâm* and *bâṭil* with *shirk* (polytheism).[172] He also gives interpretations of other theologians: *ḥaqq* is [belief in] *tawḥîd* (oneness), *'ibâda* (worship), God or the Qur'ân; *bâṭil* is worship of *aṣnâm* (idols), *shayṭân* (Satan).[173] In his commentary of these verses, Ṭabâṭabâ'î does not give an explanation of *ḥaqq* and *bâṭil*, but he does explain *ḥaqq* in his *Shi'ite Islam*:

> God has made this vast and extensive program which embraces every aspect of the countless beliefs, ethical forms and actions of mankind and takes into account all of their details and particularities, to be the "Truth" (haqq) and to be called the religion of the truth (din-i haqq).[174]

The Qur'ân contains passages in which the connotation of *ḥaqq* is *islâm*:

> If the revelation that came through the mouthpiece of the prophet is the Truth, then it follows naturally that Islâm, the religion based on this revelation, is also Truth [X:35, XVII:81].[175]

In the Shî'î version of history *ḥaqq* also plays a role. During the Umayyad era 'Alî was considered by his supporters to be 'in accordance with *ḥaqq* and guidance (*'alâ l-ḥaqq wa- l-hudâ*)'.[176] Furthermore, in a Shî'î book on the history of Karbalâ', the battle between Ḥusayn and Yazîd is also represented as one between the 'sacred cause of truth and falsehood and the devil's forces'.[177]

To make clear to his audience why the war was launched, and what the Islamic Republic was defending, Khâmini'î, in his first sermon after the war began, cited *al-Anfâl*, VIII:8 which, according to Muslim exegesis, was revealed during the battle of Badr: 'in order that He might verify the *ḥaqq* and falsify the false, even though the sinners were averse'. He translated the verse into Persian as: 'God wants to install truth (*jâ-uftâdan-i ḥaqq*) in the world and remove falsehood (*bar-uftâdan-i bâṭil*) which is bound to vanish, to be abolished completely'.[178] Throughout the war, Iranian leaders repeated Khâmini'î's words that the war was one between *ḥaqq* and *bâṭil*: '*nabard-i ḥaqq 'alâ bâṭil*'.[179] *Ḥaqq* was symbolized as a white horse trampling on a fire-spitting dragon.[180] According to Khumaynî, the war was a *jihâd* for the protection of Islam and for *ḥaqq,*[181] a *jihâd dar râh-i ḥaqq* (a *jihâd* for the sake of the truth).[182] The reference to *ḥaqq* was used not only as a justification for the war, but also as an evocative term which gave moral support to the Iranian people. Muntaẓirî, for instance, extolled the soldier on the battlefield who was prepared to sacrifice himself as a *mard-i ḥaqq wa khudâ* (a man of *ḥaqq* and God) and his opponent as a man of this world.[183] Khumaynî said that it did not matter whether the Iranians would be victorious in this world and in this war. He reminded his audience of the fact that the Prophet won and lost several wars, but that in the end the followers of the Prophet always were victorious (*ghalaba*) because ultimately *ḥaqq* was always victorious and *bâṭil* always vanished as God had promised in *al-Isrâ'* XVII:81, which is about Muḥammad's destruction of the idols in Mecca: 'the truth has come and the false has vanished; verily the false is apt to vanish'.[184] God had ordained this war, as he had the battle of Badr, in order to install *ḥaqq* and destroy *bâṭil* and only God decides the outcome of this war between *ḥaqq* and *bâṭil*.[185]

Although the war was presented as something evil brought about by perverse people and devils, at the same time it was said that the war with Iraq was the most recent in a series of conflicts between *ḥaqq* and *bâṭil* throughout history, which had already been described in the Qur'ân. The war belonged to the catastrophes to which God subjected the world with certain intentions. In order that the world should not be conquered by falsehood and *fasâd* (corruption), God had chosen some people, the *ahl-i ḥaqq*, to defend truth.[186] He made Muslims His standard bearers and ordered them to fight and give their blood for His cause.[187] In the rhetoric of the war, *ḥaqq* symbolized the struggle by the Islamic Republic for the liberation of oppressed people from their oppressors, symbolized by *bâṭil*. Those who represented *bâṭil* feared this and therefore imposed the war upon the Islamic Republic.[188] *Ḥaqq* was presented as a certainty, a goal worth fighting for. People could take the path of *ḥaqq* as a recourse. This was in contrast with *bâṭil*, which had nothing to offer and which led people to nothing. With the way *ḥaqq* was used, combining fighting for the Islamic Republic and fighting for *ḥaqq*, Iranian leaders once more emphasized the rightfulness of the Islamic revolution and the Iranian participation in and continuation of the war. The recitation of Qur'ânic verses related to wars fought by the Prophet and applied by the leaders to the Iranian situation underscored this point. This was made very clear by Âyatullâh Mahdawî Kanî, in his Friday sermon in the month of *ramaḍân*. After the battle of Badr God had revealed *al-Anfâl* VIII:41: 'and what We sent down to Our servant on the day of the *furqân*, the day the two parties met'. 'The day that the two divisions met, the day on which *ḥaqq* and *bâṭil* were separated from each other, that day is the *yawm al-furqân*. Some say that on the day of Badr the Qur'ân or verses of the Qur'ân were sent down. Good. That time when fasting Muslims fought at Badr and Khandaq, their Day of Badr was their Day of the *furqân*. The Qur'ân says that *ḥaqq* and *bâṭil* are separated on the battlefield. We give the same sign to our enemies when we separate *ḥaqq* from *bâṭil* on the battlefield when our soldiers and militiamen will show with burning bullets to our Saddamist enemies on whose side *ḥaqq* is. Hopefully it is in this month of *ramaḍân*'.[189] As we have seen before, the similarity between the situation of the Islamic Republic and that of Muḥammad's community is emphasized, since this verse is understood as referring to the separation between the newly established Muslim community and the polytheists.[190]

Notes

1. M.R. Waldman, 'The Development of the Concept of *kufr* in the *qur'ân*', in: *Journal of the American Oriental Society* 88 (1968) pp. 442-455, p. 453.

2. Louis Gardet, 'Îmân' in: *The Encyclopaedia of Islam*[2] Vol.3 p. 1171; Waldman, 'Concept of *kufr*', p. 447. See also Watt, who argues that the European equivalent for *îmân* has connotations which are inappropriate in the context of Islam. W. Montgomery Watt, 'The Conception of *îmân* in Islamic Theology', in: *Der Islam* 43 (1967) pp. 1-10, p. 1.

3. H. Ringgren, 'The Conception of Faith in the Koran', *Oriens* 4 (1951) pp. 1-20, p. 15.

4. Gardet, 'Îmân', pp. 1170, 1171.

5. 'Allâmat al-Hillî (Ibn Muṭahhar), *al-Bâb al-Ḥâdî 'ashar*, trans. by W.M. Miller (London: Royal Asiatic Society, 1928) p. 87.

6. Gardet, 'Îmân', p. 1172. Wensinck refers to *al-Nisâ'* 4:136 which has almost the same content. A.J. Wensinck, *The Muslim Creed. Its Genesis and Historical Development* (London: Frank Cass, 1965) p. 24.

7. Wensinck, *The Muslim Creed* p. 23. Also cited by W. Montgomery Watt, 'The Conception of *îmân* in Islamic Theology', p. 6. Gardet refers to the 'Tradition of Gabriel' (al-Bukhârî, *Jâmi'*, *al-îmân*, 37) which is almost identical to the above-mentioned tradition. Gardet, 'Îmân', p. 1172.

8. Jane I. Smith, *An Historical and Semantic Study of the Term Islam as seen in a Sequence of Quran Commentaries* (Missoula: Scholars Press, 1975) [Harvard dissertations in religion. no.1], pp 83, 219. Besides Sunnî commentators on the Qur'ân, she included the Shî'î commentators Abû 'l Hasan 'Alî b. Ibrâhîm b. Hâshim ibn Mûsâ ibn Bâbawayhi al-Qummî and Abû Ja'far Muhammad ibn Hasan al-Tûsî. 'Al-Qummî: *Al-dîn* [Islam] is submission through internal affirmation and self-dedication to God and to the saints, related to *îmân* in terms of degree and manifested through individual performance of God's commands'. 'Al-Tûsî: *Al-dîn* [Islam], which is obedience to God as well as requital by God in terms of man's obedience, is surrender to the guidance and command of God, distinguishable from *îmân* only in its inclusion of the performance of the specific requirements as outlined by the Prophet'.

9. Abû 'Alî al-Fadl ibn al-Hasan al-Tabarsî (d548/1153), *Majma' al-bayân fî tafsîr al-qur'ân* (Beirut: Dâr ihyâ' al-turâth al-'arabî, 1412/1992) Vol. 9-10 p. 176; and the modern interpretation of Muhammad Husayn Tabâtabâ'î (1903-1981), *Tafsîr al-mîzân* (Tehran: Muhammadî, 1363) Vol.36 pp. 209-207. Muhammad Taqî al-Muddarisî, *al-Fikr al-islâmî. Muwâjaha haḍâriyya* (Beirut: Dâr al-Jubayl, 1395/1975) p. 206.

10. al-Kulaynî, *al-Uṣûl min al-kâfî* Vol.2 (Beirut: Dâr al-ta'arruf, 1401) p. 25, nr.1.

11. al-Kulaynî, *al-Uṣûl min al-kâfî* p. 25 nr.1, p. 26 nr.4.

12. al-Kulaynî, *al-Uṣûl min al-kâfî* pp. 26-27 nr.5.

13. Wensinck, *The Muslim Creed* p. 23, 34.

14. W. Montgomery Watt, 'The Conception of *îmân* in Islamic Theology', p. 10.

15. Shaykh al-Mufîd Muhammad ibn al-Nu'mân, *Awâ'il al-maqâlât fî madhâhib al-mukhtârât* (Tabriz, 1371/1952) p. 70.

16. Martin J. McDermott, *The Theology of al-Shaikh al-Mufîd* (Beirut: Dar el-Machreq Éditeurs, 1978) p. 235, citing from Shaykh al-Mufîd's *Awâ'il al-maqâlât*, p. 15; See also Dominique Sourdel, 'L'Imamisme vu par Cheikh al-Mufid', *Revue des Études Islamiques* 40 (1972) pp. 217-296.

17. Lyman Tower Sargent, *Contemporary Political Ideologies. A Comparative Analysis* (Belmont: Wadsworth, 1993⁹) p. 3.

18. Khumaynî, *Jang wa jihâd* 31/6/59 p. 71: *'ki jang bâ îrân, jang bâ islâm ast, jang bâ qur'ân ast, jang bâ rasûl allâh ast'*.

19. See Khumaynî's speeches in the first days after the outbreak of the war, which have been published in several newspapers and collections of his speeches. For instance: *Ṣaḥîfa-yi nûr. Majmû'a-yi rahnamûdhâ-yi ḥaḍrat-i imâm Khumaynî* (Tehran: Ministry of Culture and Islamic Guidance, 1370/1991) pp. 533-536.

20. For instance, *Dar maktab-i jum'a* Mûsawî, Vol.5 20/1/61 p. 352, Mûsawî Ardabîlî, Vol.5 1/5/61 p. 105.

21. Khâmini'î, *Dar maktab-i jum'a* Vol.2 4//7/59 p. 316. See also *The Imam and the Ommat. The Selected Messages of Imam Khomeini concerning Iraq and the War Iraq Imposed upon Iran* (Tehran: Ministry of Islamic Guidance, 1981) p. 144. The same metaphor was used by Khumaynî, *Jang wa jihâd*, 11/9/60 pp. 83: '*shumâ dar râh-i khudâ dârîd jang mîkunîd, wa în 'alâmat-i îmân-i shumâ-st'. wa ânhâ dar râh-i ṭâghût dârand jang mîkunand wa în 'alâmat-i kufr ânhâ-st.*

22. Muntaẓirî, *Jang-i taḥmîlî dar bayânât-i Âyatullâh al-'uẓmâ Muntaẓirî* (Tehran: Ministry of Culture and Islamic Guidance, 1367/1988) p. 18 n.d., 27/2/61 p. 49, 2/8/59 p. 99; *Jang bâ inqilâb* p. 9.

23. *Jang bâ inqilâb* p. 9-12.

24. Âyatullâh Muḥammad Yazdî, *Dar maktab-i jum'a* Vol.4 17/7/60 p. 31.

25. Khâmini'î, FBIS *Daily Report* 29 November 1980.

26. Khumaynî, *Jang wa jihâd* 11/9/60 pp. 83-84; Khâmini'î, Friday sermon in *Iṭṭilâ'ât*, 4/7/66.

27. Gardet, 'Îmân', p. 1171.

28. English titles from *Dah sâl bâ ṭarrâḥân-i grafîk-i inqilâb-i islamî, 1357-1367*, compiled by Dâwûd Ṣâdiq 'Alî, (Tehran: Hawza-yi hunarî-yi sâzimân-i tablîghât-i islâmî, 1368/1989) Vol.2 p. 53, Vol.3 p. 189.

29. This place is commonly understood to be Jerusalem but sometimes also as referring to heaven. Rudi Paret, 'al-Burâḳ', in: *Encyclopaedia of Islam*[2] Vol.1 p. 1310. It is also the Arabic term for the Wailing Wall in Jerusalem, Rudolph Peters, *Islam and Colonialism. The Doctrine of Jihad in Modern History* (The Hague: Mouton, 1979) p. 100. In popular piety, *al-burâq* is a kind of protective symbol for travellers. According to Annemarie Schimmel, numerous presentations of the *burâq* can be found on the rear of trucks in Pakistan and Afghanistan, so as to ensure the driver a safe journey. 'Muḥammad' in: *Encyclopaedia of Islam*[2] Vol.7 p. 376.

30. Rafsanjânî, *Dar maktab-i jum'a* Vol.2 9/8/59 p. 366: *al-Tawba* IX:25: 'Allah hath already helped you on many fields, and on the day of Ḥunain when ye prided yourselves on your numbers but they did not benefit you at all, and the land, wide as it was, became too narrow for you and ye turned away in retreat. (26) Then Allah sent down His assurance upon His messenger and the believers, and sent down hosts which ye did not see, and punished those who disbelieved - that is the recompense of the unbelievers'. Yazdî, *Dar maktab-i jum'a*, Vol.4 17/7/60 p. 30: *al-Ḥajj* XXII:38: 'Verily Allah will ward off (enemies) from those who have believed Allah loveth not any unbelieving traitor'.

31. Khâmini'î, *Dar maktab-i jum'a* Vol.2 25/7/59 p. 349, 357: *Âl 'Imrân* III:173: 'To whom the people said: "The people have collected (forces) for you, so be afraid of them". But it increased them in belief'.

32. Rafsanjânî, *Dar maktab-i jum'a* Vol.7 21/5/62 p. 23.

33. Rafsanjânî, *Dar maktab-i jum'a* Vol.4/10/60 p. 158. The use of *lutf* is surprising since, according to Shî'î theology, God has to give *lutf* to people in order to help them when they are not capable of realizing the goals for which He has created them. J. ter Haar, *Volgelingen van de imam. Een kennismaking met de shi'itische islam* (Amsterdam: Bulaaq, 1995) pp. 48-49.

34. Ṭabâṭabâ'î, *Tafsîr al-mîzân* Vol.20 pp. 205-206. Al-Ṭabarsî, *Majma' al-bayân* Vol.5 pp. 174-175.

35. Âyatullâh Ṣâni'î, *Iṭṭilâ'ât*, 25/10/65.

36. Khumaynî, *Jumhûrî-yi islâmî*, 3/7/59; *Iṭṭilâ'ât*, 8/5/66; Khâmini'î, *Chahâr sâl bâ mardum* (Tehran: Ḥizb-i Jumhûrî-yi Islâmî, 1364/1985) 27/9/63 p. 372.

37. Khâmini'î, *Iṭṭilâ'ât* 3/7/65: '*ramz-i inqilâb wa jang imân-i 'umîq-i madhhabî-yi millat-i mâ*', (the secret of revolution and war is the profound belief in the religion of our nation). See also Khumaynî, FBIS *Daily Report* 28 May 1988. 'The only way to happiness is *îmân*, *jihâd* and *shahâda*', *Farhang-i jabha*, p. 31.

38. Khâmini'î, *Chahâr sâl bâ mardum* 2/10/60 p. 21; *Iṭṭilâ'ât*, 28/2/65.

39. Anonymous, FBIS *Daily Report* 13 July 1988.

40. Khumaynî, *Jumhûrî-yi islâmî*, 8/4/61.

41. Khâmini'î, *Dar maktab-i jum'a* Vol.2 4/7/59 p. 316; Yazdî, *Dar maktab-i jum'a* Vol.4 17/7/60 p. 30; 'Alî Tehrânî, Vol.7 6/8/62 p. 208. On the occasion of the *Wa-l-fajr* offensive: *al-Ḥajj* XXII:40: '...verily to help them Allah is able'. Khâmini'î, *Dar maktab-i jum'a* Vol.2 25/7/59 p. 357. Khumaynî, *Jang wa jihâd* 61/3/2, p. 286, *al-Aḥzâb* XXXIII:26: '...and cast terror into their hearts'; 20/11/61 pp. 290-1, *al-Anfâl* VIII:17: '... it was not thou but Allah who threw'.(reference to Muḥammad throwing a handful of gravel towards the enemy during the battle of Badr).

42. Friday sermon in *Iṭṭilâ'ât*, 4/7/66: Citation of *al-Saff* LXI:11-13: '(11) Ye will believe in Allah and His messenger, and strive with goods and person in the way of Allah; that is better for you, if ye have knowledge; (12) and he will forgive you your sins and will cause you to enter Gardens through which the rivers flow, and good dwelling-places in Gardens of Eden; that is the mighty success. (13) And other things which ye love - help for Allah and a near clearing-up. Give good tidings to the believers'.

43. The first part of this verse was frequently cited, a few times the whole verse. *Dar maktab-i jum'a* Vol.2 Khâmini'î, 4/7/59 p. 318; Vol.4 Imâmî Kâshânî, 13/9/60 p. 127; Vol.6 Rafsanjânî, 2/2/62 p. 240. Muntaẓirî, *Jang-i taḥmîlî* p. 13, p. 98, 59/7/11, 59/10/22. Ṭabarsî, *Majma' al-bayân* Vol.5 p. 51: 'Either victory (*ghalaba*) and booty (*ghanîma*) in this world or martyrdom with everlasting reward (*thawâb*) in the hereafter'.

44. Citation of Khumaynî's words in: *Khaṭṭ-i tawṭi'a* (Tehran: Sipâh-i pâsdârân-i inqilâb-i islâmî, 1366/1987) p. 7.

45. Prime Minister Mîr Ḥusayn Mûsawî, *Iṭṭilâ'ât*,9/9/60; War poster titled: '*Naṣr min allâh wa fatḥ qarîb*' (Help is from Allah and the victory is near),*Dah sâl bâ ṭarrâḥân-i grafik-i inqilâb-i islamî, 1357-1367* Vol.2 p. 194; *al-Naṣr* CX in several sermons: '(1) When comes the help of Allah and the victory, (2) And thou seest the people entering into the religion of Allah in crowds; (3) Then give glory with the praise of

thy Lord, and ask pardon of Him; verily He hath been prone to relent', Khâmini'î, *Dar maktab-i jum'a* Vol.3 14/9/59 p. 18, 22/3/60 p. 247.

46. Khâmini'î, *Dar maktab-i jum'a* Vol.2 4/7/59 p. 316.

47. Yazdî, *Dar maktab-i jum'a* Vol.4 17/7/60 pp. 30-31.

48. Khâmini'î, *Dar maktab-i jum'a* Vol.2/8/59 p. 355.

49. Yazdî, *Dar maktab-i jum'a* Vol.4 17/7/60 pp. 30-31; Khâmini'î, Vol.2 16/8/59 p. 375; Rafsanjânî, Vol.6 2/2/62 p. 236; 'Alî Tehrânî, Vol.7 6/8/62 p. 208. *The Imam and the Ommat* 30/9/80 p. 71.

50. Khâmini'î, *Dar maktab-i jum'a* Vol.3 p. 349/357: *Âl 'Imrân* III:173: 'To whom the people said: "The people have collected (forces) for you, so be afraid of them". But it increased them in belief'.

51. This seems contrary to Egyptian Islamists who used the term *mu'min* as the opposite of the term Muslim. These Muslims, who were opposed to Sadat, understood *mu'min* in a negative sense because it was used by government circles in *al-ra'îs al-mu'min*, an honorific title for president Sadat (cf. Johannes J.G. Jansen, 'Mu'min' in: *Encyclopaedia of Islam*[2] Vol.3, p. 555).

52. Ram, Haggay, *Myth and Mobilization in Revolutionary Iran. The Use of the Friday Congregational Sermon* (Washington: American University Press, 1994) pp. 42-43.

53. Muntaẓirî, *Jang-i taḥmîlî* p. 63. See also the citation of Khumaynî's words in: *Khaṭṭ-i tawṭi'a* p. 7. Rafsanjânî, *Dar maktab-i jum'a* Vol.4/10/60 p. 158.

54. Khâmini'î, *Dar maktab-i jum'a* Vol.2 25/7/59 p. 349, 2/8/59 p. 360, p. 369; Muntaẓirî, *Jang-i taḥmîlî* 2/4/63 p. 12; Head Central Office Pâsdârân, *Iṭṭilâ'ât*, 8/2/64; Shîrâzî, Member Defence Council, *Iṭṭilâ'ât*, 5/7/65.

55. Rafsanjânî, *Dar maktab-i jum'a* Vol.4/10/60 p. 158; Khâmini'î, *Iṭṭilâ'ât*, 13/11/62. Ṭabarsî, *Majma' al-bayân* Vol.2 p. 632. This verse refers to the battle of Uḥud. *taṣbirû*: endure the *jihâd* and what God has ordered you to; *tattaqû*: fear of disobedience to God and His Prophet.

56. For instance Khumaynî, *Iṭṭilâ'ât*, 9/9/60; Muntaẓirî, *Jang-i taḥmîlî* 2/10/60, p. 120. Mûsawî Ardabîlî, *Dar maktab-i jum'a* Vol.4 22/8/60 p. 96, 25/10/60 p. 195.

57. Khâmini'î, *Dar maktab-i jum'a* Vol.5 12/9/61 p. 386; Rafsanjânî, Vol.7 4/9/62 p. 266. According to Shî'î commentators also, this verse refers to the separation between *ḥaqq* and *bâṭil*;Ṭabâṭabâ'î, *Tafsîr al-mîzân* Vol.17 p. 89; al-Ṭabarsî, *Majma' al-bayân* Vol.4 p. 664; Abû Ja'far Muḥammad b. Jarîr al-Ṭabarî *Jâmi' al-bayân 'an tâ'wîl ây al-qur'ân* (Cairo: Dâr al-Ma'ârif, 1955-1969) Vol.13 p.487.

58. Khâmini'î, *Iṭṭilâ'ât*, 13/11/62. Mûsawî, 14/4/65-5/7/86.

59. W. Björkman, 'Kâfir' in: *Encyclopaedia of Islam*[2] Vol.4 pp. 407-9, p. 408.

60. Kulaynî, *al-Uṣûl min al-kâfî* pp. 389-390. R. Brunschvig in his article 'barâ'a' in: *Encyclopaedia of Islam*[2] Vol.1 p. 1026-1027, says that Shî'îs advocate the "repudiation" (barâ'a) of the enemies of 'Alî and his descendants. Ibn Bâbawayhi interprets the word as: 'complete dissociation from he who disobeys the religion of Allah and befriends His enemies or shows enmity towards His friends'. A. Fyzee, *A Shi'ite*

Creed. A Translation of Risâlatu'l-I'tiqâdât of Muḥammad b. 'Alî Ibn Bâbawayhi al-Qummi known as Shaykh Ṣadûq (London: Oxford University Press, 1942) p. 114. See also Etan Kohlberg, 'Barâ'a in Shî'î Doctrine', in: *Jerusalem Studies in Arabic and Islam* 7 (1986) pp. 139-175.

61. Björkman, 'Kâfir', p. 408.

62. Rudolph Peters, 'The Political Relevance of the Doctrine of Jihad in Sadat's Egypt', in: *National and International Politics in the Middle East. Essays in Honour of Elie Kedourie*, ed. by L. Lugram (London: Frank Cass, 1986) p. 271 n4.

63. Arjomand, Said Amir, *The Shadow of God and the Hidden Imam. Religion, Political Order, and Societal Change in Shi'ite Iran from the Beginning to 1890* (Chicago: University of Chicago Press, 1984), p. 243.

64. Hans Kruse, '*Takfîr* und *jihâd* bei den Zaiditen des Jemen', in: *Welt des Islams* 24 (1984) pp. 424-457, pp. 427-428.

65. Khâmini'î, *Dar maktab-i jum'a* Vol.2 4/7/59 p. 317.

66. *Jang-i taḥmîlî*, introduction by Rafsanjânî, p. 5; *Jang bâ inqilâb* pp. 9-12.

67. Khâmini'î, *Dar maktab-i jum'a* Vol.2 4/7/59 p. 317; Rafsanjânî, *Iṭṭilâ'ât*, 8/9/59; Muntaẓirî, *Jang-i taḥmîlî* p. 11, p. 37, 3/10/59, pp. 54-55, 19/3/61. Rafsanjânî, *Dar maktab-i jum'a* Vol.4 3/7/60 p. 11; Mûsawî Ardabîlî Vol.3 27/6/60 p. 414.

68. Khumaynî, *Mustaḍ'afîn, mustakbirîn* p. 23.

69. '... all non-Islamic systems of government are the system of *kufr*, since the ruler in each case is an instance of *taghut*, and it is our duty to remove from the life of Muslim society all traces of *kufr* and destroy them'. *Islam and Revolution. Writings and Declarations of Imam Khomeini*, trans. and annotated by Hamid Algar (Berkeley: Mizan Press, 1981) p. 48.

70. Khumaynî, *Iṭṭilâ'ât*, 31/9/63. Rafsanjânî, *Iṭṭilâ'ât*, 27/11/6.

71. Khâmini'î cited in the first sermon after the outbreak of the war *al-Nisâ'*:76. Vol.3, Mûsawî Ardabîlî, 27/6/60 p. 311 *al-Tawba* IX:73 'O thou prophet, strive with the unbelievers and the Hypocrites, and be rough with them; their resort is Gehenna - a bad destination'.

72. *The Imam and the Ommat* p. 144, *al-Nisâ'* IV:74-78; Khâmini'î, *Dar maktab-i jum'a* Vol.2/8/59 p. 360, *al-Tawba*, IX:12; Imâmî Kâshânî, *Dar maktab-i jum'a* Vol.3 27/6/60 p. 411: *al-Tawba* IX:12-14, 73, *Muḥammad* XLVII:4-6.

73. This seems in line with Waldman's observation that *kufr* in the late Medinan period was also associated with 'hostility to the prophet', Waldman, 'Concept of *kufr*', p. 452.

74. *Al-Ḥashr* LIX:2 (partly) '... as they made their houses desolate with their own hands', in Khâmini'î, *Dar maktab-i jum'a* Vol.2 18/7/59 p. 340; Vol.7 Rafsanjânî, 22/7/62 p. 162, was cited as referring to the cowardice of the Iraqi soldiers and the courage of the Iranian soldiers.

75. For instance Prime Minister Muḥammad 'Alî Rajâ'î, *Iṭṭilâ'ât*, 5/8/59; Muntaẓirî, *Jang-i taḥmîlî*, 27/11/64 p. 64.

76. Khâmini'î, FBIS *Daily Report* 6 June 1988.

77. Qur'ânic verse *al-Baqara* II:74: 'Then your hearts became hard after that, and they are like stones or even harder'. Rafsanjânî, *Iṭṭilâ'ât*, 31/5/66; Khâmini'î, *Iṭṭilâ'ât*, 21/3/67.

78. David Bakan, 'Some Philosophical Propadeutics toward a Psychology of War', in: *The Psychology of War and Peace. The Image of the Enemy*, ed. by Robert W. Rieber (New York: Plenum Press, 1991) pp. 41-58, p. 47.

79. FBIS *Daily Report* 26 July 1981, Statement by Ministry of Foreign Affairs.

80. Khumaynî, *Iṭṭilâ'ât*, 18/11/65; Mûsawî, *Iṭṭilâ'ât*, speech before sermon, 18/11/65.

81. Rafsanjânî, Friday sermon, *Iṭṭilâ'ât*, 1/5/67.

82. Toshihiko Izutsu, *Ethico-Religious Concepts in the Qur'ân* (Montreal: McGill University Press, 1966) pp. 166-167.

83. Fyzee, *A Shi'ite Creed* p. 107.

84. Yazdî, *Dar maktab-i jum'a* Vol.4 17/7/60 pp. 30, 31; Rafsanjânî, *Dar maktab-i jum'a* Vol.6 2/2/62 pp. 232, 236; 'Alî Tehrânî, *Dar maktab-i jum'a* Vol.7 8/6/62 p. 208; *Jang bâ inqilâb*, p. 15.

85. W. Madelung, 'Mulḥid' in: *Encyclopaedia of Islam*^{2} Vol.7 p. 546; Bernard Lewis, 'Some Observations on the Significance of Heresy in the History of Islam', in: *Studia Islamica* 1 (1953) pp. 43-63, p. 56.

86. Khumaynî, *Jang wa jihâd* 17/6/61 p. 57. Cf. *al-A'râf* VII:80; *al-Mu'min* XLI:40 and *al-Hajj* XXII:25: 'Whoever seeks in it to perpetrate deviation (*bi-ilḥâd*) wantonly, We shall make him taste a painful punishment'.

87. Khumaynî, *Ṣaḥîfa-yi nûr*, 4/7/59 p. 543.

88. According to Lewis, in the nineteenth century *ilḥâd* was used by one Ottoman historian to describe ideas from the French Revolution which were disseminated in Turkey. Lewis, 'Some Observations on the Significance of Heresy', p. 56.

89. Khumaynî, *Iṭṭilâ'ât*, 23/11/59; Mahdawî Kanî, *Iṭṭilâ'ât*, 1/7/60.

90. Muntaẓirî, *Jang-i taḥmîlî* 3/8/61 p. 156.

91. Khumaynî, *Jang wa jihâd* 29/1/59 p. 46.

92. Khumaynî, *Ṣaḥîfa-yi nûr* p. 534.

93. *The Imam and the Ommat* 28/10/80 p. 115.

94. Franz Buhl, ‘Munâfiqûn’ in: *Encyclopaedia of Islam*[1] Vol.6 p. 722.

95. A. Brockett, ‘Munâfiqûn’ in: *Encyclopaedia of Islam*[2] Vol.7 pp. 561-562.

96. Izutso, *Ethico-Religious Concepts in the Qur’ân* p. 180.

97. Haggay Ram, ‘"Islamic Newspeak": Language and Change in Revolutionary Iran’, in: *Middle Eastern Studies* 29 (1993) pp. 198-219, p. 211.

98. Khumaynî, *Iṭṭilâ‘ât*, 21/9/60: ‘these corrupt *mujâhidîn*, these hypocrites’.

99. *The Imam and the Ommat* 8/11/80 p. 125. See also *Iṭṭilâ‘ât*, 15/8/59.

100. *The Imam and the Ommat* 8/11/80 p. 125.

101. *The Imam and the Ommat* 28/10/80 p. 115.

102. Ram, "Islamic Newspeak", p. 211.

103. Brockett, ‘Munâfiqûn’, p. 562; Kohlberg, ‘The Development of the Imâmî Shî‘î Doctrine of *jihâd*’, p. 70 n42, p. 71. See also Ṭabarsî, *Majma‘ al-bayân* Vol.5 p. 67 (IX:73), Vol.10, p. 100 (LXVI:9).

104. Ṭabâṭabâ’î, *al-Mîzân*, Vol.18 pp. 289-290; Vol.38 p. 324.

105. Ṭabarsî, *Majma‘ al-bayân*, Vol.5 p. 67 (IX:73), Vol.10, p. 100 (LXVI:9).

106. Brockett, ‘Munâfiqûn’, pp. 561-562. Kohlberg, ‘The Development of the Imâmî Shî‘î Doctrine of *jihâd*’, p. 70.

107. Khumaynî, *Jang wa jihâd*, pp. 69, 84.

108. Arthur Jeffery, *The Foreign Vocabulary of the Qur’ân* (Baroda: The Oriental Institute, 1938) pp. 202-203.

109. Muntaẓirî, *Jang-i taḥmîlî* 2/10/62, 26/8/62 p. 61, 19/8/61 p. 100, 27/8/62 p. 202.

110. According to Ṭabâṭabâ’î, *al-Mîzân* Vol.4 p. 247 (2:256). Ṭâliqânî gives the same definition. M. Abedi and G. Legenhausen (eds) *Jihâd and Shahâdat. Struggle and Martyrdom in Islam,* (Houston: IRIS, 1986) pp. 51-53.

111. *Islam and Revolution* p. 154 n.41.

112. *Islam and Revolution* p. 92.

113. *Islam and Revolution* p. 147.

114. *Islam and Revolution* p. 48.

115. Muntaẓirî, *Jang-i taḥmîlî* 28/2/63 p. 164. The use of *ṭâghût* is not a novelty in the history of Shî'ism. As Kohlberg has stated, the antediluvian infidel rulers were called *ṭawâghît*, and *ṭâghût* was an abusive title for Abû Bakr and 'Umar among Shî'îs. Etan Kohlberg, 'Some Shî'î Views of the Antediluvian World', in: *Studia Islamica* 51 (1980) pp. 41-66, p. 48, citing I. Goldziher, *Gesammelte Schriften* IV pp. 295-308, p. 323.

116. Âyatullâh Rabânî Amlashî, *Dar maktab-i jum'a* Vol.4 20/9/60 p. 133.

117. Khumaynî, *Dar justujû-yi râh az kalâm-i imâm: Mustaḍ'afîn, mustakbarîn* Vol.1 (Tehran, Amîr Kabîr, 1363[2]) p. 116; *Islam and Revolution* p. 243.

118. Âyatullâh Rabânî Amlashî, *Dar maktab-i jum'a* Vol.4 20/9/60 p. 133.

119. Khâmini'î, *Dar maktab-i jum'a* Vol.2, 4/7/59 *al-Nisâ'* IV:76 'Those who have believed fight in the way of Allah, and those who have disbelieved are fighting in the way of the Ṭâghût'.

120. Muntaẓirî, *Jang-i taḥmîlî* p. 61, references to traditions of 'Alî and Ḥusayn which said that one always has to fight the *ṭâghût* in defence of the oppressed. Someone who is silent when he sees that people are oppressed or when God's bounds are transgressed is a *ṭâghût* and belongs to the oppressors. These traditions are given without a source.

121. Khâmini'î, *Dar maktab-i jum'a* Vol.2 11/7/59 p. 328, 'the battlefield of *ḥaqq* and *bâṭil*, the battlefield of Islam and the Islamic Republic with the *ṭaghûtî* systems of the world'; Vol.2 16/8/59 p. 376.

122. Khumaynî, *Jumhûrî-yi islâmî* 19/12/60, *The Imam and the Ommat*, 26 December 1980; FBIS *Daily Report*, 24 April 1983: 'You are living in an age when human values have totally disappeared, having been replaced by worldly satans and satanic values. You are living in an inhuman age, in an age when they want to bring the world under the domination of Satan'; 6 July 1988. *Iṭṭilâ'ât*, 5/8/63 Mûsawî Ardabîlî, President Court of Justice; *Jang bâ inqilâb*, p. 12.

123. Muntaẓirî, *Jang-i taḥmîlî* 59/7/4 p. 42; *The Imam and the Ommat*, 28/10/80 p. 115.

124. Rafsanjânî, *Dar maktab-i jum'a* Vol.4 3/7/60 p. 10; 10/7/60 p. 22; and 30/11/60 p. 158.

125. Khumaynî, *Jang wa jihâd* 59/1/20 p. 45, p. 49.

126. Louis Gardet, 'Fâsiḳ', in: *Encyclopaedia of Islam*[2] Vol.2 pp. 833-834, p. 833.

127. Izutsu, *Ethico-Religious Concepts* p. 157.

128. Kulaynî, *al-Uṣûl min al-kâfî* Vol.2 p. 291.

129. '*în mard-i fâsiq-i kâfir*', Khumaynî, *Jang wa jihâd* 5/10/59, p. 49.

130. Khumaynî, *Jang wa jihâd* 8/7/59 p. 128.

131. Khumaynî, *Ṣaḥîfa-yi nûr* p. 535; Muntaẓirî, *Jang-i taḥmîlî* 29/10/63 p. 62.

132. Khâmini'î, *Dar maktab-i jum'a* Vol.2 4/7/59 p. 317.

133. Khâmini'î, *Dar maktab-i jum'a* Vol.2 9/8/59 p. 367; Vol.3 21/9/59 p. 21.

134. Khâmini'î, *Dar maktab-i jum'a* Vol.2 11/7/59 p. 332; 9/8/59 p. 367/370; Mûsawî Ardabîlî, Vol.3 29/6/60 p. 413.

135. Muhsin Rizâ'î, *Iṭṭilâ'ât*, 22/9/59.

136. Khumaynî, *Jang wa jihâd* 29/1/59 p. 69.

137. Khumaynî, *Jang wa jihâd* 14/1/61 p. 73.

138. Khumaynî, *Jang wa jihâd* 31/6/59 p. 71.

139. See for instance Rafsanjânî, *Dar maktab-i jum'a* Vol.5 8/5/61 p. 124.

140. In sermons in *Iṭṭilâ'ât*, Khâmini'î, 6/11/62; 18/11/63; Rafsanjânî 26/3/63; 28/5/63; Mûsawî Ardabîlî 1/9/65.

141. In sermons in *Iṭṭilâ'ât*, Rafsanjânî, 26/4/63; Imâmî Kâshânî, 20/2/65.

142. Khâmini'î in sermon in *Iṭṭilâ'ât*, 19/11/63, 6/10/65.

143. Tabâtabâ'î, *al-Mîzân* Vol.24 p. 73 (XVI:22); Tabarsî, *Majma' al-bayân* Vol.6 p. 460 (XVI:22,23), Vol.7 p. 150 (XXIII:67). The verb *istakbara* and its derivatives occur 48 times in the Qur'ân; '*mustakbirûn*' in *al-Nahl* XVI:22,23, *al-Munâfiqûn* LXIII:5, and *al-Mu'minûn* XXIII:67.

144. Mûsawî, *Iṭṭilâ'ât*, 8/9/64; Khâmini'î, 31/1/67.

145. Khâmini'î *Dar maktab-i jum'a* Vol.2 16/8/59.

146. *Jang bâ inqilâb* p. 12-13.

147. Khumaynî, *Iṭṭilâ'ât*, 12/4/88.

148. Tabâtabâ'î, *al-Mîzân*, Vol.9 pp. 80-81 (IV:96). See also Kulaynî, *al-Uṣûl min al-kâfî*, Vol.2, traditions on the authority of the fifth and sixth *imâms*, pp. 404-406. According to Ṭabarsî, *Majma' al-bayân* Vol.3, p. 124, verse IV:96 was sent down on the day of Badr. Those who were weakened by the polytheists because of their majority and strength and because the polytheists did not allow them to believe in God or follow His messenger. Vol.4 p. 226 (VIII:26) 'their weakness weakened their power during their time in Mecca.'.

149. Rûḥullâh Khumaynî, *Kashf al-asrâr* (Tehran, n.p., n.d.) p. 258.

150. Ervand Abrahamian, *Khomeinism* (London: I.B. Tauris, 1993) p. 47. Arjomand, Said Amir, *The Turban for the Crown. The Islamic Revolution in Iran* (Oxford: Oxford University Press, 1988) pp. 95-96. Cf. Qur'ân *al-Anfâl* VIII:26 'and remember when ye were few and downtrodden in the land'; and *al-Nisâ'* IV:97 '... we were oppressed in the land'.

151. Khumaynî, *Mustaḍ'afîn, mustakbarîn*, pp. 28, 183, 184. The compilers dedicated the volume to the *mustaḍ'afîn*, 'the continuing beloved of God the Exalted, the shining faces of Islam, the dedicated supporters of the religion of God, and the real inheritors of the earth'.

152. Khumaynî recited *al-Nisâ'* partly, IV:75: '(What is wrong with you) that you fight not in the way of Allah and the oppressed, men, women, and children', *Mustaḍ'afîn, mustakbirîn* pp. 28-29.

153. Khumaynî, *Mustaḍ'afîn, mustakbirîn* p. 31.

154. Khumaynî, *Mustaḍ'afîn, mustakbirîn* pp. 126, 167, 169, 125.

155. Khumaynî, *Mustaḍ'afîn, mustakbirîn* p. 28.

156. Khumaynî, *Mustaḍ'afîn, mustakbirîn* p. 12.

157. Khumaynî, *Mustaḍ'afîn, mustakbirîn* pp. 24, 28.

158. Khumaynî, *Mustaḍ'afîn, mustakbirîn* p. 23.

159. Khumaynî, *Mustaḍ'afîn, mustakbirîn* pp. 126, 96-97, 167, 168.

160. Khumaynî, *Mustaḍ'fîn, mustakbirîn* p. 42. According to Ṭabarsî, this verse refers to the Israelites during their time in Egypt, *Majma' al-bayân* Vol.7 p. 310.

161. Khumaynî, *Mustaḍ'afîn, mustakbirîn* pp. 96, 97. Mûsawî also stressed the dichotomy of the *mustakbirûn* and the *mustaḍ'afûn*, *Iṭṭilâ'ât*, 28/11/85.

162. Âyatullâh Âzarî Qumî, *Khaṭṭ-i imâm wa wîzhgîhâ-yi ân* (The Line of the Imâm and its particulars, (Qum: Dâr al-'Ilm, n.d.) pp. 25-27.

163. Âzarî Qumî, *Khaṭṭ-i imâm wa wîzhgîhâ-yi ân* p. 25.

164. Âzarî Qumî, *Khaṭṭ-i imâm wa wîzhgîhâ-yi ân* p. 25.

165. Âzarî Qumî, *Khaṭṭ-i imâm wa wîzhgîhâ-yi ân* p. 27.

166. Khumaynî, *Mustaḍ'afîn, mustakbirîn* pp. 185, 186, 190.

167. Khumaynî, *Mustaḍ'afîn, mustakbirîn* p. 125.

168. Khumaynî, *Mustaḍ'afîn, mustakbirîn* pp. 126, 129.

169. Muntaẓirî, *Jang-i taḥmîlî* p. 66.

170. Khumaynî, *Mustaḍ'afîn, mustakbirîn* pp. 167, 168.

171. According to D.B. MacDonald (E.E. Calverley), in 'Ḥaqq' in *Encyclopaedia of Islam*[2] Vol.3 pp. 82-83, the ideas of 'right' and 'real' are expressed in pre-Islamic poetry and in Arab sayings. In the Qur'ân *ḥaqq* means 'reality', 'fact', 'truth' and 'right'. *Bâṭil* is the opposite of these meanings. Y. Linant de Bellefonds' article 'fâsid wa- bâṭil' in *Encyclopaedia of Islam*[2] Vol.2 pp. 829-832 does not give the Shî'î interpretation of *bâṭil* and refers to the concepts in the legal sense only.

172. '*ay ẓahara al-ḥaqq wa-huwa al-islâm wa-l-dîn, ay baṭala al-bâṭil wa- huwa al-shirk*'. Ṭabarsî, *Majma' al-bayân* Vol.6 p. 562.

173. Ṭabarsî, *Majma' al-bayân* Vol.4 p. 645 and vol.6 p. 562.

174. Muḥammad Ḥusayn Ṭabâṭaba'î, *Shi'ite Islam*, trans. and ed. by Seyyed Hossein Nasr, (Albany: SUNY Press, 1975) p. 154.

175. Izutsu, *Ethico-Religious Concepts in the Qur'ân* p. 97.

176. W. Montgomery Watt, 'Shi'ism under the Umayyads' in: *Journal of the Royal Asiatic Society* (1960) pp. 158-172, p. 160.

177. S.V. Mir Ahmed Ali, *Husain. The Saviour of Islam* (Qum: Shafagh Publications, 1987) pp. 176-177.

178. Khâmini'î, *Dar maktab-i jum'a* Vol.2 4/7/59 p. 316, 11/7/59 p. 326, 2/8/59 p. 356, 9/8/59 p. 366-368, p. 371. For the classical interpretation see: Ṭabarsî, *Majma' al-bayân* Vol.4 p. 645.

179. FBIS *Daily Report*, 26 July 1981; Mûsawî, *Iṭṭilâ'ât*, 9/6/64; Khâmini'î, *Dar maktab-i jum'a* Vol.3 12/10/59 p. 45; Khâmini'î, *Chahâr sâl bâ mardum* p. 372; *Jang bâ inqilâb* p. 5; Khumaynî, *The Imam and the Ommat* pp. 65, 104.

180. *Dah sâl bâ ṭarrâḥân-i grafik-i inqilâb-i islâmî*, Vol.3 pp. 17, 22, 94.

181. Khumaynî, *Jang wa jihâd* 7/10/59 pp. 11-12. Khumaynî, *Iṭṭilâ'ât*, 28/5/88; According to Aḥmad Jannatî, one of the goals of *jihâd* is 'establishment of truth and justice and destruction of falsehood and injustice', 'Defense and Jihâd in the Qur'ân' in: *Tawhîd* 1 (1404) pp. 39-58, p. 46.

182. Khumaynî, *Iṭṭilâ'ât*, 7/1/61.

183. Muntaẓirî, *Jang-i taḥmîlî* p. 99.

184. Khumaynî, *Ṣaḥîfa-yi nûr* Vol.7 p. 576. The same speech appeared in *The Imam and the Ommat* p. 104.

185. Khâmini'î, *Dar maktab-i jum'a* Vol.2 12/10/59 p. 45: 'God has worked on his promise, which is the victory of *ḥaqq* over *bâṭil* (falsehood)'.

186. Rafsanjânî, *Dar maktab-i jum'a* Vol.4 3/7/60 p. 10: *al-Baqara* II:216: 'Fighting is prescribed for you, though it is distasteful to you'; Imâmî Kâshânî, Vol.4 13/9/60 p. 125. He referred to the following Qur'ân verses: *al-Ḥajj* XXII:40: 'But for Allah's warding off the people, some by means of others, hermitages and churches and oratories and places of worship in which the name of Allah was had would have been destr-

oyed in numbers'; *al-Baqara* II:251: '...Now if Allah had not beaten off one set of the people by means of others, the land would have gone corrupt'; and *al-Mâ'ida* V:54: '... Allah will produce (another) people whom He loveth and who love Him, humble towards the believers, haughty towards the unbelievers, striving in the cause of Allah, and not fearing the blame of anyone; that is Allah's bounty which He bestoweth upon whomsoever He pleaseth; Allah is unrestricted, knowing'. Mûsawî, *Iṭṭilâ'ât*, 9/6/64.

187. Rafsanjânî, *Dar maktab-i jum'a* Vol.4 3/10/60 p. 158.

188. Khâmini'î, *Dar maktab-i jum'a*, Vol.2 16/8/59, p. 376 'It is clear and natural that the idols (*ṭawâghît*) of the world do not allow that a movement of *ḥaqq* remains in the world, therefore they want to destroy it', p. 377: 'a war started because the United States is against Islam and because it wants to suppress and suffocate the cry for *ḥaqq* by oppressed nations'. *Jang bâ inqilâb*, p. 5.

189. Mahdawî Kanî, *Dar maktab-i jum'a* Vol.6 3/4/62 p. 383. This conforms with Ṭabâṭabâ'î's explanation of this verse. *al-Mîzân* Vol.17 p. 142.

190. Ṭabarsî, *Majmâ' al-bayân* Vol.4 p. 673. Ṭabarî, *Jâmi' al-bayân* Vol.14 p. 570.

4 HISTORICAL EXEMPLARY DISCOURSE

During the Islamic revolution in Iran one of the most salient features of political rhetoric had been the re-enactment of perhaps the major event in Shî'î history, the revolt of the third *imâm*, Ḥusayn, against the Umayyad Caliph, Yazîd. Traditionally, this event was commemorated each year in drama and mourning ceremonials but now it was linked to the political realities of the day, in which Iran became Karbalâ', the place where the actual fight between Ḥusayn and his opponents took place; Muḥammad Rizâ Shah became identified with Yazîd, and the Iranian people with Ḥusayn. The identification of rulers with Yazîd had been used before by their clerical opponents as an instrument to rouse people against the Shah,[1] but during the revolution the use of 'Karbalâ' as a representation of Iranian politics was broadened to include Ḥusayn's sacrifice and martyrdom as an example for the Iranian population.

In this chapter I shall deal with various ways of referring to parts of Islamic history and historical figures during the war with Iraq. I shall first deal with the references to the wars fought by the prophet Muḥammad. Secondly, I shall pay attention to the image of 'Alî. Thirdly, the roles of Ḥusayn and Yazîd and, fourthly, the role of the twelfth *imâm* will be treated. At the end of the chapter, the names of the military operations and the slogans will be dealt with. The way the Iranian leaders referred to the past fits into to what Eickelman and Piscatori have described as 'the blurring of tradition and modernity': on the one hand the key elements of Islamic tradition are fixed, but these traditions on the other hand are being modified and manipulated because they are created, 'because the line between occurred and perceived pasts depends upon the construction, dissemination, and acceptance of authoritative historical narratives, the past of occurred events exists mostly as a pool of resources which can be drawn upon in traditional and modern settings to sanction present practice'.[2]

Initially, during the first weeks after the outbreak of the war in 1980 and after the cease-fire in 1988, the leaders made many comparisons with the wars fought by the Prophet by way of presenting the situation of Iran as one which had strong similarities to the wars of the Prophet. The picture was that of a newly established community under threat, facing the same problems as the community of the Prophet. There were numerous references to the Prophet Muḥammad, his son-in-law 'Alî and his family, but the references to Ḥusayn, the third Shî'î *imâm* and son of 'Alî outnumbered all others. References to other wars fought by Muslims or to other periods in Islamic history did not play any role of importance. All figures (Muḥammad, 'Alî, Ḥusayn) lived in the first centuries of Islam and were essential for the Shî'î religion. Other parts of Islamic history and Iranian history were disregarded. The battle of Qâdisîya (635/7), the battle in which the Arab army defeated the forces of the Persian Sasanian Empire and which prepared the way for the conquest of Persia, received some attention. But this was in reaction to the fact that Ṣaddâm Ḥusayn had declared the war to be 'a second Qâdisîya'. Iranian leaders reacted scornfully by asking why Ṣaddâm Ḥusayn had taken Qâdisîya as an example since that battle was contrary to everything Ṣaddâm represented. According to Khumaynî, the importance of Qâdisîya lay in the defeat of the unbelievers and the victory of Islam, and not in the fact that it was waged by Arabs against Persians. Qâdisîya in fact was a blessing for Persia.[3] It had liberated the deprived people of Iran from the tyrannical Sasanian regime, and had guided them to Islam.[4] After the recapture of Bustân in 1982, Imâmî Kâshânî referred to other important victories in Islamic history. He accentuated the role of Iranian fighters in recent triumphs and equated these with important victories in Islamic history. He said: 'O fighters of Islam, O beloved of the borders, O ground troops, O navy, O air force, O *sipâh* [*Pâsdârân*], O *basîj* (mobilized), O police, O fighters. You have conquered Bustân and acquired a name in history'. The recapture of Bustân belonged to the great victories of Islam, together with Khandaq, Gibraltar and the Suez Canal.[5] The nationalization of the Suez Canal is a symbol of a successful blow to imperialism. Gibraltar is an odd example. The name is a corruption of 'Jabal Ṭâriq', the name Arabs gave to Gibraltar after Ṭâriq, who invaded Spain via this point in 711. This marked the beginning of Arab rule over Spain, which lasted for almost eight centuries. The conquest, however, was made by the great enemies of the Shî'a, the Umayyad dynasty, to which the alleged murderer of Ḥusayn, Yazîd, also belonged. Furthermore this was a conquest and not a defensive war.

Historical analogies: Parallels with the wars of the Prophet

Immediately after the outbreak of the war Khâmini'î drew a parallel with the wars of the Prophet. He compared the war with Iraq to the battle of the Trench, *Khandaq*, in 5/627.[6] For Khâmini'î the comparison did not concern the manner of fighting (the Meccans laid siege to the Trench which the Prophet had dug to stop them entering Medina), but lay in the fact that both wars were fought for the same reason: to ward off the destruction of Islam and the Islamic community. Moreover, this war would also have the same outcome as the battle of the Trench, that is, a resounding victory for the forces of Islam.[7]

Another aspect of the reference to the battle of the Trench was the comparison between Ṣaddâm Ḥusayn and 'Amr ibn 'Abd Wudd, the commander of the Meccan troops. Ṣaddâm's fate would be the same as that of 'Amr. He would be killed by the forces of Islam, represented by the Iranian forces, just as 'Amr had been killed by 'Alî, the 'Commander of the Faithful'. The image of the warrior 'Alî, as one of the most heroic and brave companions of the Prophet and the person who killed one of the fiercest enemies of Islam, was an important factor in the efforts to mobilize the Iranian population. Not only had 'Alî played an important role in the outcome, but he had in fact provoked the Meccan attack at Khandaq. The battle of Khandaq originated from a conflict between 'Alî and 'Amr ibn 'Abd Wudd which had started when both were still in Mecca. It was said that 'Alî had smashed one of the idols in Mecca and this had angered the son of the high priest, 'Amr. In the ensuing fight, 'Alî killed 'Amr's son and 'Amr swore that he would take revenge. He succeeded in persuading other Meccans to attack the Muslims and this led to the battle of Khandaq.[8]

In the same sermon Khâmini'î recounted the tradition in which the Prophet, during the digging of the Trench, struck a stone with his pick-axe. Muḥammad said that in the sparks which flew from the stone he saw the palaces of *kisrâ* (Chosroes) and *qayṣar* (Caesar) which would be subdued by the forces of Islam after the war was over.[9] They represent the kings of the Sasanian and Byzantine empires, the two great powers of that time, which later really were subdued by the forces of Islam. Both became the 'poetic symbol of past glory and of fate that overtakes even mighty kings',[10] and a symbol of the tyranny and usurpation by non-Muslim rulers.[11] Khumaynî referred to the same tradition in one of his speeches to make clear that Ṣaddâm would meet the same fate as the Sasanian King Anûshîrwân (the name by which Chosroes I (531-579) was popularly known), who was defeated because of his oppressive politics.[12] For Khâmini'î and Khumaynî it was clear that this tradition was also a promise that the present superpowers (*abar-qudrat-hâ*) would be defeated by the Muslims of Iran.

The fact that the following week in the Friday sermon a parallel was drawn with the battle of Badr (2/624), where the Muslims were not in a defensive position but were the attacking party,[13] shows that the justification of the war was not based only on the fact that Iran had been attacked and was defending itself.[14] It was also based on the fact that war is ordained by God, that it is His decision and that it is beyond the power and knowledge of human beings to reason why. Khâmini'î recited Qur'ânic verse *al-Anfâl* VIII:7: 'when Allah was promising you that one of the two parties should be yours, and ye were wishing that the one without armed protection might be yours ' and 'Possibly ye may dislike a thing though it is good for you', and *al-Baqara* II:216: 'Fighting is prescribed for you, though it is distasteful to you. Possibly ye may dislike a thing though it is good for you, and possibly ye may love a thing, though it is bad for you; Allah knoweth, though ye do not know'. Khâmini'î told his audience that in anticipation of a Muslim attack, the Meccans had sent out a force to protect a caravan returning from Syria. The Muslims wanted to attack the caravan, but God commanded them to attack the armed Meccan forces. The reason for this was that God wanted them to confront the forces of *bâṭil* (falsehood), and the *shayṭânî* (satanic) and *ṭâghûtî* (idolatrous) powers in order to defeat them and install *ḥaqq* (truth) in the world.[15] It was clear from these statements that Khâmini'î equated the role of the Iranians with that of the Muslims who fought at Badr. In his eyes the Iraqis, supported by the United States, represented the modern version of the Meccans. Khâmini'î demanded from his audience the same thing that God had demanded from the Muslims at Badr; their assignment was the same. Iranians therefore had no other choice than to accept the war and support it, because criticism of the war was criticism of God and, as a consequence, criticism of Islam, the Islamic revolution and Republic.[16]

Finally, the parallel with Badr is important because the battle was a great victory for the Muslims over the powerful Meccans and meant that the status of Muḥammad was greatly enhanced and that Muḥammad's authority and power were accepted as a force to be reckoned with.[17] Muntaẓirî referred to the victory at Badr as an example of God's benevolence to those who obeyed Him and relied on Him.[18] Furthermore Minister of Foreign Affairs Wilâyatî said: 'the blessed month of Ramadan is the month of victory for Islam and the annihilation of blasphemy. ... Hopefully with your attention another Badr will happen in the new dawn of the history of Islam'.[19]

Khumaynî maintained that true followers of God sacrifice their lives for Islam. He said that the Prophet of Islam had suffered more than anyone else for the sake of Islam, yet all his sufferings are wasted today by those who neglect their duty towards Islam.[20] Furthermore, the conflict between prophets and arrogants is not limited to history but is eternal. According to God and the Prophet, *jihâd fî sabîl allâh* is the most important of the divine *aḥkâm* (principles) because *jihâd* safeguards Islamic principles. It is stated that those who do not obey the divine injunction to participate in *jihâd* can expect punishment. This is laid down in *al-Nûr* XXIV:63: 'do not set the messenger's summoning of you on the same footing amongst you as your summoning of each other; Allah knoweth those of you who slip away secretly, so let those who oppose from His affair beware lest a trial affect them or there fall upon them punishment painful'.[21]

As a rule Khumaynî presented a picture of identification of the Iranian people with the Prophet and praised them for the fact that they had taken upon themselves the responsibility to fight for the sake of Islam.

> You are the followers of the Prophet of God who endured unbearable pains for the cause of God's religion, who accepted great hardship in Mecca when he was the object of so much pressure, slanders and insults; and in Medina when so many wars were waged against him. Nevertheless, His Holiness

> and his faithful followers remained steadfast like a mountain and served Islam and the Muslims. You are the followers of the Commander of the Believers and his children who welcomed any pain and disaster for the cause of God.[22]

> You the beloved ones and great youths must know that guarding and protecting Islam, the Islamic country and religion of the truth constitute the greatest obedience towards which the prophets and great saints... have always made arduous efforts and have never stinted any sacrifice.[23]

Refuting criticism of the fact that so many people had died as a result of the war, for which the Islamic Republic itself was to blame since it had confronted the United States and its allies, Khumaynî said that the Prophet Muḥammad and his descendants 'Alî and Ḥusayn also had not submitted and compromised with the 'Abû Sufyâns', a reference to one of the fiercest enemies of Muḥammad. 'Many Muslims lost their lives in the war against the hostile Meccans, in the struggle against the enemies of 'Alî and Ḥusayn's rebellion against the tyrannical government [of Yazîd]. When all prophets who fought against criminals were wrong, then we have made the same mistake... When we speak about everything we have lost we have to think also about the things we have gained. Do all these losses outweigh what we have gained by these wars, the *iḥyâ'* (revival) of Islam'?[24] On another occasion Khumaynî said that the war was imposed on Iran because the Islamic Republic had 'committed the crime' of reviving the *sunna* of the Prophet.[25] Âyatullâh Mahdawî Kanî, the former prime minister, implicitly said that the Islamic Republic was in the same position as the Prophet by arguing that the war with Iraq had the same meaning as the battle at Badr and the battle of the Trench, that is, separating *ḥaqq* from *bâṭil* (see Chapter 3).[26]

A compelling example of the Islamic past was made by Muntaẓirî when he referred to the soldiers during the Prophet's expedition to Tabûk in 9/630. He warned Iranians not to waste anything and to pay strict attention to sobriety and moderation. According to him, the hardship of the soldiers of Tabûk was such that one day two soldiers had to share one date between them in order to get some food. Is it dignified, Muntaẓirî asked his audience, for someone who adheres to Islam to waste or to practice usury when these soldiers have lived in so much hardship in order that Islam may survive?[27]

The war showed God's relationship with the people, He had fulfilled His promise by assisting them in the war. In return they had to keep their promise by obeying the command of God, otherwise God's mercy would disappear and this would become clear at the Day of Resurrection.[28] Khâmini'î drew a parallel with the battle of Uḥud in 3/625 and that of Ḥunayn (10/630) to make this clear.[29] This parallel however had a function different from those with the battle of Badr or the battle of Khandaq. Badr and Khandaq were obvious examples of victory for Muslims and therefore selected as encouragement for Iranian soldiers. The parallel with Uḥud, Tabûk and Ḥunayn had more of a moral function. According to Khâmini'î, the Muslims had suffered considerable losses during these battles as a result of the immoral attitude of some Muslims. The story was told to Iranians as an object lesson in overconfidence, greediness and disunion.

Historical analogies: The lessons of 'Alî

The figure of 'Alî ibn Abî Ṭâlib, son-in-law of Muḥammad and the first Shî'î *imâm*, has always had a profound influence on Iranians. 'Alî is the popular hero of Iran par excellence. Not only does he play an important role in rituals and popular social beliefs but his words and political and military deeds are used as a source for Shî'î legal procedure, at the same time legitimizing these procedures.[30] In Iran, 'Alî is seen both as a pious and unworldly man, representing Islam, good and virtue, and as a man of action fighting for social justice.[31] The *Nahj al-balâgha* (Path of Eloquence), a collection of ethical and moralizing aphorisms, sermons and letters mostly pertaining to 'Alî's caliphate, is regarded by Shî'îs as an authentic work of 'Alî. For them this work is second in importance after the Qur'ân and has a position of immense authority.[32]

It does not, therefore, come as a surprise that Iranian leaders referred to the speeches and letters of 'Alî as laid down in the *Nahj al-balâgha* to legitimize their war policy. In the war rhetoric, 'Alî's image was used as a role model which gave guidelines and precepts and as a compelling example, both for the government (how to act) and for Iranians (how to behave). Muntaẓirî for instance in one of his speeches said that according to 'Alî, one had to take a hostile position against the oppressor and the *ṭâghût* and to help the oppressed.[33] 'If we belong to 'Alî's party and are his supporters, then we must not be silent in the face of this attack on Islam and Muslims, but rather as His Holiness ordered in the *Nahj al-balâgha*, defend Islam, the Qur'ân and our sanctuaries'.[34] On the occasion of the birthday of 'Alî, Khumaynî said that following the example of 'Alî the whole nation was in favour of the war and like 'Alî all Iranians regarded it as their duty to safeguard Islam and Islamic principles and fight against those who wanted to reduce Islam to blasphemy and polytheism.[35]

Besides references to 'Alî as brave warrior, Iranian leaders referred to 'Alî's admonitions in order to mobilize the Iranian population. In his first sermon after the start of the war Khâmini'î referred to sermons 27 and 51 and letter 47 from the *Nahj al-balâgha* in which *jihâd* and sacrifice were exalted.[36] A few months later, he cited a letter from 'Alî to his Governor in Egypt, Malik al-Ashtar, in which 'Alî advised Malik not to enter peace negotiations when these implied submission, reconciliation with unbelief, heresy and aggression.[37]

'Alî's instructions and advice during the battle of Ṣiffîn (37/657) when his met the forces of the rebellious governor of Syria, Mu'âwiya, were used as an important source for mobilization and for justification of the war. Imâmî Kâshânî, for instance, drew a parallel with this battle. The situation at Ṣiffîn had become difficult for 'Alî's troops when Mu'âwiya cut them off from their water-supply by blocking access to the Euphrates. Kâshânî said that Iran's enemies had put Iran in the same position as 'Alî by their attack, by blocking the Euphrates.[38] Like 'Alî the Iranians had two options: drench their swords with the enemy's blood and quench their thirst with water, or submit to humiliation, defeat, misfortune and punishment. Two months later (July 1982) Mûsawî Ardabîlî used the same sermon to justify Iran's invasion of Iraq.[39] He said that the Iranian population had opted for the first advice 'Alî had given, that is, they wanted to drench their swords in Ṣaddâm's blood. Mûsawî Ardabîlî denied that Iran's role had changed from a defensive to an aggressive one, since Ṣaddâm was still attacking Iranian cities. He continued by asking whether it was an option for Iran to say that the army would not fight on the other side of the border, and that it was all right for them [Ṣaddâm and Ba'th] to send aircraft to bomb Iranian cities. According to Ardabîlî, 'Alî had already given the answer to this rhetorical question by saying that people who fight on their own ground will not find salvation and courageous Muslims must not allow their enemy to fight on their territory. The aggressor must be defeated on his own ground.[40] The fact that the Iranian leaders referred to the battle of Ṣiffîn in order to encourage people to continue fighting is in fact paradoxical since that battle ended in arbitration, which was not mentioned by the leaders.

The Karbalâ' paradigm

The Karbalâ' paradigm, because of its emotional appeal based on the martyrdom and sacrifice of Ḥusayn, his family and supporters, played a fundamental role in the war rhetoric throughout the war. Before going into detail about the way Ḥusayn and the battle of Karbalâ' were used in the war rhetoric, I will give a brief historical outline of what happened in 61/680 and the way Ḥusayn's revolt and death were interpreted by Shî'îs.

After the death of the first *imâm*, 'Alî, in 40/661, his son Ḥasan, the second *imâm*, abandoned all claims to the caliphate and accepted Mu'âwiya as the new Caliph. For the rest of his life he abstained from political activities. Shî'î sources say that his abdication from the caliphate for the remainder of Mu'âwiya's life was the result of his political awareness and his desire to avoid useless bloodshed, and not because of feebleness or cowardice in the face of Mu'âwiya's military strength.[41] Ḥasan died in 49/669 and his younger brother Ḥusayn was chosen as the new *Imâm*. It seems that he considered Mu'âwiya's rule a *fait accompli* because he did not revolt against the Caliph.[42] Ṭabâṭabâ'î says that this was because Ḥusayn was bound by his brother's treaty with Mu'âwiya.[43] After the death of Mu'âwiya in 60/680 two developments made him decide to oppose the new Caliph, Yazîd. On the one hand it was the ever increasing pressure on him by the Kûfans, who did not accept any other leader than someone from the house of the Prophet. On the other hand, it was Yazîd's behaviour which led to Ḥusayn's decision to come into action. Many Muslims regarded Yazîd's accession to the caliphate as an outrage because he was openly disrespectful of the principles and laws of Islam. When he demanded Ḥusayn's *bay'a* (pledge of allegiance), the latter refused to give it.[44] Although he knew that Muslim ibn 'Aqîl, whom he had sent to Kûfa to assess the situation there, had been killed, and although he was warned that the people of Kûfa were not to be trusted in their support, Ḥusayn brushed aside warnings and set out for Kûfa with his family and a handful supporters. On the command of the Governor of Kûfa, 'Ubayd Allâh ibn Ziyâd, Ḥusayn and his followers were prevented from entering the city. On 2 *muḥarram* 61/680 they were stopped by a military unit on the plain of Karbalâ' in present-day Iraq, surrounded, and cut off from the water of the Euphrates. Ḥusayn tried to negotiate a settlement, but his adversaries left him no other choice than to pay allegiance to Yazîd or to die of thirst. On 10 *muḥarram* (known as *'âshûrâ'*) the confrontation between Ḥusayn and his followers and Ibn Ziyâd's army, which was much superior in numbers, took place. In the unequal fight, all the men on Ḥusayn's side including himself were killed. The women and Ḥusayn's only surviving son, 'Alî, were taken as prisoners to Yazîd's court in Damascus.[45]

According to Veccia Vaglieri, the Shî'î texts on the purpose of Ḥusayn's deliberate sacrifice are clear:

> to 'revive the religion of his grandfather Muḥammad', 'to redeem it', and 'save it from the destruction into which it had been thrown by the behavior of Yazîd', furthermore, he wished to show that the conduct of the hypocrites was shameful and to teach the peoples the necessity of revolt against unjust and impious governments (*fâsiḳs*), in short he offered himself as an example (*uswa*) to the Muslim community.[46]

The identification of rulers with Yazîd had already been used by clerical opponents as an instrument to rouse people against the Shah, but the politicizing of Ḥusayn's example as the champion of the Islamic cause was to a great extent influenced by the much-debated publication of *Shahîd-i jâwîd* by Ni'matullâh Ṣâliḥî Najaf-âbâdî. In this work, the writer stated that Ḥusayn's uprising was a 'wholly rational and fairly well-planned attempt at overthrowing Yazîd', proven by the fact that Ḥusayn had sent Muslim ibn Aqîl to Kûfa in order to assess the amount of support there. His uprising was not motivated by any prescience that it was God's will that he would be martyred, a view prevalent under more traditional Shî'î theologians. He furthermore refuted the traditional idea that Ḥusayn's sacrifice was a 'unique and inimitable event in history, above the capacity of the common run of human beings'.[47] On the contrary, Ḥusayn's sacrifice was an example for Muslims to follow.

In popular Shî'î piety, Ḥusayn's martyrdom was interpreted in more than one way. One interpretation sees Ḥusayn, like the other *imâms*, as an intercessor who mediates between God and man. Ḥusayn is capable of granting people a place in Paradise.[48] Participation in the annual rituals and commemoration services, such as the passion play *ta'ziya* during *muḥarram* during which the event of Karbalâ' is commemorated, is thought to be essential for obtaining a place in Paradise.[49] This interpretation of Ḥusayn's martyrdom led to quietism and political accommodation since people transferred Ḥusayn's role as intercessor to political, social and economic life as well, and made themselves dependent on those in power in order to achieve their goal or obtain things.[50] However, during the revolution, the activist interpretation of the Karbalâ' event became the most effective symbolic instrument in the opposition to the Shah. Ḥusayn's position as an intercessor was not important but the person of Ḥusayn, his sacrifice for the cause of Islam, his struggle against tyranny, has become an example for Iranians to follow. The activist interpretation of Ḥusayn's martyrdom had gained the upperhand in 1978 when traditional mourning processions during *muḥarram* were suspended and substituted by political marches.[51]

The Karbalâ' paradigm was used extensively after the installation of the Islamic Republic in order to keep revolutionary fervour alive. During the suppression of ethnic unrest in Kurdistan, when army units were dispatched to Kurdish areas, the value of martyrdom was stressed in Friday sermons. Prayer leaders also made it clear that grief and lamentation for the martyrs of the revolution was misplaced because martyrdom was unsurpassable. People should rather take the martyrs as an example to follow.[52]

In the war rhetoric, references to Ḥusayn and Karbalâ' were almost commonplace. The fact that Karbalâ' is situated in Iraq was used by Iranian leaders as a major incentive to mobilize people for the war effort. Slogans such as '*râh-i Karbalâ' az Mihrân mîguzarad*' (the road to Karbalâ' passes through Mihrân) and '*râh-i Quds az Karbalâ' mîguzarad*' (the road to Jerusalem passes through Karbalâ') were heard repeatedly. Road signs on the battlefield gave the remaining distances to Karbalâ' and Jerusalem.[53]

It is not surprising that at a time when Ḥusayn and his struggle for the cause of Islam were presented as a model for the Iranian people, Yazîd, the alleged murderer of Ḥusayn and notorious for his un-Islamic attitude and criminal record, was one of the nicknames for Ṣaddâm Ḥusayn, which belongs to Rank's category of 'intensifying the enemy's 'bad' through association and identification.[54] In the sermons it was almost commonplace to call Ṣaddâm Ḥusayn 'Ṣaddâm-i Yazîd'.[55] The leaders emphasized that Ṣaddâm Ḥusayn's purpose with this war was identical to that of Yazîd, Mu'âwiya and the rest of the Umayyad dynasty: the destruction of Islam and a return to the pre-Islamic era of the Jâhilîya.[56] On several occasions Ṣaddâm was compared to Abû Jahl, one of the fiercest enemies of the Prophet. Khumaynî said on the occasion of *ghadîr khumm*, the anniversary of the nomination by Muḥammad of 'Alî as his successor, that asking to make peace with Ṣaddâm was as absurd as asking the Prophet to make peace with Abû Jahl.[57] In his first speech after the outbreak of the war, Khumaynî attacked Ṣaddâm Ḥusayn for invoking the names of 'Alî and Ḥusayn and said that Ṣaddâm could not be regarded as a Muslim since he and the Ba'th had been excommunicated by Muḥsin al-Ḥakîm, the highest religious authority in Iraq. His invoking the names of 'Alî and Ḥusayn had the sole purpose of deceiving the people.[58] Imâmî Kâshânî also attacked Ṣaddâm Ḥusayn for claiming that he was a descendant of Ḥusayn, the third *imâm*. He emphasized that Ṣaddâm Ḥusayn, following the Shah, misused Islam for the purpose of propaganda and demagogy. Imâmî Kâshânî asked his audience whether Ṣaddâm Ḥusayn would have attacked the land of the eighth *imâm* if he really was a Muslim.[59] The rejection by the Iranian leaders of every connection Ṣaddâm Ḥusayn could have with those historical Islamic figures who served as an example or were glorified, again is an example of how they maximized the evil side of their enemy and how they tried to degrade Ṣaddâm Ḥusayn in the eyes of the Iranian population.

As I have shown above, Iranian leaders from the beginning equated the war with Iraq with the battles the Prophet and 'Alî fought, such as those at Badr and Khandaq. Leaders justified the war by trying to convince the Iranian population that the Islamic Republic was in the right because the war it fought had the same intention as those of the Prophet and 'Alî: the preservation of Islam and the installation of *ḥaqq* and the annihilation of *kufr* and *bâṭil* (see Chapter 3). Ḥusayn's struggle is seen in the same light; his sacrifice was for the installation of *ḥaqq* and justice and for the safeguarding of Islam.[60] The comparison which leaders made between the Islamic Republic and Ḥusayn and his supporters on the one hand, and, on the other, the identification of Ṣaddâm with Yazîd, were intended to show that the Islamic Republic was assigned the same task as the third *imâm*, safeguarding and reviving Islam and fighting against oppression and tyranny.[61] Again, a world view was presented in which Iran's badness, in the form of participation in a war - which by definition is bad, as the Iranian leaders themselves did not hesitate to stress - [62] was minimized, redefined and turned into a greater goodness.

Khumaynî on one occasion said that all the propaganda and conspiracies against the Islamic Republic could not hide *ḥaqq*.

> You are in the right just like the *imâm*, Lord of the Martyrs, was in the right and became superior with so few in number. Although he was mar-

tyred together with his sons, he revived Islam and brought disgrace on Yazîd and the Umayyad dynasty.[63]

Another version of this text is followed by the sentence: 'You are the Shî'ites following the same Lord'.[64] It was expected of the courageous nation of Muslims of Iran to opt for continuation on the path of Ḥusayn and his sister Zaynab. Furthermore, Iranians were prepared to die because they were a nation which knew that martyrdom, guidance, generosity and sacrifice were the reason for their eternal life.[65] 'The nation of the Party of God of Iran will never submit while on the path of *imâm* Ḥusayn... Our young men at the battlefronts become martyrs in order to realize the goals which Ḥusayn laid down in his will. Ḥusayn's uprising was aimed at stopping the plundering acts of the oppressors and the violation of the rights of Muslims. We follow this path and like Ḥusayn we are present on the global battlefield'.[66] Ḥusayn's legacy to the soldiers was the responsibility to safeguard Islam against different forces which wanted to obliterate it.[67] The Islamic Republic was a follower of the path of Ḥusayn (*payraw az râh-i Ḥusayn*).[68] Furthermore, 'the sacrifice of 'Alî Akbar, 'Alî Asghar [two sons of Ḥusayn killed at Karbalâ'] and *imâm* Ḥusayn, is valuable for the continuation of Islam. At the present time, thousands of our youths, younger than the helpers of *imâm* Ḥusayn, are willing to sacrifice themselves for the continuation of Islam and the strengthening and consolidation of the revolution'.[69]

The leaders emphasized that the Karbalâ' event was a model and an example for Iranian men and women, the young and elderly to follow. People in Iranian society acted in the same way as the Muslims at Karbalâ'. Soldiers regarded the night of *'âshûrâ'*, the night of Ḥusayn's death, as the most suitable night to fight.[70] Muntaẓirî said: 'You are like those people who defended *imâm* Ḥusayn in Karbalâ'. You are like his companions because your intention is pure.[71]

The Iranian leaders not only equated the war with Karbalâ' but represented the war as a re-enactment of Karbalâ': 'Today is the day of Husayn's *'âshûrâ'*. Today Iran is Karbalâ'... Today is the day of resistance'.[72] 'Oh courageous fighters, today the bloodstained Ḥusaynî banner of Karbalâ'î-yi Iran is entrusted to your peace-seeking hands. Your attacks and brave resistance on the battlefield open the path to Jerusalem through Ḥusayn's Karbalâ'... Ḥusayn's question whether there is an assistant to defend Islam has been answered by you'.[73] Iranian soldiers were equated with Ḥusayn's followers who fought with him at Karbalâ': 'We see the same thing now as we know from the companions of *imâm* Ḥusayn who expected to appear in Paradise... a front like the front of *imâm* Ḥusayn... you are sons of Ḥusayn'.[74]

Towns and cities which were badly damaged in the war were renamed in the cause of propaganda, For instance Khûnînshahr (City of blood) for Khurramshahr and Karbalâ'-yi Sûsangird (City of those who love martyrdom) for Sûsangird.[75] In the last years of the war when the financial costs became an almost intolerable burden for the government, the National Bank advertised in newspapers asking people to support the war financially with the slogan '*kullu yawm 'âshûrâ', kullu maqâm Karbalâ*' '(every day is *'âshûrâ'*, every place is Karbalâ') which had been a very popular slogan during the revolution. In 1362/1983, the Karbalâ' paradigm at one time was used to explain why the war had been imposed on the Islamic Republic. Karbalâ' was of fundamental importance to Iran, Rafsanjânî said, and therefore Iranians had to start a struggle against tyranny (*ṭughyân*). It was not acceptable to Iranians that a tyrant such as Ṣaddâm should have his government in a place where Ḥusayn was buried, where his revolt took place and where the centre of Alî's government was located. It was only natural that the effects of the Islamic revolution were expected and feared there. In anticipation of this, the war had been started by the Iraqi regime.[76]

In the war rhetoric, the Karbalâ' paradigm, compared to the examples of Badr and Khandaq, had another function besides justification. Ḥusayn's martyrdom was the example *par excellence* to mobilize people for the war. In almost every speech, Iranian leaders highlighted Ḥusayn's voluntary acceptance of martyrdom and sacrifice for the preservation of Islam, or spoke about the willingness of so many Iranians to follow Ḥusayn's example. For instance, Khâmini'î said on the occasion of the first *'âshûrâ'* after the outbreak of the war: 'Every one of the soldiers who, yearning for *jihâd*, went to the front like the soldiers of Ḥusayn ibn 'Alî during *'âshûrâ'* is longing to sacrifice himself... the spirit of *'âshûrâ'*, of *muḥarram*, the Ḥusaynî spirit shows itself in our youths everywhere along this broad front... in the month of *muḥarram* blood must become victorious over the sword, and so it will be'.[77] This last sentence was often heard in the war rhetoric. Ḥusayn's blood and that of the soldiers who had died in the war with Iraq were evocative symbols in the war. According to Khumaynî, the Islamic Republic was irrigated with the blood of the martyrs and Islam will survive with their blood.[78] He said that all martyrs could be full of pride since they had followed the example of the prophets and *imâms* who had sacrificed their lives in the cause of God.[79] Among the slogans written on billboards which had been put in the war zones for propaganda purposes were texts like: 'Blood is victorious over the sword'; 'the sword does not bring victory, it is blood which brings it'; 'the blood of martyrs decides over the fate of the Islamic revolution'; furthermore: 'the blood of the Lord of the Martyrs brings the blood of all Islamic nations to the boil'; 'swim in the sea of blood until you reach the shore of *ḥaqq*'.[80] As said above, after the liberation of Khurramshahr, the town was renamed 'khûnîn-shahr' (City of blood).[81] The water of the fountain at *Bihisht-i zahrâ*, Tehran's main cemetery was coloured red, symbolizing the blood of all those who were killed in the war and revolution.

In the first years of the war, prayer leaders related stories about heroic acts by Iranians or their willingness to sacrifice themselves or their families. The daily *Iṭṭilâ'ât*, for instance, published an article about a family whose four sons had become martyrs. The father had said that there was no sorrow in the family since he had raised the boys to serve Islam and the best way to do this was by becoming martyrs. The mother's reaction was to say: '*innanâ lillâhi wa innanâ ilayhi râji'ûna*' 'to God we belong and to God we will return', from *al-Baqara* II:156).[82] In later years these vivid reports disappeared and leaders confined themselves saying that the Iranian population was incomparable in its preparedness to sacrifice. But references to Ḥusayn's willingness to sacrifice himself and remarks reminding the public that this was the duty of all Iranians remained during the whole war (Chapter 2). Those who had died as a result of the war, especially those who had fallen on the battlefield, were thanked in speeches and commemorated on special memorial days. Time and again, leaders stressed the *shahâda ṭalabî* the 'martyrdom-seeking nature' of the Iranian population. Testaments of 'martyrs' which all emphasized their willingness to sacrifice for the cause of Islam and obedience to Khumaynî's leadership, were published in newspapers and cited in sermons and speeches.[83] But, especially after 1985 as a result of a shortage in manpower, the leadership had to urge people to keep supporting the war or to be prepared to go to the front and during the *'âshûrâ'* of the following year, newspapers emphasized in their headings that *'âshûrâ'* motivated large numbers of people to go to the front. The numerous references to Karbalâ', to *'âshûrâ'* and to Ḥusayn's sacrifice, in combination with the urging of people to mobilize, show that the *miranda*, the emotive symbols of the third *imâm*, played a fundamental role in the mobilization of the Iran-Iraq war, as they had been before in the early Ṣafawid time as a motivation for military action.

The Karbalâ' event was also used to justify the dispatch of minors to the battlefield. Rafsanjânî told his audience the story of the children of soldiers killed at Karbalâ'. These children put on a shroud, took up their father's sword and were ready to sacrifice themselves. Ḥusayn forbade a child to take part in the fighting, but the child responded that his mother had sent him, saying that she wanted to be in the same position on the Day of Resurrection as mothers of other children who had become martyrs. When the child was killed the mother hurled his head to the enemies. Rafsanjânî added, addressing his enemies: 'Monsters, we are not as weak as you, we can not so easily be discouraged by all the things we have seen in God's cause. This is our Karbalâ'.[84] Rafsanjânî said that commanders forbade families to send children under seventeen or sixteen to the front, but this did not restrain children, he added. Then he asked whether these children could be considered as minors in view of their (adult) attitude. Khumaynî also did not hesitate to glorify the willingness of children to make themselves martyrs. He related a story about a twelve-year-old boy who had thrown himself with a hand grenade in front of an Iraqi tank. Khumaynî called the boy '*rahbar*' (guide; Khumaynî himself was the *rahbar* of the Islamic Republic).[85]

As stated above, it was thought that lamentation and participation in rituals and commemoration services for Ḥusayn were rewarded with a place in Paradise. But during the war, leaders made it clear that a sure way to obtain a place in Paradise was through sacrifice and martyrdom. They supported this by reciting *Âl 'Imrân* III:169: 'Count not those who have been killed in the way of Allah as dead, nay, alive with their Lord, provided for'.[86] Khumaynî asked his audience: 'Why should we be distressed when we become martyrs, go to the kingdom of heaven and are to receive the mercy of the *ḥaqq-i ta'âlâ* (God)? Why be sorrowful when our friends become martyrs and are freed from the fetters of this world and receive God's mercy?'[87]

During the war, Ḥusayn was not presented only as a role model for Iranians, as an instructor who gave political advice and lessons in moral conduct. According to Muntaẓirî, on his way to Karbalâ' Ḥusayn had said that the messenger of Islam had said clearly that those who are silent in times of *ẓulm* (oppression) of the people and aggression against divine bounds are among the oppressors and *ṭâghût*.[88] On another occasion, Muntaẓirî warned his audience to listen to Ḥusayn: 'Someone who experiences some iniquity or act of aggression from some devil or tyrant but prefers to remain silent and indifferent without moving or reacting in the least against that iniquity and tyranny, it is right when God Almighty unite such person with the selfsame tyrant on the Day of Judgement'.[89] Âyatullâh Ṣâni'î on the occasion of *'âshûrâ'* referred to Ḥusayn also as a teacher of political lessons: 'The nation of the Party of God of Iran follows Ḥusayn's political guidelines as laid down in his will'.[90] Like the Prophet and 'Alî, Ḥusayn was taken as an example for the Islamic Republic of how to act regarding peace settlements. Ḥusayn's refusal to give his pledge of allegiance (*bay'a*) to Yazîd was presented as a strong motivation for the leaders not to seek reconciliation with Iraq:

> It is Ḥusayn's assertion that neither he himself, nor any other person in his place or position may ever give his allegiance or make a reconciliation with Yazîd or any person in his place with the same character.[91]

The role of the twelfth imâm

The twelfth *imâm* played a role in the war rhetoric as well. Central in Imâmî Shî'î doctrine is the belief that the twelfth *imâm*, Muḥammad ibn Ḥasan, did not die, but has been concealed by God and is now in occultation (*ghayba*). Shî'îs divide his occultation into two periods. The first is the Lesser Occultation after his disappearance in 260/874 in which he remained in contact with his followers through four special representatives or agents (known as *bâb*, *safîr*, or *nâ'ib al-khâṣṣ*). This period lasted until 329/941 when the last agent died. On that date the Greater Occultation started, which has lasted until our time. A central theme in this doctrine is that 'God has bestowed upon the Holy Community the gift of an infallible guide at all times, a guide who is to govern all affairs in the temporal realm and, therefore, safeguard its welfare'. In the Shî'î view these guides are the *imâms*.[92] Although he is no longer in contact with his followers, the twelfth *imâm* is considered to be the *ṣâḥib al-zamân* (Lord of the Age) who still guides the community and is in control of the affairs of the believers. He is endowed with special knowledge and has inherited the knowledge of his eleven predecessors, Muḥammad and the earlier prophets.[93] The essence of the doctrine of the occultation of the twelfth *imâm* is the expectation that he will appear as the *mahdî* (guided one) shortly before the Day of Judgement. The *mahdî* will fight against the enemies of Islam and he will put an end to injustice and tyranny and fill the earth with justice and equity.[94] In general, the term *mahdî* is not used very often by Shî'ìs, who instead use the term *al-qâ'im* (he who will rise and rule).

In order to mobilize as many people as possible, Iranian leaders made use of messianistic expectations of the Iranian population by stressing that participation in the war effort would hasten the appearance of the hidden *imâm*.[95] The war was presented as part of a programme of active preparation for the appearance of the hidden *imâm*; the war would pave the way for his return. In the speeches it was suggested, albeit implicitly, that the appearance of the *mahdî* would occur in the Islamic Republic. According to Khâmini'î, 'it is our conviction that this is the *mamlakat-i imâm-i zamân*' (the State of the Lord of the Age).[96] Repeatedly Iran was called the '*kishwar-i baqîyat-i allâh*'(the land of the Remnant of God),[97] '*millat-i imâm-i zamân*'(the nation of the Lord of the Age), *kishwar-i ṣâḥib-i zamân* (the land of the Lord of the Age).[98] Soldiers at the battlefront were referred to as '*sarbâzân-i ḥaḍrat-i walî-yi 'aṣr*' (the soldiers of the Lord of the Age.[99] One of the slogans of the war was 'The evening of the attack is the evening of the manifestation of the *mahdî*'.[100]

Radio Tehran cited Shîrâzî, Commander of the ground forces, on the relation of the war and the hidden *imâm*:

> He expressed the hope that the Islamic combatants of Iran would soon be able to hold joint prayers at Karbala along with the oppressed Iraqi nation. This, according to him, would be a start of the fulfillment of the world-wide mission of the Iranian soldiers against international colonialism and despotism and at the same time it would be an attempt to eliminate the Zionist regime, paving the way for the liberation of holy al-Quds. Thus, he

> added, God willing, the ground would be prepared for the appearance of imam mahdi, the absent imam.[101]

This presentation of the war as an extra stimulus for the reappearance of the Hidden *imâm* was also an indirect way to justify the war since it maximized the positive side of the war. Iranian leaders alternated eschatological notions about the twelfth *imâm* as the *mahdî* with references regarding the twelfth *imâm* as the *walî-yi 'aṣr* or *ṣâḥib al-zamân*. As the Lord of the Age he is considered to be the *imâm* of this time who has divine knowledge, who guides the community and is in control of the affairs of the believers. Devotion for the Lord of the Age is an important aspect of Shî'î piety.[102] Iranian leaders frequently referred to this devotion in their speeches. They translated divine guidance into 'spiritual support' for soldiers by stressing that God supported them through the presence of the *imâm-i 'aṣr* on the battlefront, praying for them and helping them: '*ḥaqq-i ta'âlâ* (Almighty God) is with you, and the powerful arm of the Remnant of God, which is God's arm, is with you'.[103] This picture was the ultimate sacralization of the war since God was on the side of the Iranian soldier. Occasionally, stories were told of soldiers who had really seen a manifestation of the *mahdî* and even spoken to him.[104] These statements are more in line with popular religion than with Twelver Shî'î dogma, which stresses his absence.

Most of the time, however, his presence was regarded as a spiritual presence giving extra support:

> I am convinced that the holy presence of the *walî-yi 'aṣr*, who was present and gave his help during all our great struggles through long years, will also be here in this war which was imposed on us by the mercenaries of arrogance and imperialism... The Lord of the Age sees all this beloved and pure blood; he will certainly pray for all of them [the soldiers] and we must likewise never lessen our inclination to, attention for and connection with the *walî-yi 'aṣr*; we must ask God's help and ask this great man [*mahdî*] for intercession. We ask the Creator through the blessing of the holy presence of the *baqîyat-i allâh* to support and guide, make strong and full of confidence the brave and courageous soldiers on this battlefield, on which we are engaged in struggle with *ẓulm* (tyranny) and worldwide *istikbâr* (arrogance).[105]

> I call on all zealous young people and the fruitful segments of the Islamic country to rush to the fronts and join the ranks of the troops of the holy al-Mahdi and thereby to rob the last breath from the lives of the Saddamists, because the victorious hand of justice is with you. Just as He, graciously

> granted you the blessings of His hidden succor and His special considerations to this day and in all scenes, He will henceforth also remain your friend and companion. He will never leave you alone.[106]

On the occasion of the *ḥajj* in 1987: 'we have achieved victory thanks to reliance upon the weapon of *îmân*, reliance on God and the prayers of the *baqîyat-i allâh*.[107] The burden of war could only be endured thanks to God's hidden benevolence, the special attention of the great saints of religion (*awliyâ'*) and the prayers of the *baqîyat-i allâh*.[108] Victory would be obtained with the help of God, and the prayer of *baqîyat-i allâh* would help in *îmân* (belief) and *tawakkul* (confidence).[109] Together with 'Alî, Ḥusayn, Mûsâ ibn Ja'far, the seventh *imâm*, *al-Jawâd* ('the generous', the reference to the ninth *imâm*), 'Alî al-Hâdî, the tenth, and al-'Askarî, the eleventh *imâm* (reference to them is made because they are all buried in Iraqi soil), the Hidden *imâm* was presented as an intercessor between God and the Iranian people: he could put in a good word for them, he could appeal for help from God, and through him God would supply the Islamic Republic with generosity, help and mercy.[110] Kâshânî put this request to the Hidden *imâm*: 'Guide us, accompany us, intercede for us, accompany us to God, precede us and plead for us with God.[111] Furthermore, Khâmini'î told his audience: 'I am convinced that the blessings and mercy of the Creator, His grace and kindness will increase because of the presence of the Lord of the Age, the rightful *imâm*, the promised *mahdî*, at our battlefronts, among our youths'.[112]

Schmidtke has observed that Khumaynî and his followers reinterpreted the doctrine of *intiẓâr* (expectation of the *mahdî*). She argues that Khumaynî claimed certain tasks which were assigned to the *mahdî* for himself and that the 'aggressive' *jihâd*, although Khumaynî never said this explicitly, is one of those tasks.[113] This seems in line with the following examples. According to *khaṭṭ-i tawṭi'a*, Khumaynî explained the saying *shî'atunâ ahlu l-fatḥ wa-l-ẓafar* (our party is one of triumph and victory) by Ja'far al-Ṣâdiq, the sixth *imâm*, by saying that all superpowers should know that we (the Iranians) until the last person, the last home and the last drop of blood would stand for the *i'tilâ'* (ascension) of the word of God and contrary to their expectation a government of neither West nor East would be erected in most countries of the world.[114]

As we saw in Chapter 2, Khumaynî never was assigned the *imâm*'s task of declaring an offensive *jihâd*. He said: 'when we say we want to export our Revolution we mean we would like to export this spirituality which dominates Iran... We do not intend to attack anyone with swords or other arms'.[115] Although in the war rhetoric statements such as 'this is a *jihâd* in God's cause, a divine war like the *ghazawât* of the messenger of Islam' were occasionally made, most references to *jihâd*, including those of Khumaynî, had a defensive character.[116] The references to an aggressive *jihâd* must be regarded as more symbolic than realistic, made to arouse militant feelings.

The leaders of the Islamic Republic borrowed a revolutionary interpretation of *intiẓâr* from Shari'atî, who distinguished between 'positive' and 'negative' waiting. He no longer interpreted the notion of *intiẓâr* as a passive waiting for the appearance of the *mahdî* who would install justice, but as the responsibility of every person to prepare for his return. The leaders of the Islamic Republic also reserved an active role for the people who were capable of hastening the return of the *mahdî* by paving the way for a just society through revolutionary activity against oppression and tyranny.[117] Âyatullâh Murtaḍâ Muṭahharî, whose ideas also influenced the revolutionary movement in Iran, like Sharî'atî distinguished between two kinds of *intiẓâr*. He favoured a 'constructive' instead of a 'destructive' waiting. According to him, the destructive waiting considers the appearance of the *mahdî* only possible after an explosion of social injustice whereas the constructive waiting for the *mahdî* regards the appearance of the *mahdî* as the ultimate and victorious phase of the struggle between the righteous and the unrighteous ones.[118]

Khâmini'î explained the meaning of *intiẓâr* on the occasion of the *mahdî*'s birthday. He said that the peculiarities of the appearance (*ẓuhûr*) of the *mahdî* can to a certain extent also be found in the Islamic revolution; since the revolution is for the whole of mankind, the Islamic Republic is fighting against the great powers of this world, and the revolution has crushed all materialistic expectations. The revolution has brought forward the appearance of the *mahdî* and has brought his revolution a step nearer since the revolution is realizing the purpose of the *mahdî*'s revolution by installing justice (*'adâla*) throughout the world. *Intiẓâr* is the expectation of the rule of the Qur'ân and Islam. Khâmini'î continued by saying that installing justice is assigned to the Islamic Republic because those who are oppressed and who want justice and the return of the *mahdî* are incapable of realizing this themselves. Furthermore, the Islamic Republic is the country of the *imâm-i zamân*, the Lord of the Age. The Islamic revolution is his revolution since it is the revolution of Islam. Every step taken for the continuity of this revolution is a step nearer to the appearance of the *mahdî*.[119]

Imâmî Kâshânî refuted the idea that history showed a development towards total *fasâd* (decay), *ẓulm* (oppression) and *bâṭil* (falsehood) and that therefore it was useless to strive and sacrifice for the installation of *ḥaqq* (truth). The divine revelations (Torah, Gospel and Qur'ân) had already underlined that this thought was wrong and had emphasized the idea that the world was proceeding towards justice, humanity and integrity and that every person can contribute to this development.[120] He then cited a tradition from the *Sunan* by the Sunnî Ibn Mâja: *yakhruju nâsun min al-mashriqi fa-yabta'ûna li-l-mahdî ay sulṭânihi*[121] (people will come from the East and they are subordinated to the authority of the *mahdî*). The meaning of this tradition was that a group of people from the East would rise and would prepare the world for the rule and government of the *mahdî* before he himself would rise.[122] He continuby saying that Iranians were working to prepare for the government of the Lord of the Age.[123]

The war rhetoric of the Iranian leaders showed a deviation from the traditional doctrine of *intiẓâr* just as did the rhetoric during the revolution. The appearance of the *mahdî* was not expected when the earth was filled with injustice in order that he might install justice. On the contrary, the appearance of the hidden *imâm* would occur once the Islamic Republic had installed justice. The war was presented as a means to achieve this. Khumaynî was very clear on this subject. For instance, on the occasion of the birthday of the *mahdî* in 1988 he emphasized that it was wrong to think that the world must be full of *ẓulm* and *jawr* (oppression and coercion) as a condition for the appearance of the *munjî* (saviour), the Lord of the Age. It could not be true that Muslims had to pray to Ṣaddâm, the United States and the Soviet Union to fill the world with oppression in order that the *mahdî* could appear and install justice. Waiting for his appearance was not a reason to neglect one's duty (*taklîf-i shar'î*) to end *ẓulm* and *jawr*. Government was an instrument to combat oppression and to stop oppressors. People had to cooperate and make possible the appearance of the hidden *imâm*. When the Islamic government did not exist, oppressors would have free play.[124] The Islamic Republic had always behaved very considerately and justly in the war, this in contrast to Ṣaddâm. Iran obeyed the Qur'ânic injunction of *al-Mâ'ida* V:8: 'O ye who have believed, be furnishers of justice as witnesses for Allah, and let not the hatred of a people incite you not to act fairly', and: *al-Baqara* II:190: 'do not provoke hostility'. He continued, 'We have not exceeded our bounds. As the Lord of the Believers made history and enlightened the pages of history with justice, hopefully we shall also present this enlightened revolution on the doorstep of the Lord of the Age'.[125]

In a few instances, Khumaynî was referred to as the *nâ'ib* or even as the *nâ'ib buzurg-wâr* (great deputy) of the Lord of the Age.[126] This manner of speaking is an implicit reference to *nâ'ib al-khâṣṣ*, the special representative of the Hidden *imâm*. Traditional Shî'î doctrine accepts only four representatives, who after the disappearance of the twelfth *imâm* acted as his deputies. After the last one died in 329/941, the *'ulamâ'* as a whole came to be regarded as *nâ'ib 'âmm* (general representative) of the Hidden *imâm*. Imâmî Kâshânî went even further when he elevated Khumaynî to the same level as the Lord of the Age by calling Khumaynî his *rafîq* (companion, friend).[127]

Expectations of the return of the Lord of the Age were exploited in times of hardship by the leaders. One week before the acceptance of Resolution 598 by Iran,

Imâmî Kâshânî, speaking about the shooting down of the Iranian airbus and the fact that the United Nations and other international organizations had not reacted as they should have, and the Islamic Republic stood alone in protecting the oppressed of this world, said that according to the Islamic traditions, the reason for the delayed manifestation of the Lord of the Age was that the people first must understand that there was only salvation in times of real hardship, something which could be observed in Iran at that moment [since the *mahdî* had not appeared].[128]

The way the Iranian leaders treated the principle of *intiẓâr* suggests that they were trying very hard to discourage millenarian expectations among the Iranian people. Their interpretation of the principle in fact seemed to be contrary to the whole idea of *intiẓâr* since with their interpretation they implicitly refuted its messianic essence. Iranian leaders characterized passiveness and quietism regarding oppression and tyranny as a very negative attitude and contrary to Shî'î doctrine. They refuted the idea that people had to endure oppression and tyranny and that the installation of justice and equity was postponed until the appearance of the *mahdî*. Since, according to the leaders, the *mahdî* would appear after justice was installed and his appearance did not depend on the amount of oppression and tyranny, one might be tempted to ask what role remained for the *mahdî*. The whole denial of the messianic character of the twelfth *imâm* is in fact not very surprising. During the revolution, the notion of the *mahdî* who would appear to end *ẓulm* (oppression) and to re-establish justice and a just state had relevance in the resistance against the Shah, who was regarded as a *ẓâlim* (oppressor). After the revolution, however, this whole notion lost its relevance since the mission of the *mahdî* was fulfilled by the very goals of the Islamic Republic itself. References to millenarian expectations played a role in the rhetoric after the revolution, but the function of these references was not to encourage the expectation of his appearance to install an ideal state; millenarian expectations were exploited to legitimize the Islamic Republic and Khumaynî's leadership, since these were presented as conducive to the appearance of the Hidden *imâm*. The slogan heard in demonstrations organized by followers of the Line of the *imâm*, the official policy in the Islamic Republic,[129] 'O God, O God, keep Khumaynî until the Revolution of the *mahdî*', was also used on billboards at the front and was chanted during speeches. Other slogans in the same vein were: 'Loving the *mahdî* is impossible without loving Khumaynî' and 'O God, hasten the appearance of the *mahdî* in Khumaynî's era and government'.[130]

The names of military operations

If one looks at the Iranian military operations during the war it becomes clearer that only selected aspects of Islamic history played a role in the war rhetoric, in particular those parts of history which are important for Shî'îs. Of the 95 operations Iran launched, only six did not receive a name which referred to Islamic history.[131]

These six were named after the regions in which they took place. The other titles (several operations received the same name, for instance Karbalâ'î), had an Islamic or a more specific Shî'î context. With these titles, the Iranian leadership maximized and intensified its own 'goodness' through association and identification with for Shî'îs positive or emotionally charged connotations. Ten operations were named after Islamic historical figures, the Prophet and his relatives: *Muḥammad rasûl allâh*; the first *imâm* Alî: *Imâm 'Alî* and *Mawlâ-yi mutaqîyân* (Lord of the pious, an honorific title for 'Alî); the twelfth *imâm* and *mahdî*: *Imâm mahdî* and *Ḥaḍrat-i mahdî*; Fâṭima, Alî's wife and mother of Ḥusayn and Ḥasan: *Umm al-Ḥusayn*; the third *imâm* Ḥusayn: *Ḥusayn ibn 'Alî* and *Thâr allâh* (God's avenger).[132]

Another slogan was named after the eighth *imâm*, 'Alî al-Riḍâ: *Thâmin al-a'imma*; and *Muslim ibn 'Aqîl*, Ḥusayn's cousin who was sent to Kûfa by Ḥusayn to assess how strong was the support of the Kûfans for his cause. During his stay in Kûfa he was killed at the command of 'Ubayd Allâh, the Governor of Kûfa. Muslim is venerated in popular Shî'î piety because he was the first of the martyrs of Karbalâ' but also for his moral uprightness and bravery, which are dramatized in Shî'î popular piety.[133]

Three names referred to Ḥusayn's death (see below): *Muḥarram*, *'Âshûrâ'î* and *Karbalâ'î*. The town named after the plain where Ḥusayn, the third *imâm*, met his death, is situated south of Baghdad. But the operations called *Karbalâ'î* had only limited strategic objectives; for example, the first was launched in order to liberate the city of Mihrân.[134] Two operations were named after victorious battles during the reign of Muḥammad: *Badr*[135] and *Khaybar* (see below). Khamini'î said that the latter received the name Khaybar because the Islamic Republic fought not only the Iraqis but also the Zionists. The war therefore had strong resemblance to the Prophet's attack on the Jewish citadels of Khaybar in 7\628. Khamini'î said: 'Hopefully, with God's help, we will vanquish these citadels like the citadel of Khaybar.[136]

Two other operations were called *Ramaḍân*, the month in which the battle of Badr took place; both were launched during *ramaḍân*. Several operations received the titles of Qur'anic *sûra*'s or verses: *al-Fatḥ* (XLVIII); *Fatḥ-i mubîn* ('clear victory' in XLVIII:1, this first verse of the *sûra* was probably revealed after the battle of Badr);[137] *Ẓafar* ('victory' in *fatḥ* XLVIII:24) (7); (*Wa-l-fajr* (in LXXXIX:1) (10); *Maṭla'-i fajr* ('the rising of dawn' in *al-Qadr* XVIIC:5) and *sûrat al-naṣr* ('help', CX) (9).

A few operations were named after Jerusalem; *Quds* and *Bayt al-muqaddas*. In the war rhetoric, the liberation of the third most important Muslim city from the 'Zionist occupiers' was frequently mentioned as one of the goals of the Islamic Republic (see Chapter 5). One would expect these operations to have been launched after the Iranian invasion of Iraqi territory in July 1982 because Iranian leaders justified the invasion as necessary for the liberation of Jerusalem, but in fact they took place in 1985 and 1988 and had only limited objectives. Two other operations which were called *Ṭarîq al-Quds* (the road to Jerusalem) at the end of November 1981 and *Taḥrîr al-Quds* (the liberation of Jerusalem) in the spring of 1984 also had only limited objectives. These titles did not and could not refer to strategic or military aims; they only served as an extra stimulus for the Iranian soldiers because of the emotional and evocative value these words had for an Iranian audience.

Only one operation referred to God, albeit indirectly, *al-Qâdir* 'the powerful', one of God's attributes. One operation was named after Khumaynî: *Khumaynî rûḥ-i khudâ* (60/3/21) 'Khumaynî the spirit of God', a play on his first name, '*Rûhullâh*'. Another operation was called *Shahîd Madanî*, (60/6/28) 'martyr Madanî', after Asadullâh Madanî, Khumaynî's representative in Tabrîz, who was killed by a hand grenade in September 1981, an attack for which the *mujâhidîn-i khalq* were held responsible.[138] Interestingly, one operation was named *Shahîd Faḍlullâh Nûrî* (60/2/25) after Shaykh Faḍlullâh Nûrî, who was hanged in 1909 for his anti-constitutional activities. Nûrî was one of the leaders of the constitutional movement at the beginning of this century. He believed that the constitution should be in accordance with the *sharî'a* (the principle of *mashrûṭa-yi mashrû'a*, constitution in conformity with the sacred law). Khâmini'î, on the occasion of the commemoration of Nûrî's death, glorified him for taking this position.[139] In 1907, however, Nûrî rejected the whole idea of constitutionalism and said that the constitution was contrary to Islam, one of the reasons being that the constitutionalists had tried to tamper with the *sharî'a*.[140] According to Abrahamian, history is turned inside out in the Islamic Republic, since Nûrî is considered to be the forerunner of the anti-monarchical movement whereas he in fact favoured the monarchy.[141] There are more occasions on which history is turned inside out in Iran with respect to the constitution of the Islamic Republic, when we consider the *fatwâ* Nûrî issued on the subject of the constitution: 'Constitutionalism is against the religion of Islam... it is not possible to bring this Islamic country under a constitutional régime except by abolishing Islam. Therefore, if any Muslim attempts to impose constitutionalism upon us Muslims, his attempts will be taken as destructive to the religion. Such a person is a apostate'.[142]

The impact of the glorious past of Islam becomes even clearer from the slogans most operations received.[143] It is not clear what function the slogans had; the idea probably was that they should be chanted by soldiers and mobilization forces. Of these official 68 slogans two had Qur'ânic verses as titles and referred to God: *al-Ṣaff* LXI:13: *Naṣr min allâh wa- fatḥ qarîb*; *Âl 'Imrân* III:173: *Ḥasbunâ allâhu wa-ni'mat al-wakîl* ('it is on Allah that we count, and good the trustee'). Seven slogans referred to God and twelve to the Prophet. One slogan was the *shahâda*, the declaration of faith: *Lâ ilâha ilâ allâh wa- Muḥammadun rasûl allâh*. Most slogans, however, referred to the Shî'î *imâms* and their families. Several slogans referred to 'Alî, such as *Yâ 'Alî adriknî*[144] (help me) and *Yâ mawlâ-yi muttaqîyân*. Many slogans referred to Ḥusayn: *Yâ sayyid al-shuhadâ'* (Lord of the Martyrs, one of Ḥusayn's titles), *Yâ Ḥusayn al-maẓlûm* (O Ḥusayn the oppressed) and *Labbayka yâ Ḥusayn* (in thy service, Ḥusayn). The twelfth *imâm* was often mentioned in slogans and the sixth, seventh and eighth *imâm* occasionally. According to Ram, in the Friday sermons the image of the *imâms* was no longer that of quiescent heroes but of militant and revolutionary figures who opposed tyranny and were committed to a just Islamic government. Even the second *imâm*, Ḥasan, was portrayed as a revolutionary who fought against Mu'âwiya. This is not in line with traditional Shî'î accounts. According to Shî'î historians, Ḥasan reached a compromise with Mu'âwiya as a result of his political acumen and not, as Western historians believe, as an act of cowardice.[145] With the exception of 'Alî, Ḥusayn and the *mahdî*, however, the figures of the *imâms* did not play a role of importance in the war rhetoric. Only occasionally was reference made to other *imâms*. For instance, in late 1984 Kâshânî said that the Islamic Republic would be victorious as a result of the Shî'î school of Islam and loyalty to the *imâms*.[146] Another example is that of army divisions named after *imâms*, such as the division *Imâm Ja'far al-Ṣâdiq*, *Imâm Ḥasan*, which existed side by side with divisions named after Muḥammad, 'Alî, Ḥusayn, the twelfth *imâm* and Fâṭima.

Two operations received slogans after Ḥusayn's half-brother 'Abbâs, standard-bearer and commander of the troops at Karbalâ'. According to Shî'î hagiography, he played a heroic role at Karbalâ' and he is regarded as the supreme fighter.[147] In the war rhetoric, the figure of 'Abbâs served as a model for bravery and courage but people were also compared to him. Kâshânî compared the Iranian fighters to 'Abbâs. The whole population of Iran was devoted to its soldiers, who were, like 'Abbâs, standard-bearers of Islam, fighting in a *jihâd* for the defence of Islam and Muslims, and who would bring honour to Islam and history.[148]

Fâṭima, daughter of the Prophet, wife of 'Alî and mother of Ḥusayn and Ḥasan, did not play a role in the war rhetoric, but the slogans of the operations which refer to her outnumber all others. In the rhetoric of the Islamic Republic, Fâṭima is portrayed as the personification of the ideal Islamic woman. This image consists of two characteristics: her perfect motherhood, since she is the mother of Ḥusayn and Ḥasan, and her ideal matrimonial attitude because of her obedience, devotion and contentedness towards her husband. Her image functions as a role model for Iranian women; even her birthday is declared Women's Day (20 jumâdâ al-âkhir) in Iran.[149] Another ideal model for women propagated by the Islamic Republic is Fâṭima's daughter Zaynab, sister of Ḥusayn and Ḥasan. Zaynab is venerated as a brave and courageous woman, since she defended Ḥusayn's cause at Yazîd's court in Damascus, where she had been taken as a prisoner after the battle of Karbalâ'. The two images, one of an obedient, servile woman and one of a politically combative woman, led to much confusion, as it was not always clear which model should be followed.[150] Zaynab did not play a role in the war rhetoric any more than did Fâṭima, but occasionally her name was used. Two slogans of operations invoked her name and a para military force made up of women was named after her.[151]

Not only military operations received religious names but divisions as well. For example: *lashkar-i Muḥammad rasûl Allâh*, and *lashkar-i sayyid al-shuhadâ'*, *sipâh-i Muḥammad*, *sipâh-i 'aẓîm-i mahdî*, *sipâh-i tawḥîd*, *sipâh-i imâm-i Ḥusayn*. In 1987, even the names of military exercises in the Gulf had a religious dimension: *Labaykka yâ imâm* (in thy service, O imâm), *dhû l-fiqâr* (the name of the famous two-pointed sword owned by Muḥâmmad and 'Alî), and *shahâda* (martyrdom).

Iranian leaders sacralized the war, by identification with historical figures who are venerated or, in contrast, despised much in Shî'î belief, but also by association with historical Islamic events in order to make clear that the war with Iraq had strong resemblances to these events.

Notes

1. According to Algar, clerical opponents identified the Qajar shahs with the Umayyad caliphs and even suggested that the Qajars were their offspring. Hamid Algar, *Religion and State in Iran 1785-1906. The Role of the Ulama in the Qajar Period* (Berkeley: University of California Press, 1969) p. 252; Gustav Thaiss, 'Religious Symbolism and Social Change: The Drama of Husain' in: *Scholars, Saints, and Sufis*, ed. by N.R. Keddie (Berkeley: University of California Press, 1972) pp. 349-366, pp. 360-365.

2. Dale F. Eickelman and James Piscatori, *Muslim Politics* (Princeton: Princeton University Press, 1996) pp. 28-29.

3. Khumaynî, *Jang wa jihâd*, 60/9/8, p. 279; *Iṭṭilâ'ât*, 2/6/62.

4. *Jang bâ inqilâb* p. 14.

5. Imâmî Kâshânî, *Dar maktab-i jum'a* Vol. 4 13/9/60 p. 127.

6. Khâmini'î *Dar maktab-i jum'a* Vol.2 4/7/59 pp. 315-323. Azodanloo in his translation of this passage incorrectly assumes that the comparison in this sermon is with the battle of Badr in 2/624. Apparently he confuses this sermon with the sermon of 11/7/59 in which the comparison is made with Badr, *Dar maktab-i jum'a* Vol.2 pp. 325-335. There is ample evidence that in the sermon of 4/7/59 the comparison is with Khandaq. Firstly, Khâmini'î referred to 'Amr ibn 'Abd Wudd (al-'Âmirî) as the commander of the Meccan troops and not to Abu Jahl, the commander of the Meccan troops at Badr. Secondly, the tradition of the conquest of the Sasanian and Byzantine empires was connected with Khandaq and not with Badr. Heidar Ghajar Azodanloo, *Discourses of Mobilization in Post-revolutionary Iran* (Unpublished Ph D thesis, University of Minnesota, 1992), p. 77 and pp. 115-122. Although there is enough evidence to suggest that Khâmini'î is referring to the battle of Khandaq, he started his sermon with the recitation of Qur'ân verse *Âl-'Imrân*, III:13 (11) ('Ye have already had a sign in two parties which met, one fighting in the way of Allah, another unbelieving, who saw them with their eyes twice as many as they were; Allah supporteth

with His help whom He willeth'). According to Abû Ja'far Muḥammad b. Jarîr al-Ṭabarî, *Jâmi' al-bayân 'an tâ'wîl ây al-qur'ân* (Cairo: Dâr al-Ma'ârif, 1955-1969) Vol.6 p. 231; and Abû 'Alî al-Faḍl ibn al-Ḥasan al-Ṭabarsî, *Majma' al-bayân fî tafsîr al-qur'ân* (Beirut: Dâr ihyâ' al-turâth al-'arabî, 1412/1992) Vol.2 p. 534, this verse was revealed during the battle of Badr. Ṭabâṭabâ'î holds that it was probably revealed after the battle of Badr or Uḥud, Muḥammad Ḥusayn Ṭabâṭabâ'î, *Tafsîr al-mîzân* (Tehran: Muḥammadî, 1363/1984) Vol.5 p. 181.

7. Khâmini'î, *Dar maktab-i jum'a*, Vol.2 4/7/59 p. 316. In 1987, Rafsanjânî compared the manner of fighting during the battle of the Trench with that of the Iranian population during the War of the Cities, *Iṭṭilâ'ât*, 15/1/66.

8. Rudi Paret, *Die legendäre Maghazi-Literatur. Arabische Dichtungen über die muslimischen Kriegszüge zu Mohammeds Zeit* (Tübingen: Mohr, 1930) p. 34.

9. Actually, Khâmini'î combined two events connected with Khandaq. The first story is about the palaces of the kings in power at that time which would fall into the hands of the Muslims. The second story has the same subject, but here Muḥammad promised the fortunes of Kisrâ and Qayṣar to some of his followers, the hypocrites (*munâfiqûn*) who had doubted a successful outcome of the battle.

10. M. Morony,'Kisrâ' in: *Encyclopaedia of Islam*[2] Vol.5 p. 185.

11. Bernard Lewis, *The Political Language of Islam* (Chicago: University of Chicago Press, 1988) p. 55.

12. Khumaynî, *Iṭṭilâ'ât*, 10/9/64.

13. W. Montgomery Watt, *Muhammad at Medina* (Oxford: Clarendon Press, 1956) pp. 10-11.

14. Khâmini'î, *Dar maktab-i jum'a* Vol.2 11/7/59, pp. 325-335.

15. Khâmini'î, *Dar maktab-i jum'a* Vol.2 11/7/59 pp. 325-335.

16. See also Azodanloo, *Discourses of Mobilization*, p. 29.

17. Watt, *Muhammad at Medina*, p. 15.

18. Muntaẓirî, *Jang-i taḥmîlî dar bayânât-i âyatullâh al-'uẓmâ Muntaẓirî* (Tehran: Ministry of Culture and Islamic Guidance, 1367/1988), p. 56, 19/9/61.

19. FBIS, *Daily Report*, Speech in Islamic Parliament, 22 June 22 1982.

20. Khumaynî, *Iṭṭilâ'ât*, 21/11/60

21. Khumaynî, *Iṭṭilâ'ât*, 10/5/66.

22. Khumaynî, *Iṭṭilâ'ât*, 23/11/63.

23. Khumaynî, *Iṭṭilâ'ât*, 4/9/60.

24. Khumaynî, *Iṭṭilâ'ât*, 4/10/61.

25. Khumaynî, *Iṭṭilâ'ât*, 10/5/66.

26. Mahdawî Kanî, *Dar maktab-i jum'a* Vol.6 3/4/62 p. 383.

27. Muntaẓirî, Friday sermon *Jang-i taḥmîlî*, 4/8/59 p. 104.

28. Khâmini'î, *Dar maktab-i jum'a* Vol.3 12/10/59 pp. 45-46; *Yâ'Sîn* XXXVI:60: '... did I not enjoin you, o ye children of Adam, that ye should not serve Satan'.

29. Khâmini'î, *Dar maktab-i jum'a* Vol.2/8/59 p. 362; 9/8/59 p. 365; Vol.3 12/10/59 pp. 45-46.

30. Manochehr Dorraj, *From Zarathustra to Khomeini. Populism and Dissent in Iran* (Boulder: Lynne Rienner, 1990) pp. 60-61.

31. Dorraj, *From Zarathustra to Khomeini* p. 61.

32. J.ter Haar, *Volgelingen van de imam. Een kennismaking met de shi'itische islam* (Amsterdam: Bulaaq, 1995) p. 40-41.

33. Muntaẓirî, *Jang-i taḥmîlî* 2/10/62 p. 61.

34. Muntaẓirî, *Jang-i taḥmîlî* 29/10/63 p. 63.

35. Khumaynî, *Iṭṭilâ'ât*, 5/1/65.

36. Cf. Khâmini'î, *Dar maktab-i jum'a* Vol.2 4/7/59 p. 319: sermon 27 (partly): 'Verily, the *jihâd* is one of the doors of Paradise which God has opened to His special friends'; sermon 51 (partly): 'Death in your life makes you subjugated and life in your death makes you subjugators'; and letter 47 (partly): 'God, God, [to] the *jihâd* with your possessions, your souls and your tongues'; Mûsawî Ardabîlî, *Dar maktab-i jum'a* Vol.3 27/6/60 p. 413.

37. Khâmini'î, *Dar maktab-i jum'a* Vol.3 21/1/60 p. 167.

38. Imâmî Kâshânî, *Dar maktab-i jum'a* Vol.4 10/3/61 pp. 389-390. It seems likely that Kâshânî used the blocking of the Euphrates as a symbol for the Iraqi occupation, but it should also be remembered that the long-standing conflict over the Shaṭṭ al-'Arab, the confluence of the Euphrates, Tigris and Karun rivers, was one of the causes of the Iran-Iraq war.

39. Mûsawî Ardabîlî, *Dar maktab-i jum'a* Vol.5 22/5/61 pp. 147-148.

40. Mûsawî Ardabîlî, *Dar maktab-i jum'a* Vol.5 22/5/61 p. 149. This last advice is not a part of 'Alî's sermon and Ardabîlî does not give any other reference.

41. Werner Ende, *Arabische Nation und islamische Geschichte. Die Umayyaden im Urteil arabischer Autoren des 20. Jahrhunderts* (Beirut: Orient Institut, 1977) pp. 153-162.

42. L. Veccia Vaglieri, '(al)-Ḥusayn b. 'Alî b. Abî Ṭâlib' in: *Encyclopaedia of Islam*[2], Vol.3 pp. 606-615, p. 607; See also S.H.M. Jafri, *The Origins and Early Development of Shi'a Islam* (Qum: Ansariyan, n.d.) pp. 199-205.

43. Tabâṭabâ'î, Muḥammad Ḥusayn, *Shi'ite Islam*, trans. and ed. by Seyyed Hossein Nasr (Albany: SUNY Press, 1975) p. 196.

44. Mahmoud Ayoub, *Redemptive Suffering in Islam. A Study of the Devotional Aspects of 'Âshûrâ in Twelver Shi'ism* (The Hague: Mouton, 1978) pp. 94-95; Ṭabâṭabâ'î, *Shi'ite Islam*, p. 197; Moojan Momen, *An Introduction to Shi'i Islam* (New Haven: Yale University Press, 1985) p. 27-29.

45. Ayoub, *Redemptive Suffering in Islam*, pp. 109-112.

46. L. Veccia Vaglieri, '(al)-Ḥusayn b. 'Alî b. Abî Ṭâlib', p. 614. The speech by 'Abdul-Ḥasan Banî Ṣadr on the occasion of *'âshûrâ'* 1359/1980 presents this line of reasoning, *Iṭṭilâ'ât*, 28/8/59.

47. Hamid Enayat, *Modern Political Islamic Thought* (London: Macmillan, 1982) pp. 190-194.

48. Thaiss, 'Religious Symbolism and Social Change, p. 357, citing G. von Grunebaum, *Muhammadan Festivals*.

49. Peter Chelkowski, 'Popular Shi'î Mourning Rituals', in: *Al-Serât*, Vol.12 (1986) pp. 209-226, p. 209.

50. Mary Hegland, 'Two Images of Husain: Accommodation and Revolution in an Iranian Village', in: *Religion and Politics in Iran. Shi'ism from Quietism to Revolution*, ed. by Nikki R. Keddie (New Haven: Yale University Press, 1983) pp. 218-235, pp. 221-225.

51. Michael M.J. Fischer, *Iran. From Religious Dispute to Revolution* (Harvard: Harvard University Press, 1980) p. 213.

52. Haggay Ram, *Myth and Mobilization in Revolutionary Iran. The Use of the Friday Congregational Sermon* (Washington: American University Press, 1994) pp. 68, 72.

53. *Farhang-i jabha* pp. 39-40.

54. Hugh Rank, *The Pep Talk. How to Analyze Political Language* (Park Forest: Counter-propaganda Press, 1984) p. 28.

55. To give but a few examples: Khâmini'î, *Dar maktab-i jum'a* Vol.2 4/7/59 p. 317; Vol.3 17/11/59 p. 94; Khumaynî, *Iṭṭilâ'ât*, 18/11/65; Muntaẓirî, *Jang-i taḥmîlî* 7/10/65 p. 167.

56. Mûsawî Ârdabîlî, *Dar maktab-i jum'a* Vol.5 1/5/61 p. 111.

57. Khumaynî, *Iṭṭilâ'ât*, 8/8/59.

58. Khumaynî, *Ṣaḥîfa-yi nûr* p. 534.

59. Imâmî Kâshânî, *Dar maktab-i jum'a* Vol.6 29/11/61 p. 93.

60. Muntaẓirî, *Jang-i taḥmîlî* 7/10/65 p. 167.

61. Muntaẓirî, *Jang-i taḥmîlî* 7/10/65 p. 167; Khumaynî, *Iṭṭilâ'ât*, 23/11/63.

62. Rafsanjânî, *Dar maktab-i jum‘a* Vol.4 3/7/60 p. 10.

63. Khumaynî, *Dar justujû-yi râh az kalâm-i imâm: Shahîd wa shahâda. Az bayânât wa i‘lâmiya-hâ-yi imâm Khumaynî az sâl 1341 tâ 1361* Vol.4 (Tehran: Amîr Kabîr, 1370/1991) p. 36.

64. Khumaynî, FBIS *Daily Report* 9 March 1982.

65. Khumaynî, *Iṭṭilâ‘ât*, 18/11/65.

66. Ṣâni‘î, *Iṭṭilâ‘ât*, 25/6/65.

67. Khâmini'î, *Chahâr sâl bâ mardum* (Tehran: Ḥizb-i jumhûrî-yi islâmî, 1364/1985) 10/7/63 p. 352.

68. Rafsanjânî, Friday sermon *Iṭṭilâ‘ât*, 15/6/65.

69. Khâmini'î, Friday sermon *Iṭṭilâ‘ât*, 5/7/65 (on the occasion of War Week).

70. Rafsanjânî, *Dar maktab-i jum‘a* Vol.7 22/7/62 p. 167; *Nutuq-hâ-yi qabal az dustûr-i ḥujjat al-islâm wa-l-muslimîn Hâshimî Rafsanjânî riyâsat-i majlis-i shûrâ-yi islâmî*, (Tehran: Majlis-i shûrâ-yi islâmî, 1362) 2/7/60 p. 51.

71. Muntaẓirî, *Jang-i taḥmîlî* 24/11/59 p. 59.

72. Khumaynî, FBIS *Daily report* 31 March 1988.

73. Muntaẓirî, *Jang-i taḥmîlî* 22/6/60 p. 119, 23/4/61 p. 55, 13/11/61.

74. *Nutuqhâ-yi qabal az dastûr* p. 26.

75. *Farhang-i jabha* p. 28.

76. Rafsanjânî, *Dar maktab-i jum‘a* Vol.7 1/7/62 p. 112.

77. Khâmini'î, *Dar maktab-i jum‘a* Vol.2 23/8/59 p. 387.

78. Khumaynî, *Shahîd wa shahâda* p. 34.

79. Khumaynî, *Shahîd wa shahâda* pp. 31-36.

80. *Farhang-i jabha* pp. 21, 29, 37.

81. According to Khumaynî in the introduction to *Khurramshahr az âsâra tâ âzâdî* (Khurramshahr from Captivity to Liberation) (n.p. Daftar-i nashr-i farhang-i islâmî, 1363/1984)

82. *Iṭṭilâ‘ât*, 5/10/61.

83. See for an analysis of these testaments: Dawud Gholamasad, ‘Weltanschauliche und sozialpsychologische Aspekte der iranischen Kriegsführung. Einige sozialpsychologische Aspekte des Martyriums der iranischen Kriegsfreiwilliger - eine Auswertung ihrer Testamente’ in: *Orient* 30 (1989) pp. 557-569; Gholamasad, ‘Heiliger Krieg und Martyrium bei den iranischen Schiiten im Golfkrieg, 1980-1988’ in: *Kriegsbegeisterung und mentale Kriegsvorbereitung*, ed. by M. van der Linden and G. Mergner (Berlin: Duncker & Humblot, 1991) pp. 219-230; Werner Schmucker, ‘Iranische Märtyrertestamente’ in: *Die Welt des Islams* 27 (1987) pp. 185-249.

84. Rafsanjânî, *Dar maktab-i jum‘a* Vol.7 22/7/62 p. 168.

85. Khumaynî, *Shahîd wa shahâda* p. 27.

86. Khumaynî, *Shahîd wa shahâda* p. 19; Khumaynî, *Iṭṭilâ‘ât*, 3/7/65 (War Week). According to Ṭabarsî this verse was revealed for the martyrs of Badr. *Majma‘ al-bayân* Vol.2, p. 675.

87. Khumaynî, *Shahîd wa shahâda* p. 20.

88. Muntaẓirî, *Jang-i taḥmîlî* 2/10/62 p. 61.

89. Muntaẓirî, *Iṭṭilâ‘ât*, 28/12/64.

90. Ṣâni‘î, *Iṭṭilâ‘ât*, 25/6/65.

91. Article on Ḥusayn in weekly front edition of *Iṭṭilâ‘ât*: *Iṭṭilâ‘ât-i jabha*, 15/6/66 p. 7.

92. Introduction to Chapter 1, S.H. Nasr et.al. (ed.), *Expectation of the Millennium. Shi‘ism in History* (Albany: SUNY Press, 1989) p. 2.

93. A.A. Sachedina, *Islamic Messianism. The Idea of the Mahdi in Twelver Shi‘ism* (Albany: SUNY Press, 1981), p. 20.

94. Khâmini’î, *Dar maktab-i jum‘a* Vol.3 29/3/60 p. 250.

95. According to Wilhelm E. Mühlmann, ‘Chiliasmus oder Millenarismus ist eine kollektive Einstellung, die auf einen glückseligen Endzustand der Menschheit, im speziellen: auf ein "Tausendjähriges Reich" ("Millennium") gerichtet ist’, ‘Chiliasmus’ in: *Wörterbuch der Soziologie* ed. by W. Bernsdorf (Stuttgart: Enke Verlag, 1969) p. 156.

96. Khâmini’î, *Dar maktab-i jum‘a* Vol.2 16/8/59 p. 382.

97. This title of the twelfth *imâm* is derived from *Hûd* XI:86: ‘That which is left by God’. According to a tradition in *Kamâl al-dîn* by Ibn Bâbûya, someone had asked the eleventh *imâm*, after the birth of the twelfth *imâm*, what proof there was that this boy was an *imâm*. The child himself then said: ‘I am the *baqîyat allâh* on earth and His avenger against His enemies’ (quoted by Sachedina, *Islamic Messianism* p. 74).

98. Khumaynî, *Jang wa jihâd* p. 144. Khumaynî, *Iṭṭilâ‘ât* 7/2/67.

99. Muntaẓirî, *Jang-i taḥmîlî* 22/2/60 p. 88, 19/2/61 p. 122; *Farhang-i jabha* p. 44.

100. *Farhang-i jabha* p. 44.

101. Shîrâzî, FBIS *Daily Report* 17 July 1982.

102. Sachedina, *Islamic Messianism* pp. 180-181.

103. Khumaynî, *Iṭṭilâ'ât*, 23/11/63.

104. Kâshânî, *Dar maktab-i jum'a* Vol.4 10/2/61 p. 392.

105. Khâmini'î, *Dar maktab-i jum'a* Vol.2 16/8/59 p. 383.

106. Khumaynî, FBIS *Daily Report* 5 February 1987.

107. Khumaynî, *Iṭṭilâ'ât-i jabha*, 10/5/66.

108. Muntaẓirî, *Jang-i taḥmîlî* 22/2/60 p. 88, 4/3/61 p. 122, 22/11/61 p. 124.

109. Khumaynî, *Iṭṭilâ'ât*, 28/5/88.

110. Imâmî Kâshânî, *Dar maktab-i jum'a* Vol.5 21/8/61 p. 351.

111. Imâmî Kâshânî, *Dar maktab-i jum'a* Vol.4 10/2/61 p. 393.

112. Khâmini'î, *Dar maktab-i jum'a* Vol.2 16/8/59 p. 383.

113. Sabine Schmidtke, 'Modern Modifications in the Shi'i Doctrine of the Expectation of the Mahdi (Intiẓar al-Mahdi): The Case of Khumaini', in: *Orient* 3 (1987) pp. 389-406.

114. *Khaṭṭ-i tawṭi'a* (Tehran: Sipâh-i pâsdârân-i inqilâb-i islâmî, 1366/1987) p. 51.

115. Cited in Farhang Rajaee, *Islamic Values and World View. Khomeyni on Man, the State and International Politics* (Lanham MD: University Press of America, 1983) p. 83.

116. Khâmini'î, *Dar maktab-i jum'a* Vol.2/8/59 p. 356.

117. Ram, *Myth and Mobilization* pp. 162-163.

118. Abdolali Faridzahdeh, *Die Umwandlung des shiitischen Islams in die politische Ideologie des Chiliasmus und Nativismus* (Unpublished Ph D thesis 1987) p. 115.

119. Khâmini'î, *Dar maktab-i jum'a* Vol.3 60/3/29, p. 250-251.

120. Imâmî Kâshânî, *Dar maktab-i jum'a* Vol.5 21/3/61 p. 20.

121. The tradition in Ibn Mâja's *Sunan* reads: '*yakhruju nâsun min al-mashriqi fa-yuwaṭṭi'ûna li-l-mahdî ya'nî sulṭânihi*'(people come from the East and they prepare the way for the authority of the *mahdî*), Ibn Mâja, *Sunan* (n.p. Dâr iḥyâ' al-kutub al-'arabîyya, 1373/1953) Vol.2 p. 1368.

122. Imâmî Kashânî, *Dar maktab-i jum'a* Vol.5 p. 21. This tradition does not occur in the collections of al-Bukhârî and Muslim.

123. Imâmî Kashânî, *Dar maktab-i jum'a* Vol.5 p. 24.

124. Khumaynî, *Iṭṭilâ'ât*, 15/1/67-4/4/88. The same line of reasoning can be found in his New Year speech, *Iṭṭilâ'ât*, 7/1/61.

125. Mahdawî Kanî, *Dar maktab-i jum'a* Vol.6 3/4/62 p. 384.

126. Muntazirî, *Jang-i taḥmîlî* 19/2/61 p. 121, 3/4/61 p. 123, 22/11/61 p. 124. Imâmî Kâshânî, *Dar maktab-i jum'a* Vol.5 p. 24.

127. Imâmî Kâshânî, *Dar maktab-i jum'a* Vol.5 p. 23, 24.

128. Imâmî Kâshânî, Friday sermon, *Iṭṭilâ'ât* 25/4/67.

129. Said Amir Arjomand, *The Turban for the Crown. The Islamic Revolution in Iran* (Oxford: Oxford University Press, 1988) p. 152.

130. *Farhang-i jabha* p. 25, 28, 36.

131. Information from *Kârnâma-yi 'amalîyât-i sipâhiyân-i islâm dar hasht sâl-i difâ'-i muqaddas* (Tehran: Markaz-i farhangî-yi sipâh-i pâsdârân-i inqilâb-i islâmî, 1373/1994[3]; *Gudharî bar du sâl jang* (After two years of war) (n.p., Daftar-i siyâsî-yi sipâh-i pâsdârân-i inqilâb-i islâmî, n.d.).

132. One of the slogans at the front was: 'From Jamarân to Huwayza, from Huwayza to Karbalâ' we come, From Khumaynî, *rûḥ allâh* to Ḥusayn, *thâr allâh* we come', *Farhang-i jabha* p. 24. *Thâr allâh* was also the name of a patrol group, founded after the revolution, whose role it was to deal with counterrevolutionary activities. Arjomand, *Turban for the Crown* p. 172. According to 'Alî Sharî'atî, *thâr Allâh* denotes the vendetta which rests from the time of the murder of Abel on the shoulders of the prophets and the *imâms*, who are all *thâr Allâh*. This vendetta will last until the ultimate vengeance by the hand of the *muntaqim* (Avenger or *mahdî*) on the *ṭâghût*, or the tribe of Cain, who was responsible for the first murder in history. *Thâr Allâh* is also part of the prayer called *ziyârat wârith*, a prayer in which greetings are sent to Ḥusayn as the heir of the prophets and previous *imâms*, M. Abedi and G. Legenhausen (eds.) *Jihâd and Shahâdat. Struggle and Martyrdom in Islam* (Houston: IRIS, 1986) pp. 255-263.

133. Mahmoud Ayoub, *Redemptive Suffering in Islam. A Study of the Devotional Aspects of 'Âshûrâ' in Twelver Shi'ism* (The Hague: Mouton, 1978) p. 102.

134. '*Hadaf-i 'amalîyât: âzâdsâzî-yi shahr mihrân wa irtafâ'ât-i manṭiqa*' (Goal of the operations: liberation of Mihrân and the heights in the area, *Kârnâma-yi 'amalîyât-i sipâhiyân-i islâm dar hasht sâl-i difâ'-i muqaddas*, p. 74. See also: Anthony H. Cordesman and A.R. Wagner, *The Lessons of Modern War* Vol.2 (Boulder: Westview, 1990), pp. 227-228.

135. The October War of 1973 also received the name 'Operation Badr', Rudolph Peters, 'The Political Relevance of the Doctrine of Jihad in Sadat's Egypt', in: *National and International Politics in the Middle East. Essays in Honour of Elie Kedourie*, ed. by L. Lugram (London: Frank Cass, 1986) p. 271 n4.

136. Khâmini'î, *Iṭṭilâ'ât*, 6/12/62.

137. Bell, *The Qur'ân* p. 519.

138. David Menashri, *Iran. A Decade of War and Revolution* (New York: Holmes and Meier, 1990) p. 191.

139. *Dar maktab-i jum'a* Vol.7 14/5/62 p. 12.

140. Said Amir Arjomand, 'The Ulama's Traditionalist Opposition to Parliamentarianism: 1907-1909', in: *Middle Eastern Studies* 17 (1981) pp. 174-190, p. 179; Vanessa Martin, *Islam and Modernism. The Iranian Revolution of 1906* (London: I.B. Tauris, 1989) p. 165.

141. Ervand Abrahamian, *Khomeinism* (London: I.B. Tauris, 1993) p. 97.

142. Abdul-Hadi Haeri, 'Shaykh Fazl Allâh Nûrî's Refutation of the Idea of Constitutionalism', in: *Middle Eastern Studies* 13 (1977) pp. 327-339, p. 338.

143. Information also from *Kârnâma-i 'amalîyât-i sipâhiyân-i islâm dar hasht sâl-i difâ'-i muqaddas*.

144. According to the *Lughat-namâ* by 'Alî Akbar Dihkhudâ (Tehran: Dânishgâh-i Tehrân, 1328) Vol.5 p. 1557, *adriknî* is a prayer and an appeal for help.

145. Ram, *Myth and Mobilization* p. 49, 54. See also Momen, *An Introduction to Shi'i Islam* p. 27.

146. Imâmî Kâshânî, Friday sermon, *Iṭṭilâ'ât*, 2/9/64: *'jumhûrî-yi islâmî az barakat-i iftikhâr-i madhhab-i tashî' wa iradâ bi asitân-i muqaddas 'â'ima-i aṭâr bi pîrûz rasîd'*.

147. Peter Chelkowski, 'From Maqâtîl Literature to Drama', in: *Al-Ṣerâṭ* 12 (1986) pp. 227-264, p. 232.

148. Imâmî Kâshânî, *Dar maktab-i jum'a* Vol.4 13/9/60 pp. 127-128.

149. Faridzahdeh, speaking about the changed image of Fâṭima during the revolution, misinterpreted an article by Adele Ferdows on Khumaynî and his ideas on women, by saying that Khumaynî propagated a new role for Iranian women on the basis of Fâṭima's image as a politicized woman who had equal status to men. The import of the article which he cited, however, is that Khumaynî's interpretation of Fâṭima's image and the role women should have in Iran did not deviate from traditional ideas that the status of women is inferior to that of men. Abdolali Faridzahdeh, *Die Umwandlung des shiitischen Islams* p. 151, citing Adele Ferdows, 'Shariati and Khomeini On Women', in: *The Iranian Revolution and the Islamic Republic*, ed. by N.R. Keddie (n.p., Middle East Institute, 1982). She says: 'On the question of education for women, although Khomeini supports it, he clearly defines the content of that education in limited terms as that which would prepare women to be mothers, housekeepers, and devout Muslims'. Furthermore: 'He [Khumaynî] represents the conservative traditionalist school of Shi'i *fiqh* and *hadith* transmitted by the clerics before him for centuries', pp. 79, 81.

150. Shahla Haeri, *Law of Desire. Temporary Marriage in Shi'i Iran* (Syracuse: Syracuse University Press, 1989) p. 226 n31.

151. Val Moghadam, 'Women, Work, and Ideology in the Islamic Republic', in: *International Journal of Middle East Studies* 20 (1988) pp. 245-263, p. 227.

5 ISLAMIC SOLIDARITY AND RELIGIOUS NATIONALISM

We have seen that the Iranian leaders presented the war between Iran and Iraq as a war with a wider scope, forming part of the longstanding conflict between the two sides of Islam and *kufr* (unbelief) and not just as a regional one between two neighbouring countries. This chapter will deal with the way Iranian leaders presented the character of the Islamic Republic as a major cause for the outbreak of the war. They argued that the superpowers had imposed the war on the Islamic Republic in order to stop the spreading of the ideas of the revolution, which had universal appeal for mankind. This chapter will also look at how the leaders envisaged the position of the Republic within Islam and the Islamic world and the role the war played therein. The leaders presented the war as part of a struggle fought by the Islamic Republic to liberate those Muslim states which either had non-Muslim governments or were occupied by non-Muslim states. Thus, although the war was presented as one between Islam and *kufr*, the Islamic Republic took up a central position. This raises the question whether and in which form nationalism played a role in the rhetoric of the Iranian leaders, and the last part of this chapter will deal with this question.

Muslim solidarity: The universalist appeal of the revolution

The ideas about the revolution of Khumaynî and his followers during the revolution and after the establishment of the Islamic Republic tended to be universalist, not only as a reaction to the secular nationalist ideas of the last Shah, but also because the revolution in Iran, which was presented as an Islamic revolution, was seen as an example for other people, especially other Muslim nations, to follow.[1] It was presented as a revolution with universal aspects, a revolution for the whole of mankind, not for Iran alone. Leaders expressed their ideas by speaking about the 'export of the revolution', by which they meant the propagation of Islam through the spreading of the ideas, the spirit and the enthusiasm of the revolution.[2]

Throughout the war, the Iranian leadership justified the war on the basis of this universal aspect of the Islamic revolution. They presented the war as a conspiracy of the Superpowers and their allies, especially those in the Persian Gulf. Fear of the revolution had brought about their cooperation against the Islamic Republic, and they aimed to bring down the Islamic Republic in order to stop the export of the revolution and the spreading of the message of Islam to other countries.[3] In his first speeches after the outbreak of the war Khumaynî referred to the war as one between *islâm* and *kufr*, thus making it clear that the war was not limited to a territorial dispute but in fact was a struggle of much larger dimensions.

The revolution had succeeded in reinstalling 'true' Islam, the real and genuine Islam of which the arrogant and imperialist powers were afraid, not only because it had made of Iran a country independent from these powers but also because Iran had taken it upon itself to realize the major goal of Islam: to spread Islam over the whole world among oppressed people. Both developments were contrary to the interests of the arrogant (*mustakbir*) and imperialist powers of this world. When the Iranian leaders spoke about interests they meant both ideological interests (enforcing a 'Western' way of thinking), and economic interests (the fact that Iran was one of the largest oil-producing and -exporting countries made the United States wish to control it). According to Khumaynî, war had been initiated by the United States to continue the time of dependency on foreigners, of corruption (*fasâd*) and of oppression (*ẓulm*) of the deprived and of stealing the natural resources of Iran, which belonged to these deprived and not to the privileged classes.[4] Thus, although the war was started by Iraq, the Iranian leaders were convinced that Iraq had acted not independently, but at the request of the United States. It was clear that the war was imposed by the United States as a last resort to bring the Islamic revolution to its knees, to reinstall imperialist power in the region and to end the threat posed by the Islamic revolution to imperialist interests.[5] On the occasion of the *ḥajj* in 1987, Khumaynî said that the war had been imposed on Iran because it had committed the crime of replacing the *ṭâghûtî* system of the Shah by Islam, because it had revived the *sunna* of the Prophet,[6] because it worked to fulfil the instructions of the Qur'ân, because it propagated unity among all Muslims, because it fought against the arrogant in defence of the rights of the deprived of this world, because it fought against Zionism, and because it had cancelled the enslaving contracts of the Pahlavi regime with the world-devourer America.[7] The Islamic Republic was in the same situation as Muḥammad and his community, since war was imposed on both in order to stop the 'divine mission' of spreading the message of Islam.[8] Repeatedly it was said that the war was the result of a conspiracy set up by the superpowers, Israel and their allies, in collaboration with the states in the Gulf region which were afraid that the Islamic revolution would be exported to their countries.[9]

Muslim solidarity: Iraq

Despite their animosity towards 'the West', the modern nation-state and the existence of separate Islamic states (formed under Western influence) were and are accepted by Iranian leaders: 'To love one's fatherland and its people and to protect its borders are both quite unobjectionable, but nationalism, involving hostility to other Muslim nations, is something quite different'.[10] Separate nations and countries were also accepted on the basis of Qur'ânic verse: 'O you people. We have created you of a male and a female and made you in nations and tribes that you may recognize each other. Verily the most honoured of you with God is the one of you who has the most *taqwâ* (pious virtue)' (49:13).[11] Furthermore, 'Iran has its own government, Iraq has its own government, Egypt has its own government, but they all are together under the banner of Islam'.[12] Pan-Islamic ideas in the war rhetoric were mainly expressed through statements in which solidarity with Muslims in other countries was shown; statements that Iran was prepared to help 'oppressed' Muslims. The leadership made it clear that they cared about such people. But the leadership were more sympathetic to some Muslims than to others: they paid much attention to the Palestinian question and the Israeli invasion of South Lebanon which affected the Shî'îs there, but the Soviet invasion of Muslim Afghanistan was not an issue in the war rhetoric. It is outside the scope of this study to see whether and to what extent the Islamic Republic interfered in the affairs of these countries, but we shall return to this since the justification of the war was partly based on Iran's concern for them.

The leaders said that the Islamic states in the region had taken part in the conspiracy to bring down the Islamic revolution, but at the same time these states were reminded of their Islamic duty to help Iran. As we saw in Chapter 2, the Iranian leaders referred to *al-Ḥujurât* XLIX:9: 'If two parties of the believers fight, set things right between them, and if one of the two parties oppresses (*baghat*) the other, fight the one which is oppressive until it returns to the affair of Allah'. It was clear that in this verse that other Islamic countries were obliged to support the Islamic Republic; because once a Muslim country had been attacked by another Muslim country, other Muslim countries were obliged to intervene on behalf of the attacked party and to fight until the oppressing party again accepted God's authority. The Muslim countries in the region clearly had neglected their duty.[13] The non-Arab Muslim countries were not criticized by Iran, probably because they lie outside the Iran-Iraq region.

The Iranian leaders paid much attention to the Iraqi population but were very ambiguous in their attitude. They made clear that they were concerned about the fate of the Iraqi population since the Iraqis had suffered as much as the Iranians from the Iraqi leaders and from the war which, after all, had been imposed on the Iraqi population as well. The leaders emphasized that they considered it their duty to help the Iraqis: 'The nation of Muslims of Iraq worries that such a treacherous and bad government has control over it. We know that we have the duty to help this deprived (*maḥrûm*) brotherly nation. Today is the day of this aid'.[14] Furthermore: 'in our region, where lives a vulture like Ṣaddâm, who shows his claws the way he does, is there another obligation for us than to give our whole heart to save and defend the Iraqi nation *(milla)* and to accept martyrdom for the salvation of an oppressed *(maẓlûm)* nation?'[15] Considering their war aims with regard to Iraq, leaders said they never had the intention of annexing Iraq. Iranian soldiers helped Iraqi *mujâhidîn* (those who participate in a *jihâd*, a term used by Muntaẓirî to denote Iraqi insurgents) and protected the Iraqi nation from the decayed Ba'th regime and the unbeliever Ṣaddâm. They did this because it was their duty prescribed by Islam and not because they were interested in Iraqi territory. Iran itself had plentiful resources given by God.[16]

But in their speeches the leaders sometimes went further than merely speaking about solidarity with the Iraqis. When they speculated about Iraq's future after Ṣaddâm, they showed a preference for a greater role of Islam in Iraqi politics. Muntazirî said that once the Iraqi population was liberated, they could choose a government, but it should be an Islamic one.[17] Khumaynî said that once the Iraqi nation had liberated itself from the oppressing party and was connected with the Iranian nation, a government would be installed in Iraq which was in accordance with the 'Islamic hope' of the population.[18] Moreover, when Rafsanjânî said that there would never be any question of annexation, he also said, 'We will allow the Iraqi nation to establish their desired government at a time when we may have the upper hand there'.[19] As I have shown, before the war the export of the revolution had been one of the aims of the Islamic Republic. But during the war the export of the revolution to Iraq and the establishment of an Islamic government with the help of Iran was part of the justification of the war:

> But after the enemy has returned within his own borders, then it is our duty (*taklîf*) and obligation (*waẓîfa*) to exert ourselves until the nation of Iraq is delivered from the evil of the oppressive (*ṭâghûtî*) powers and an Islamic government and republic have been founded.[20]

The meaning of *ṭâghût* in the war rhetoric differs from the Qur'ânic meaning of 'idol', something worshipped other than God. Here, the term must be understood in Khumaynî's interpretation, as 'oppressive governments and all illicit forms of powers that have revolted against divine government in order to establish monarchy or some other form of rule'.[21] Thus *ṭâghût* denotes the Superpowers and their allies, the driving forces of the Iraqi regime who have passed all bounds of tyranny and despotism.

In July 1982, Iranian forces occupied Iraqi territory notwithstanding the leadership's former statements that Iran had no interest in annexing Iraqi territory. The occupation was justified on several grounds. 'To go into Iraq is not an attack but defence of Islam and the Islamic country'.[22] This defence of Islam was frequently focused on the liberation of Jerusalem, the third holiest city in Islam: 'O all those who fight with *al-Aqṣâ* [the mosque on the Temple Square] and Jerusalem in mind, we do not dispute Iraqi territory or that of other Islamic countries, we dispute unbelief'.[23] After the liberation of Bustân in 1982, the city was unofficially renamed

Shahr-i ṭarîq-i quds (the City on the way to Jerusalem). Another motive for the occupation of Iraqi territory given in the war rhetoric was the liberation of the Iraqi people, since Iran had no political, governmental, territorial or economic interest in Iraq and was not planning any violation of international law. Iran had crossed the border to liberate the Iraqi population and give them peace in order that they could choose and establish their own government.[24] Shîrâzî, Commander of the ground forces presented the overthrow of Ṣaddâm's regime as one reason for the occupation.[25] Besides these three main reasons, there were other, minor ones. Occupation of Iraqi territory was part of an intensification of the war in order to be able to terminate the war as soon as possible. Ending the war did not serve the interests of Iran's enemies, especially imperialists and superpowers who wanted to prolong the war in order to be able, for instance, to test new weapons.[26] Rafsanjânî wanted to extract compensation for war damage from Iraq and the superpowers. The Islamic Republic in fact did not want any money from these enemies but war-damaged areas had to be rebuilt.[27]

Muslim solidarity: Palestine and Lebanon

On 6 June 1982 the Israeli army invaded Lebanon in order to crush the growing Palestinian power there, which the Israeli government considered a danger to the stability and safety of Israel. The Iranian regime regarded Israel as one of its most important enemies, and the rejection of the existence of Israel and the continuation of the war until Palestine and Jerusalem were be liberated, were recurring features in the rhetoric. Zionism had a negative connotation similar to imperialism, both being considered excesses of Western politics.[28] The prayer leaders in July 1982 intensified their statements about continuation of the war until Palestine was be liberated as a result of the recent victories which had bolstered Iranian self-confidence.[29] But the recapturing of Iranian territory and cities (Bustân on 30 November 1981 and khurramshahr on 23 May 1982) had already been going on for some months and during that time the propaganda against Israel had not changed. It was after the Israeli invasion of South Lebanon that the propaganda against Israel intensified considerably and became one of the aspects of the justification of, and mobilization for, the war.

A few days after the invasion, Imâmî Kâshânî depicted it as an element in a complex and intricate conspiracy, in which all enemies of the Islamic Republic featured. He told his audience that the Israeli invasion did not stand on its own but was part of a conspiracy set up by Begin, Ṣaddâm and their Arab allies like Ḥusnî [Mubârak, President of Egypt], King Ḥusayn and Khâlid [King of Saudi Arabia] to rescue the Ba'th regime of Iraq, and Israel. The other part of the conspiracy was Ṣaddâm's recent offer to withdraw the Iraqi forces from Iranian soil in order to send them to Lebanon to support their Arab brethren and fight the Israeli forces. But, Kâshânî said, Ṣaddâm and the Ba'th did not really want to defend their Arab brethren in South Lebanon. The withdrawal was just an excuse for their loss of face in Iran after their military defeats, and the invasion of Lebanon was planned in order to continue the war with Iran but now under the pretext of helping the people of South Lebanon. In reality they would fight there against the Iranian forces. They knew that Iran was sympathetic towards the *mustad'afûn* (oppressed people) and that it would therefore turn its attention to South Lebanon and send its forces there to defend its people. Imâmî Kâshânî said that the conspirators wanted to kill two birds with one stone: Iraq could continue the war against the Islamic Republic, and Israel was safe from the forces of the Islamic Republic who had to turn their attention from the liberation of Jerusalem to the liberation of South Lebanon. Iran, however, was not taken in by their plot and Imâmî Kâshânî warned Israel that it could not protect itself against the forces of Islam.[30]

A week later Rafsanjânî told his audience that the war with Iraq had in fact been imposed upon the Islamic Republic by the United States in order to protect Israel. When the Shah was deposed, Israel had lost its most important economic and political ally in the region and became isolated. America had planned this war with the idea of preventing the establishment of an anti-Israeli power in Iran. Rafsanjânî added that Iranians fought this war basically with Israel in mind. The war would therefore not end once Iraq was defeated but continue until Iranian forces stood in the heart of Israel.[31] Ironically, Ṣaddâm Ḥusayn had made use of the same justification for the attack on Iran just after the outbreak of the war: 'This glorious hour for the Iraqi Army is preparing it to liberate Palestine: victories against Iran are paving the road to Jerusalem'.[32]

Nationalism: the theoretical background

In order to assess the nature of the statements which glorified the Iranian Republic and its outstanding position within Islam, a theoretical background of the relation between religion, nationalism and national identity is needed. Nationalism is defined by Gellner as a 'theory of political legitimacy, which requires that ethnic boundaries should not cut across political ones, and, in particular, that ethnic boundaries within a given state - a contingency already formally excluded by the principle in its general formulation - should not separate the power-holders from the rest'.[33] Nationalism is based on the existence of a state and a nation bound by a culture, defined by Gellner as a system of ideas and signs and associations and ways of behaving and communicating.[34] Nationalism came to manifest itself in the industrial age, an age in which the high culture is no longer linked to a faith and a church.[35] Thus, in Gellner's view, nationalism replaces religious bounds.

This view has been contested by several people. Van der Veer, for instance, has argued that in many societies a clear division between the old traditional and the new modern society (which according to Gellner is the only natural environment for nationalism) does not exist. Van der Veer, instead, argues that India is an example of a society where a modern society invades the traditional society, where nationalism and religion are combined.[36] Arjomand observed that 'the possibility of politicization of religious identity is also especially strong in the Middle East, as Islam has always been and remains a primary basis of communal identity and loyalty'.[37] Hossein Razi argues that, while there exists a relationship between nationalism and Islam in the Middle East, it is a complex one.[38] Gellner later also came to the conclusion that Islam is the big exception to the 'secularization theory', which asserts that religious faith and observance decline in a scientific-industrial society.[39] The fact that populations in the modern world adhere to Islam is the result of the modern world itself: urbanization, political centralization, incorporation in a wider market, and labour migration, direct people away from the illiterate traditions of folk religion towards the urban Islam of the theological scholars, the 'High Islam'. He describes 'High Islam' as a 'formally (theologically) more "correct" Islam', oriented towards puritanism and scripturalism and which values order, sobriety, rule-observance and learning.[40] Gellner illustrates his thesis with the revolution in Iran. He says that Khumaynî, in order to mobilize the Iranian population, made use of 'Low Islam' or 'Folk Islam', which is characterized by saint cult and emotional excess, but he directed Shî'î Islam towards a 'High Islam' in which stress was no longer on the glorification of saints and martyrs but upon implementation of the divine law.[41]

As we have seen, religion does play a role of importance in the Islamic Republic. The emphasis which the Iranian leaders laid on the observance of divine law by Iranians, is in line with Gellner's conviction that Khumaynî turned Iranian Shî'ism into a puritanic and scriptural religion based upon the implementation and observance of divine law. With regard to the war rhetoric, I agree with Gellner only partly. When we look at the way the Iranian leaders justified the war, it is true that they referred to this 'High Islam', because they emphasized the importance of observing Islamic duties, such as the duty to take part in the *jihâd* for the defence of Islam, and made the Qur'ân and Shî'î traditions central in their rhetoric. But the situation is different when we look at the way the leaders tried to mobilize people for the war. The reason for the major attention paid in the speeches to sacrifice and martyrdom for the cause of Islam cannot only be that sacrifice on God's path is prescribed by Islamic law, thus being part of 'High Islam', or simply, as Gellner stated, because it was effective in rousing people, as it was during the revolution. The excessive attention to the example of Ḥusayn's martyrdom in the cause of Islam both during the revolution and in the war must be that this expression of 'Folk Islam' is still part of Iranian Shî'ism, both for the religious leaders and for the population, otherwise it would not have had such an effect.

Another aspect of nationalism in Iran is the alleged inherent and mutual dependence between Shî'ism and Iranian nationalism. According to Enayat, this is an incorrect assumption since 'there is nothing in the theoretical principles of Shî'ism to make it more amenable to ethnic or racial particularism than Sunnism'. The fact that the Prophet and his family, who after all are of Arab origin, occupy a central position in Shî'î belief, clearly clarifies this point. The popular belief in Iran, expressed in passion plays, which stresses the blood ties between the Iranians and the family of the Prophet through the marriage between Shahrbânû, daughter of the last Sasanian king, and Ḥusayn, grandson of Muḥammad, is in Enayat's eyes an expression of loyalty to the family of the Prophet, rather than an expression of Iranian superiority.[42] His view is sustained by the rhetoric of the Iranian leaders during the war. Iran's superiority was stressed by the leaders but on the basis of the fact that the Islamic Republic was completely in line with the teachings of the Prophet and 'Alî, whereas references to Iranian Shî'ism did not play a role.

Iran and nationalism

In pre-revolutionary Iran, the Pahlavi shahs had tried to enforce a nationalism in which stress was laid on a pre-Islamic Persian culture and on the idea of continuity between the Pahlavi monarchy and the pre-Islamic Persian empires.[43] The Persian language was presented as the unifying element which would bind the different ethnic minorities, who make up almost half of the population of Iran, into one nation. After the proclamation of the Islamic Republic, the new leaders tried to enforce a national identity based on Islam. This enforcement found expression mainly in school textbooks, since the Islamic leaders regarded the 'uncorrupted' children as a more important target than the older generation 'indoctrinated by the shah'.[44] One look at the sermons, statements and speeches of the leadership suffices to show that the leadership tried very hard to convince the whole of Iranian society that its national identity was also an Islamic one. The different ethnic minorities, among them Sunnî Muslims, were seen as part of the Islamic Iranian nation on the basis that Muslim society is one and cannot be divided. This argument was used by the new leaders of the republic in their rejection of demands for autonomy by the ethnic minorities.[45] However, the ban on the use of languages other than Persian, as had been the case under the Pahlavis, was abolished. The religious minorities hold a special status in the Islamic Republic. In the constitution, it is stated that Zoroastrians, Jews, Assyrians and Armenians are members of the accepted religions and are part of the Iranian nation. They are entitled to their own representatives in the Majlis. The acceptance of the religious minorities evokes memories of the concept of the *dhimma*, the special status which the members of the accepted religions, the *ahl al-kitâb* (People of the Book), who were living in Muslim society, received.

The distinction between secular and religious elements is also manifest in Ram's view on the development of the Iranian nationalist sentiment. He says that in the second year of the war nationalist sentiment became more intense 'although it was camouflaged by Islamic themes'.[46] This raises the question of whether a strict distinction between 'national' and 'religious' identity is valid and useful in the case of Iran or, indeed, of other Muslim countries. As we have seen, this distinction between nationalism and religion was denied by van der Veer. In Iran, patriotic sentiments were almost exclusively combined with references to Islam and these were made from the beginning of the war, for instance in slogans such as 'Defence of Islam and the country (*kishwar*) is an obligation for everybody', 'defence of Islamic ideals and the borders of the country'.[47] 'In this war we are in fact defending our Islamic and Iranian identity, our territorial integrity and honor'.[48] This is also Menashri's view: 'As opposed to the regime of the shah, which bases Iranian nationalism on an essentially secular perception rooted in Iran's pre-Islamic history, Khomeini's perception of Iranian identity sees Islam as the decisive cohesive element'.[49] In my view, the remarks about national borders and territory have more to do with a shift from a revolutionary attitude to a more pragmatic stance, and a shift from pan-Islamic sentiments to national religious sentiments, than with a change from religious to more secular nationalist and patriotic sentiments.

Other scholars have emphasized the relation between Iran's identity and Islam. 'A devotion to the nation of Iran and a devotion to Islam can coexist in the same individual',[50] an'religion and nationalism have always interacted in Iran and have shaped its national identity and character'.[51] Large parts of the Iranian population supported Khumaynî during and after the revolution because he fought for the restoration of traditional Islamic values and against the cultural dislocation of Iranian society. Already during the revolution a certain type of Iranian nationalism played a role which had nothing to do with the nationalism propagated by Muḥammad Rizâ Shah. In this nationalism an Islamic Iranian national identity was set against the secular national identity envisaged by the Shah which was based upon pre-Islamic Persian culture. This form of nationalism was also strongly anti-imperialist as a reaction to the cultural and political dominance of the United States in Iran, described by Khumaynî as 'imperialist nationalism' whose goal it was to destroy the unification of all Muslims through the establishment of separate nations.[52] This anti-imperialist attitude classifies Khumaynî as belonging to what is called 'Third World nationalism', whose key political discourse is 'anti-imperialism' and 'the problematic of dependency', signifying political, economic, cultural and social dependency on the West and loss of the indigenous identity.[53] Others have called this the 'authenticity discourse', which means that the core of this attitude is the belief that the retrieval of an authentic identity is a requirement for independence on all fronts from Western domination.[54] In my view, this last term is more fitting, because remarks about the policy of the Islamic Republic as completely in line with the teachings of the prophets, of the Prophet Muḥammad and of 'Alî, have a central place in the rhetoric.

Nationalism: Religious nationalism in the Islamic Republic

Although the Iranian leadership continuously emphasized that the war was part of a universal conflict between Islam and *kufr* and that the attack on the Islamic Republic was in reality an attack on Islam, they did not hesitate to glorify the Iranian Republic.[55] 'This nation brought about a revolution and suffered reprisals for that'.[56] Khumaynî addressed his audience in similar words. He repeatedly said that the Iranian people had to understand that making revolution naturally had consequences, such as conspiracies and this war. For the sake of the revolution, these consequences had to be accepted.[57] Already from the beginning of the war, the leadership made it clear that Iran was attacked because of the Islamic revolution. Although the war was characterized as a war between *islâm* and *kufr*, *ḥaqq* and *bâṭil*, the Islamic Republic took up a central position in this rhetoric. It was clear that *islâm*, as presented by leaders, was 'their' *islâm*, *islâm* as understood and observed in the Islamic Republic. The relationship between the nation (*milla*), about which the leaders spoke constantly, and the Islamic Republic was established as a result of the efforts of the Iranian nation.[58] Khumaynî and others emphasized that the nation again had to do its utmost, this time to defend the Republic. 'The motive of the nation and the Armed Forces of Iran is to defend Islam and the noble Koran in the interests of Muslim solidarity and the oppressed of the world','the Islamic Republic is a trust given by the Almighty to the Iranian nation; all of us, young and old, women and men, are responsible for guarding this trust' and 'you, the honorable nation who want to defend God's religion and to be the guardian of the country of the Lord of the Time'.[59] Furthermore, 'Our beloved nation, committed to Islam, is determined to continue the war until its martyrdom and until its reunion with God'.[60] Other remarks to the effect that the Iranian nation was God's chosen nation were included: 'today you have a national duty towards your country, and you have an Islamic duty toward the protection of Islam. Islam is entrusted to you'[61] and 'God supports this nation, he is all-powerful and makes this people capable of fighting and defeat those strong satanic powers... Those who perform their duties for God will become victorious'.[62] These statements, which emphasized the close relationship between the Iranian nation and God, must be regarded as the ultimate form of sacralization.

Defence of Iran's territory and defence of the Islamic revolution existed side by side because they were part of a whole. 'We are ready to fight to our last drop of blood for the protection of the borders of our land and our revolution';[63] Âyatullâh Mahdawî Kanî spoke about *istiqlâl* (independence) and *tamâmiyat-i arḍî-yi kishwar* (territorial integrity of the country).[64]

Nationalist remarks by leaders had a religious basis and focused on the idea that Iran was the Islamic country par excellence. Rafsanjânî: 'We know that one of the characteristics of Islam which crystallized from the struggles of the society of the Muslims of Iran, was a mentality of self-sacrifice and generosity which is not present to this day in any other society or revolution'.[65] The Iranian nation was presented as unique nation because its mentality was *jang-âwar* (militant) and *fidâ-kârî* (self-sacrificing) to a degree that was unprecedented: 'With a few exceptions from the dawn of Islam there is no one in the history of Islam who can be compared to our youths';[66] 'There is nothing in history which is equal to us'; 'This transformation which has taken place in Iran is unparalleled';[67] 'A magnificent power without precedent'.[68]

The war was presented as a part of an important mission entrusted to the Iranians in the same way as it had been entrusted in the past to Muslims:

> You, the Muslim nation, should perform your historical mission and your responsibility towards human society as the architects of this lasting phase of history. In a word, you should perform your Islamic duty in a befitting manner. Your actions and decisions today will shape not only the destiny of the people of the present age, but even the lives of future generations. So rush towards the fronts in order to crush your aggressive enemies. In the end, victory will belong to the believers.[69]

> We who finish the work of the prophets and the most distinguished Messenger have to struggle until Islam and justice are established.[70]

Iranians had at their disposal the same power which throughout history had made the prophets of God victorious over waves of idols. They had at their disposal the staff of Moses and his white hand. For them, even fire was cold and pleasant.[71] Although this was not said explicitly, the comparison with Moses was made to demonstrate that Iran had also received a special mission to instruct and guide the arrogant powers of this time as Moses had instructed Pharaoh. The Iranian nation (*milla*) had received God's signs for the very same reason. This seems to be a continuation of the notion in Shî'î piety 'that prophetic history continuously repeats itself, hence the analogy between Moses and his people and Muhammad and his people'.[72] In his *Ḥukûmat-i islâmî*, Khumaynî regularly referred to Moses and his determination to overthrow the illegitimate government of Pharaoh as an example for Muslims to follow, and not as something which was beyond the capacity of human beings.[73] Contrary to expectation, the Iranian leaders did not associate Ṣaddâm Ḥusayn with Pharaoh as had been the case before and during the revolution when the Shah's government was equated with that of Pharaoh.[74] In Egypt, too, President Sadat's murderer had identified him with Pharaoh.[75] After all, the presentation of Ṣaddâm Ḥusayn in the war rhetoric brings to mind the Qur'ânic image of Pharaoh as a tyrant who belongs among the *mufsidîn* (corrupt ones) and who is arrogant (*istakbara*)(*al-Qaṣaṣ* XXVIII:4, 39),[76] which descriptions were also used of Iran's enemies.

There was almost no speech dealing with the war which did not glorify the martyrdom and self-sacrifice of the Iranian population. 'Where in the world do you witness the resistance of forty million people against the attacking enemy? Today, even our children in the cradle grow up with soldiers' tunes about worldwide arrogance'.[77] Before sending them to the front, mothers held the Qur'ân above their children's head and said a farewell prayer.[78] During the 'War of the Cities' in 1365/66 (1987), the glorification of the population was even more intense; prayer leaders drew parallels between the courage of Iranian people and that of the early Muslims.[79]

Although the prominent place leaders reserved for the Iranian nation was mainly for mobilization purposes, there was also an element of justification in it, since the attitude of the population was described in such a manner that it had to be understood by the audience as sanctioning the policies of the regime. The population was presented by leaders as a nation willing to do its utmost in this war, which was meant to show that the continuation of the war had met with widespread approval. During the whole war the leaders almost constantly spoke in the first person plural, referring not to the regime but to the whole nation. They said so explicitly in 1983/1362: 'We do not defend Islamic honour or our revolution because we are a government but because we are a nation. This power that we feel in ourselves is belief in God'.[80] The Iranian nation even guided the leadership in their actions: 'These efforts and holy war will continue until we achieve the conditions which we have set and which have been endorsed throughout the world as just. Our nation, followed by its obedient government will not retreat one inch from this position'.[81] 'Our nation as the vanguard of the Islamic movement has prepared itself to forge ahead with all its might and assets, and will not turn back from its chosen path, along which it sees and enjoys divine support and God's succour and guidance'.[82] The Muslim people of Iran were determined to continue the war until the very end.[83]

One of the most conspicuous features of the war rhetoric was remarks which equated the rule of the Islamic Republic with that of the Prophet: 'the system of the Islamic Republic is the system of the most honourable Messenger. From the death of the most honourable Messenger until now, there has not existed an Islamic movement like today and this is the movement of the most honourable Messenger. Therefore, worldwide arrogance has exercised all its power for the annihilation of this movement'.[84] Khumaynî went even further when he said:

> I claim that nothing like the nation of Iran, the Parliament of Iran, the state apparatus of Iran, the President of Iran, the Judicial Council, the Council of Guardians and the whole nation of Iran has ever existed, from the beginning of world history until the present time. The best era of Islam was the era of the noble Messenger... but what did people then do with the Messenger... when he ordered them to participate in a war, they did not go but made excuses... With the exception of a handful at the beginning of Islam, no one can be compared with our Pâsdârân and our armed forces, who stay upright with all these difficulties and troubles, with martyrdom and sacrifice, torture and misfortune.[85]

The leaders even went so far as to give a more favourable picture of the population of the Islamic Republic than of the Muslim subjects during the governments of 'Alî, Ḥasan and Ḥusayn. The reason for this, Rafsanjânî said, was that the people today supported the government; they were the very foundation of this government, whereas the followers of 'Alî and Ḥasan had not been loyal to their governments and had not participated in government as well as the people of today. At the time of the first *imâm* the people did not understand his *'adâla* (justice), their belief was weaker than that of today's Iranians.[86] In praising the Iranian population for the observance of their Islamic duty, Khumaynî compared them favourably to the people of the Ḥijâz at the time of God's Messenger who had not obeyed his order to go to the battlefronts, and the people of Kufa and Iraq during the era of 'Alî and Ḥusayn who had disobeyed 'Alî and deserted Ḥusayn. Indirectly it was also a critical reference to the Saudi people of this time, who had neglected their Islamic duty, and to the Iraqi people, who had not risen en masse against Ṣaddâm Ḥusayn.[87]

This is remarkable, since these views contradict the view which prevails among Muslims, that Muḥammad established an ideal and perfect Islamic society.[88] Without the guidance of the Prophet, or an *imâm*, and thus lacking the necessary knowledge to create an ideal state, man can only strive to emulate in an imperfect form Muḥammad's perfect society.[89] Nevertheless, the leaders did not hesitate to stress that Iranian society was perfect. However, one has to keep in mind that these statements were part of the war rhetoric and were made in the course of the war.

Nationalism: milla, mîhan *and* umma

In the speeches the notion of *milla* played an important role. The original meaning of the word, 'religion', changed semantically to 'people' or 'nation'.[90] In Iran, this change was brought about in the period leading to the constitutional revolution. In the constitutionalist discourse, *milla* signified all Iranians, regardless of professional, social or religious status, 'a unified force and the source of sovereignty, invested with the right to determine the policies of the government through its representatives to the *Majlis*'.[91] The name *Majlis-i shûrâ-yi millî* (National Consultative Assembly) given to the first Iranian Parliament in 1906 must be understood in this sense. The Parliament of the Islamic Republic, at first, was also called *Majlis-i shûrâ-yi millî* at a time when the different parties (national-liberals, communist and socialist) who had been engaged in the revolution still shared power. In its first session, in spring 1980 the Majlis renamed itself *Majlis-i shûrâ-yi islâmî*[92] replacing the word *millî* (national), which for the Iranian leaders must still have had a secular connotation. But they continued using the notion of *milla* in the modern political meaning of nation. 'Iran is a prime example of national unity, for instance the unity between Shî'îs and Sunnîs and the unity between *milla* and the *dawla* (state apparatus)'.[93] Khumaynî spoke about the Arab nation, the Turkish,[94] the Iranian nation and the American nation.[95] But leaders also made it clear in numerous remarks that the prime element of the culture of the Iranian *milla* was Islam. 'A nation who has found its own way, the way of the *ṣirâṭ al-mustaqîm*' (the straight path, i.e. Islam).[96] Other examples were; 'We thank God that this nation, the whole country, men, women, children and aged people, is serving Islam';[97] 'The nation wants Islam and wants Iran to become Islamic;[98] 'This nation whose uprising is analogous to the uprisings of the prophets and the *imâms*, a nation whose motive for rising was Islam and *îmân*'.[99] 'The nation of Muslims of Iran'.[100] Moreover, Khumaynî depicted the Iranian *milla* as identical to the kingdom of the Hidden *imâm* or the *imâm-i zamân* and the *walî-yi 'aṣr* (the Lord of the Age) and the *baqiyat-i Allâh* (the Remnant of God).[101] Leaders used the notion *millat-i ilâhî* (divine nation),[102] and *millat-i ḥizbullâhî*, referring to *al-Mâ'ida* V:56 and *al-Mujâdala* LVIII:22 in which the believers are associated with 'the Party of God', which is promised victory and prosperity.[103] Furthermore, one of the slogans in the war was: 'The banner "there is no God but God", which is the symbol of the great nation of Iran, will wave until eternity'.[104]

References to *milla* should be seen in the light of efforts to mobilize the Iranian people and give them moral support, especially by stressing Iran's special relationship with God. Khâmini'î said: 'God Almighty has promised that when a nation takes a decision and acts upon that decision unwaveringly, then that nation's victory is certain. It might be delayed or brought forward by a few days but there is no doubt that this objective will be obtained'.[105] But he also enjoined people to exert themselves in God's cause because 'this was His condition for the victory of truth over falsehood and a condition for the continuation of the nation's relationship with God'.[106] 'God gave His support to this holy revolution and this deprived nation that is defending its rights.[107]

Two terms often used in the speeches were the Persian word *mîhan* and the Arabic word *waṭan,* which both mean fatherland. While *mîhan* has patriotic connotations and the term was used by the Pahlavi dynasty in a secular context, *waṭan* has a religious connotation.[108] Richard states that one would expect

Khumaynî to prefer the term *waṭan*, but in the war rhetoric I could not find any examples which confirmed his view; in fact, *waṭan* was rarely used. Imâmî Kâshânî once spoke of loyalty to the Islamic revolution, water and earth, land, *waṭan* and *mamlaka*.[109] Rafsanjânî used the term in a neutral sense: 'We have to take care that in ten years there are universities everywhere on our ground, in our *waṭan*',[110] but also as the Persian equivalent of 'national home', when he spoke about the Balfour declaration and the promise of a Jewish state or national home: *dawla yâ waṭan-i millî-yi yahûd*.[111] Instead of *waṭan*, Khumaynî and other leaders regularly spoke about *mîhan*. But they combined this term with religious notions: 'The honour of religion and *mîhan*';[112] 'It is an 'Islamic and a *mîhanî* (patriotic) duty' to go to the battlefront';[113] 'defence of Islam and beloved *mîhan*';[114] 'the Islamic fatherland';[115] 'those who sacrifice themselves for the Qur'ân and the beloved *mîhan*'.[116] Khâmini'î spoke frequently in the same vein during his Friday sermon: 'with martyrdom for God's cause, religion and the fatherland';[117] and: 'go and defend your honour and pride, your revolution and your fatherland';[118] 'in order to fight for God's cause and for the freedom and independence of this beloved fatherland';[119] 'brothers who are at the battlefield confronting the enemies of Islam, revolution and beloved fatherland'.[120] Yazdî, President of the Supreme Court also spoke about Islam in a patriotic sense: 'this is an Islamic and *mîhanî* duty'.[121]

There is another term that must be dealt with in this context, *umma*. According to Ayalon, in the Arab world, *umma* has acquired the modern meaning of nation-state besides the traditional meaning of community of believers.[122] This seems to be the case in the Islamic Republic as well. In the Iranian war rhetoric, *umma* was like *milla* used for the Iranian nation: 'Our combative and model ummah is at present engaged in this great and fateful battle';[123] 'Muslim Iranian Ummah, arise for Satan has arisen against you'.[124] *Umma* was also used to describe the Iranian religious community of believers: 'The *umma* of the *ḥizb allâh* of Iran',[125] and for those who were gathered together for the Friday congregational service. Although one of the major themes of the revolution was the propagation of Islam and the universality of the revolution,[126] it was also clear from the speeches that the Iranian leaders accepted the concept of independent states and that they, in this war, were not striving for a state based on a greater Islamic *umma* in which all Muslims would be united. And although the title (*imâm-i umma*) for Khumaynî could lead to ambiguity since it could bear the implication that he was the leader both of the Iranian Muslims and of Muslims outside Iran, in the rhetoric of the war Khumaynî was in fact only important as the leader of the Iranian *umma* under attack: 'The Imam shares with the ummah the bitterness and the sweetness, … and the ummah too finds itself committed to obey and follow the orders of the imam'.[127]

Nationalism: The religious minorities

We have seen that the Muslims of Iran received much attention in the war rhetoric. But what about the religious minorities? They supported the Islamic regime in an effort to seek the protection of Khumaynî, and the Jews, Assyrians and Armenians, were legally recognized as religious minorities.[128] The Bahais were considered to be heretics and were persecuted for this reason. The Christian Armenians were presented as forming part of the Iranian nation and Iran's culture, and, although they were not Muslims, the Iranian leaders spoke with respect about them because of their heroic role in several battles (see also Chapter 2). When considering the abovementioned concept of *dhimma*, this is not surprising. However, the Iranian leadership's attitude towards the Christian Armenian minority was different from the attitude towards the other religious minorities who were accepted by the Iranian leadership. The Jewish community did not receive any positive attention in the war rhetoric, probably because the Iranian leaders were not certain of the loyalty of the Jewish community to the government, but the fact that Israel was regarded as one of the major enemies of Iran and Islam certainly played a role in the different attitude towards the Jewish community. Rafsanjânî glorified the Armenian martyrs and their families and said that they had a honourable place in Iranian society.[129] One of the days of War Week 1988 was dedicated to the Armenian 'martyrs' of the war. *Iṭṭilâ'ât-i jabha* at Christmas 1987 published an interview with an Armenian priest who did not hesitate to stress that the Armenians were part of the Iranian *mamlaka* (land) and that they were willing to fulfil their duty to it. He said that Armenians had been present on the battlefield from the start of the war and that Armenian soldiers fought shoulder to shoulder with their Muslim brethren and sacrificed their blood in the 'holy defence of the honourable *milla* of Iran under the leadership of the *imâm-i umma*'. He spoke in the same vein about the war as the Iranian leadership, in the sense that the war was a conspiracy by worldwide arrogance and its allies against the Islamic revolution. He even used the term *fitna* to describe the war in the Gulf. The war was not a war between two nations, but a conflict between two opposite movements, on the one hand a nation which under the leadership of the clergy, who had sublime religious motives, strove to wipe out *fasâd* (moral decay) and to continue the divinely inspired government, and, on the other, worldwide arrogance which oppressed and plundered nations. Furthermore, he asserted that no believer in the great teachings of the divine messengers could remain indifferent to the conflict which had been imposed on *ḥaqq* by *bâṭil*.[130] *Iṭṭilâ'ât-i jabha* went so far as to portray the loyalty of the Armenians by publishing pictures of an Armenian priest on the battlefield, against a background of soldiers bearing flags with the Muslim creed written on them.[131] It must be stressed that this report was in 1988, when popular support was diminishing and voluntary mobilization had declined considerably. So this article may also have had the function of mobilizing the Armenians for the war effort and obtaining support from them.

Iranian nationalism versus Arabism

In his war rhetoric towards his own population and those of other Arab states, Ṣaddâm Ḥusayn had presented the war as a means to defend the interests of the (pan-Arab) 'Arab nation'.[132] Iranian leaders, in contrast, said that the war was not between Arabs and Iranians but between *islâm* and *kufr*, since the war had been imposed on the Iraqi and Iranian populations by a regime of unbelievers. Moreover, if it was a war between Arabs and Persians, why had Ṣaddâm Ḥusayn started the war in Khûzistân and inflicted many casualties and damage on this province, which had many Arabic-speaking people?[133] According to *Jang bâ inqilâb*, the war was started by Iraq in order to stop the Islamic revolution in Iran and to preserve the Arab character of Islam. It was clear, the source continued, that the people who had begun this war were not genuine Muslims, otherwise they would have pointed their guns towards Israel in order to liberate the Palestinian people instead of waging war on Iran.[134]

Nationalist sentiment and the antagonism between Arabs and Iranians played a minor role in the war rhetoric, especially in the comparison between Iran on the one hand and Iraq and other Arab states on the other in the Islamic sphere. Two sermons focused on Salmân Fârisî, a companion of the Prophet who was of Persian origin.[135] One of the prayer leaders said that the Prophet was once asked who were the people, mentioned in *al-Mâ'ida* V:54: 'Allah will produce (another) people whom He loveth and who love Him, humble towards the believers, haughty towards the unbelievers, striving in the cause of Allah, and not fearing the blame of anyone; that is Allah's bounty which He bestoweth upon whomsoever He pleaseth; Allah is unrestricted, knowing'. Muḥammad thereupon struck Salmân on his shoulder and said: 'This Salmân and the persons who are with him who are as Salmân and are Persians'. Rafsanjânî expressed himself in the same vein as Kâshânî. He recited *al-Mâ'ida* V:54 and *al-Nisâ'* IV:133: 'He will remove you, O ye people, and bring forward others', and explained that the Prophet had told the Arabs that when they acted in a manner God did not approve of, he would take their *iqtidâr* (power) and *'ilm-i islâm* (knowledge of Islam) and give these to another people. When the Prophet had expressed this, he had laid his hand on Salmân's shoulder. Rafsanjânî added: 'I think that today the Islamic Republic is the interpretation and substantiation of this noble verse'.[136]

Khumaynî himself occasionally became involved in Arab-Persian rivalry for which he reproached Ṣaddâm Ḥusayn: 'If we look at historical records, and if Ṣaddâm goes through these records or if he has any knowledge of history, he will notice that Iraq is part of Iran. Madâ'in (Ctesiphon) is ours; it belongs to Iran. There is evidence for this. The great palace of Kisrâ (Chosroes) exists in what is now Baghdad, but since we are followers of Islam and since we respect previous agreements, we have no intention of violating what now belongs to Iraq'.[137] This is a remarkable observation, since throughout the war Iranian leaders maintained that they regarded the Sasanian dynasty, to which Chosroes belonged, as usurpers who tyrannized the Iranian population. Statements of this kind were rare in the Iranian war rhetoric. On the whole, the Iranian leaders disregarded pre-Islamic Iranian history or spoke with contempt about this period. As we have seen, Khumaynî called the battle of Qâdisîya, the battle in which the Arab Islamic army defeated the forces of the Persian Sasanian Empire and which prepared the way for the conquest of Persia, a blessing.[138] On another occasion he referred to a tradition of the Prophet which was about the destruction of the Sasanian palace. This palace was the centre of oppression and the Sasanian king Anûshîrwân was one of the cruellest kings.[139]

Expressions of nationalism were almost always combined with references to Islam. Their function was to justify the war, to mobilize the Iranian people for the war effort; and, by stressing the Islamic identity of the Iranian nation, the leadership tried to safeguard unity within the state and loyalty to the new religious leaders. These expressions were also a reaction to Arab Muslim countries which had not taken Iran's side in the conflict. Nationalist statements stressed the interdependency of the Islamic revolution and the Iranian nation and sometimes these statements had a chauvinistic bias, to the effect that the Islamic character of Iran was set off favourably against Arab states.

As I showed in Chapter 3, immediately after the outbreak of the war Khumaynî sacralized the war by saying that it was one between Islam and *kufr*. During the rest of the war the relationship between Islam and Iran moved centre stage in the rhetoric of Khumaynî and other leaders. Iranians were presented as the real heirs to the family of the Prophet, by references to abiding by the law of Islam and the observance of Islamic duties, rather than by referring to the popular belief that the Shî'î *imâms* have Iranian blood.

Notes

1. Khâmini'î, *Chahâr sâl bâ mardum* (Tehran: Ḥizb-i jumhûrî-yi islâmî, 1364/1985) 21/11/60 p. 42, in a speech to foreign visitors on the anniversary of the victory of the Islamic revolution. Yann Richard, 'The Relevance of "Nationalism" in Contemporary Iran', in: *Middle East Review* (1989) pp. 27-36, p. 33.

2. Farhang Rajaee, 'Iranian Ideology and World view: The Cultural Export of Revolution' in: *The Iranian Revolution and its Global Impact*, ed. by John L. Esposito (Miami: Florida International University Press, 1990) pp. 63-80, p. 69.

3. *Jang bâ inqilâb* pp. 5, 9; Muntaẓirî, *Jang-i taḥmîlî* p. 49.

4. Khumaynî, *Iṭṭilâ'ât*, 23/11/63. Khumaynî, especially, repeated time and again that the war was part of a worldwide conspiracy of arrogance and imperialism to destroy Islam. See *Ṣaḥîfa-yi nûr* Vol.7 pp. 533-579; *Jang wa jihâd* pp. 17-41.

5. Khâmini'î, *Dar maktab-i jum'a* Vol.2, 4/7/59, p. 317, 18/7/59 p. 341, 2/8/59 p. 356. Khâmini'î, *Chahâr sâl bâ mardum* p. 219; *Jang bâ inqilâb*; *Jang-i taḥmîlî, armaghân-i shûm-i qadrathâ-yi shayṭânî* (Tehran: *Sitâd-i buzurkhdâsht-i panjumîn sâlkhard-i pîrûz-i inqilâb-i islâmî*, 1362). *Faith versus Aggression. al-Îmân yuqâwimu al-i'tidâ'* (Tehran: Ministry of Islamic Guidance, 1982).

6. There is a tradition in Islam that at the beginning of every Islamic century someone will arise and revitalize the religion. This person is called *mujaddid*. There is general consensus among Shî'î's over who this figure was in some centuries, but not for other centuries. For the fifteenth century he gives Khumaynî with a question mark. Moojan Momen, *An Introduction to Shi'i Islam* (New Haven: Yale University Press, 1985) pp. 205-206.

7. Khumaynî, *Iṭṭilâ'ât*, 10/5/66.

8. Muntaẓirî, BBC *Summary of World Broadcasts* 29 August 1985.

9. Muntaẓirî, *Jang-i taḥmîlî* p. 36, 43. Rafsanjânî, *Dar maktab-i jum'a* Vol.7 1/7/62 pp. 110-118; Friday sermon, *Iṭṭilâ'ât*, 12/3/63 and Khâmini'î, *Iṭṭilâ'ât*, 19/3/64, Banî Ṣadr, *Iṭṭilâ'ât*, 1/7/59.

10. *Islam and Revolution. Writings and Declarations of Imam Khomeini*, Trans. and annotated by Hamid Algar (Berkeley: Mizan Press, 1981) p. 302. This seems to be in line with religious nationalists in general. See Mark Juergensmeyer, *The New Cold War? Religious Nationalism Confronts the Secular State* (Berkeley: University of California Press, 1993) pp. 6-7. See also Jacob Landau, *The Politics of Pan-Islam. Ideology and Organization* (Oxford: Clarendon Press, 1990) pp. 257-260.

11. Introduction to *The Imam and the Ommat. The Selected Messages of Imam Khomeini concerning Iraq and the War Iraq Imposed upon Iran* (Tehran: Ministry of Islamic Guidance, 1981) p. 1.

12. Khumaynî, *Ṣaḥîfa-yi nûr. Majmû'a-yi rahnamûdhâ-yi ḥaḍrat-i imâm Khumaynî* (Tehran: Ministry of Culture and Islamic Guidance, 1370/1991) Vol.7 p. 547.

13. Khumaynî, *Jumhûrî-yi islâmî*, 29/7/59.

14. Khâmini'î, *Dar maktab-i jum'a* Vol.2 4/7/59 p. 318; see also 2/8/59 p. 356, 16/8/59 p. 374.

15. Rafsanjânî, *Dar maktab-i jum'a* Vol.3 12/4/60 p. 274 .

16. Muntaẓirî, *Jang-i taḥmîlî* p. 61.

17. Muntaẓirî, *Jang-i taḥmîlî* 66/1/28 p.131.

18. Khumaynî, *Jang wa jihâd* 31/3/61 p. 115.

19. FBIS *Daily Report* 28 August 1986.

20. Khâmini'î, *Dar maktab-i jum'a* Vol.2 11/7/59 p. 333.

21. Khumaynî, *Islam and Revolution* p. 92.

22. Khumaynî, *Iṭṭilâ'ât*, 22/1/62; See also Muntaẓirî, *Jang-i taḥmîlî* p. 34 and Mûsawî, *Iṭṭilâ'ât* 27/4/61.

23. Muntaẓirî, *Jang-i taḥmîlî* p. 34, p. 55; Khumaynî, *Jumhûrî-yi islâmî* 8/4/61-29/7/82; Rafsanjânî FBIS *Daily Report* July 18th, 1982; Wilâyatî, Minister of Foreign Affairs) FBIS *Daily Report* July 8th, 1982.

24. Rafsanjânî, *Dar maktab-i jum'a* Vol.5 p. 128; Khumaynî, *Iṭṭilâ'ât*, 31/1/64.

25. FBIS *Daily Report* 22 June 1982.

26. Rafsanjânî, *Dar maktab-i jum'a* Vol.5 8/5/61 pp. 122-128.

27. Rafsanjânî, *Dar maktab-i jum'a* Vol.5 8/5/61 p. 128; FBIS *Daily Report* 18 July 1982.

28. Rafsanjânî, *Dar maktab-i jum'a* Vol.4 3/7/60 p. 10; Mûsawî Ardabîlî, *Dar maktab-i jum'a* Vol.4 20/1/61 p. 253.

29. Haggay Ram, *Myth and Mobilization in Revolutionary Iran. The Use of the Friday Congregational Sermon* (Washington: American University Press, 1994) p. 212.

30. Imâmî Kâshânî, *Dar maktab-i jum'a* Vol.5 21/3/61 pp. 25-26. He recited *Ibrâhîm*, XIV:26: 'And a corrupt word is like a corrupt tree which is bodily removed from off the earth and has no fixity'. See also Khumaynî, *Jang wa jihâd* p. 95 and p. 115, *Iṭṭilâ'ât* 1/4/61-22/6/82; and Shîrâzî, Commander of the ground forces, FBIS *Daily Report* 7 July 1982; for the same views on this conspiracy.

31. Rafsanjânî *Dar maktab-i jum'a* Vol.5 28/3/61 p. 43 he repeated Ibrâhîm, XIV:26.

32. Shahram Chubin and Charles Tripp, *Iran and Iraq at War* (London: I.B. Tauris, 1988) p. 144, citing BBC *Summary of World Broadcasts* 30 September 1980.

33. Ernest Gellner, *Nations and Nationalism* (Oxford: Blackwell, 1983) p. 1. This definition was used by E.J. Hobsbawm in his *Nations and Nationalism since 1780* (Cambridge: Cambridge University Press, 1990) p. 9.

34. Gellner, *Nations and Nationalism* pp. 6-7.

35. Gellner, *Nations and Nationalism* p. 141.

36. Peter van der Veer, *Religious Nationalism. Hindus and Muslims in India* (Berkeley: University of California Press, 1994) pp. 14-15.

37. Said Amir Arjomand (ed.), *From Nationalism to Revolutionary Islam* (London: Macmillan, 1984) p. 4.

38. G. Hossein Razi, 'Legitimacy, Religion, and Nationalism in the Middle East', *American Political Science Review* 84 (1990) 1, pp. 69-91, p. 82.

39. Ernest Gellner, *Postmodernism, Reason and Religion* (London: Routledge, 1992) p. 5.

40. Gellner, *Postmodernism, Reason and Religion* pp. 11, 15.

41. Gellner, *Postmodernism, Reason and Religion* pp. 17-18.

42. Hamid Enayat, *Modern Islamic Political Thought* (London: Macmillan, 1982) p. 121.

43. M. Reza Ghods, *Iran in the Twentieth Century. A Political History* (Boulder: Lynne Rienner, 1989) p. 7.

44. Mostafa Vaziri, *Iran as Imagined Nation. The Construction of National Identity* (New York: Paragon House, 1993) p. 199.

45. David Menashri, *Iran. A Decade of War and Revolution* (New York: Holmes and Meier, 1990) p. 198.

46. Ram, *Myth and Mobilization* pp. 215-217.

47. Muntaẓirî, *Jang-i taḥmîlî* 2/8/59 p. 59; Mûsâwî, FBIS *Daily Report* 7 July 1987; Raja'î, *Iṭṭilâ'ât*, 8/8/59.

48. Wilâyatî, FBIS *Daily Report* 21 March 1982.

49. David Menashri, 'Khomeini's Vision: Nationalism or World Order?' in: *The Iranian Revolution and the Muslim World*, ed. by D. Menashri (Boulder: Westview Press, 1990), pp. 40-57, p. 54.

50. Richard Cottam, *Nationalism in Iran* (Pittsburgh: University of Pittsburgh Press, 1964) p. 156.

51. Shireen Hunter, *Iran and the World. Continuity in a Revolutionary Decade* (Bloomington, Indiana University Press, 1990) p. 10.

52. Khumaynî, *The Imam and the Ommat* p. 139.

53. See Mehrdad Mashayekhi, 'The Politics of Nationalism and Political Culture' in: *Iran. Political Culture in the Islamic Republic*, ed. by S.K. Farsoun and M. Mashayekhi (London: Routledge, 1992) p. 93.

54. Emmanuel Sivan, *Radical Islam. Medieval Theology and Modern Politics* (New Haven: Yale University Press, 1985) p. 69; Dale F. Eickelman and James Piscatori, *Muslim Politics* (Princeton: Princeton University Press, 1996) p. 33.

55. Khumaynî, *Iṭṭilâ'ât*, 15/10/63; Muntaẓirî, *Jang-i taḥmîlî* p. 11; Khâmini'î, *Dar maktab-i jum'a* 59/7/11, p. 328.

56. Khâmini'î, *Dar maktab-i jum'a* Vol.3 21/9/59 p. 20; *Jang bâ inqilâb* p. 9.

57. Khumaynî, *Iṭṭilâ'ât*, 19/6/63.

58. Khumaynî, *Jumhûrî-yi islâmî*, 4/9/60.

59. Khumaynî, FBIS *Daily Report* 25 November 1981

60. Khumaynî, *Iṭṭilâ'ât*, 16/5/65.

61. Khumaynî, *Iṭṭilâ'ât*, 3/10/63.

62. Khumaynî, *Jumhûrî-yi islâmî*, 4/9/60.

63. Khâmini'î, *Dar maktab-i jum'a* Vol.3 21/1/60.

64. Âyatullâh Mahdawî Kanî, *Dar maktab-i jum'a* Vol.6 14/2/62 p. 276.

65. (*mâ mîdânîm ki yikî az mushakhkhiṣât-i islâm dar mubârazât-i jâmi'a-yi muslimân-i Irân tabalwur piydâ kard, rûḥiyya-yi fidâ-kârî wa îthâr bûd ki dar hîch jâmi'a wa dar hîch inqilâbî bâ în ab'âdish wujûd nadâsht)* Rafsanjânî, *Dar maktab-i jum'a* Vol.3 6/6/60 p. 372 .

66. Khumaynî, *Jumhûrî-yi islâmî*, 16/9/59.

67. Khumaynî, *milla, umma* p. 236.

68. *yik nîrû-yi a'ẓîm wa bî-sâbiq*: Khâmini'î, *Dar maktab-i jum'a* Vol.2 18/7/59 p. 341.

69. Statement from War Information Headquarters, BBC *SWB* 18 April 1988.

70. Khumaynî, *Iṭṭilâ'ât*, 19/6/63.

71. Khâmini'î, *Dar maktab-i jum'a* Vol.2 2/8/59 p. 360. The staff and the white hand belonged to the nine signs Moses received from God to show God's omnipotence to the Pharaoh who had become arrogant and presumptuous. With the fire God had drawn the attention of Moses. There are several places in the Qur'ân in which these two signs of God are mentioned. The reference to the fire is also borrowed from the Qur'ân, *al-Anbiyâ'* XXI:69 'O fire be coolth and peace to Abraham'. The passage speaks about the rescue of Abraham from the fire into which his heathen compatriots had thrown him and which Abraham endured. Rudi Paret, 'Ibrâhîm', in: *Encyclopaedia of Islam*[2] Vol.3 pp. 980-981.

72. Mahmoud Ayoub, 'The Speaking Qur'ân and the Silent Qur'ân: A Study of the Principles and Development of Imâmî Shî'î *tafsîr*', in: *Approaches to the History of the Interpretation of the Qur'ân*, ed. by Andrew Rippin (Oxford: Clarendon Press, 1988) pp. 177-198, p. 196.

73. Khumaynî, *Ḥukûmat-i islâmî. Majmû'a-yi darshâ-yi rahbar-i shî'îyân-i jihân taḥta 'unwân: 'wilâyat-i faqîh'* (n.p., n.p., 1391/1971) p. 186.

74. Khumaynî, *Ḥukûmat-i islâmî* p. 40.

75. Gilles Kepel, *Le Prophète et pharaon: Les Mouvements islamistes dans l'Égypte contemporaine* (Paris: La Découverte, 1984) p. 204.

76. Heribert Busse, 'Herrschertypen im Koran', in: *Die islamische Welt zwischen Mittelalter und Neuzeit*, ed. by U. Haarmann und P. Bachmann (Beirut: Orient Institut, 1979) pp. 56-80, p. 69.

77. Khâmini'î, *Dar maktab-i jum'a* Vol.6 p. 218.

78. Rafsanjânî, *Iṭṭilâ‘ât*, 18/6/65.

79. Âyatullâh Ṣâni‘î, Friday prayer leader in Qum, Friday sermon, *Iṭṭilâ‘ât*, 25/11/65, the newspaper did not give specific examples. Rafsanjânî, *Iṭṭilâ‘ât*, 15/1/66, compared the people who had built shelters during the War of the Cities to the Muslims during the battle of Khandaq.

80. Khâmini'î, *Dar maktab-i jum‘a* Vol.6 26/1/62 p. 218.

81. Mûsawî, *Iṭṭilâ‘ât*, 31/5/61.

82. Rafsanjânî, *Iṭṭilâ‘ât*, 28/7/66.

83. Khumaynî, *Iṭṭilâ‘ât*, 17/1/64.

84. Kâshânî, *Dar maktab-i jum‘a* Vol.4 10/2/61 p. 391: *‘niẓâm-i jumhûrî-yi islâmî-yi irân ast ki niẓâm-i piyghambar-i akrâm ast wa ba‘da az riḥlat-i rasûl-i akram tâ aknûn ḥarakat-i islâmî mithl-i imrûz piydâ nashudi wa în ḥarakat-i piyghambar-i akram ast wa lidhâ-st istikbâr-i jihânî tamâm-i nîrû-yash-râ barâ-yi maḥw în ḥarakat guzâshti-st’.*

85. Khumaynî, *Iṭṭilâ‘ât*, 7/1/61-27/3/82: *‘mithl-i millat-i îrân...az ṣadr-i târîkh-i ‘âlam tâ ḥâlâ nabûdi.*

86. Rafsanjânî, *Dar maktab-i jum‘a* Vol.5 pp. 83-92.

87. Khumaynî in his last will, *Jumhûrî-yi islâmî*, 2/3/67.

88. Yvonne Yazbeck Haddad, *Contemporary Islam and the Challenge of History* (Albany, SUNY Press, 1982) pp. 7, 8.

89. Thomas Naff, ‘Towards a Muslim Theory of History’, in: *Islam and Power*, ed. by A.S. Cudsi and A.Dessouki (London: Croom Helm, 1981) p. 26. Cf. Chapter 4: The Islamic Republic had paved the way for the appearance of the Hidden *imâm* since many of his aims had been realized in Iranian society.

90. F. Buhl (C.E. Bosworth) ‘Millat’ in: *The Encyclopaedia of Islam*[2] Vol.7 pp. 60-61. See also Ami Ayalon, *Language and Change in the Arab Middle East. The Evolution of Modern Political Discourse* (New York: Oxford University Press, 1987) pp. 19-21.

91. Mohamad Tavakoli-Targhi, ‘Refashioning Iran: Language and Culture during the Constitutional Revolution’, in: *Iranian Studies* 23 (1990) pp. 77-101, p. 98.

92. Said Amir Arjomand, *The Turban for the Crown. The Islamic Revolution in Iran* (Oxford: Oxford University Press, 1988) p. 165.

93. Khumaynî, *Dar justujû-yi râh az kalâm-i imâm. Milla, umma. Az bayânât wa i‘lâmiya-hâ-yi imâm Khumaynî az sâl 1341 tâ 1361* (Tehran: Amîr Kabîr, 1362/1983) 9/10/60 p. 544.

94. Khumaynî, *Kayhân*, 21/10/60.

95. Khumaynî, *Milla, umma* 1/10/58 p. 426.

96. Khumaynî, *Iṭṭilâ'ât*, 23/11/59; *Jumhûrî-yi islâmî*, 8/4/6.

97. Khumaynî, *Jumhûrî-yi islâmî*, 4/9/60.

98. Khumaynî, *Milla, umma* 1/3/59 p. 29.

99. Khumaynî, *Milla, umma* 26/7/60 p. 37.

100. Khumaynî, *Jang wa jihâd* p. 177.

101. Khumaynî, *Jumhûrî-yi islâmî*, 8/4/61; Khumaynî, *Milla, umma* 4/2/58 p. 506; Khâmini'î, *Dar maktab-i jum'a* Vol.2 16/8/59 pp. 382-383.

102. Nâṭiq Nûrî in the Iṣfahân Friday sermon, *Iṭṭilâ'ât* 7/1/61.

103. Khumaynî, *Jumhûrî-yi islâmî*, 8/4/61; Mûsawî, FBIS *Daily Report*, 25 February, 1986. The *Ḥizb Allâh* movement in Lebanon took its name from these verses.

104. *Farhang-i jabha* p. 32.

105. Khâmini'î, FBIS *Daily Report*, 22 September 1986, interview on the occasion of War Week.

106. Khâmini'î, *Dar maktab-i jum'a* Vol.3/11/59 p. 68: *al-Mâ'ida* V:54 (partly): 'O ye who have believed, if any of you draw back from their religion, Allah will produce (another) people whom He loveth and who Love Him'; *Muḥammad* XLVII:39 (partly) '... if ye turn away, He will substitute for you another people; and then they will not be like you'; p. 73 *al-Tawba* IX:39 (partly) 'If ye do not march out He will inflict upon you a painful punishment, and will substitute (for you) another people'.

107. Rafsanjânî, speech to Parlement, *Iṭṭilâ'ât*, 29/2/66.

108. Yann Richard, 'The Relevance of "Nationalism" in Contemporary Iran', p. 28.

109. Imâmî Kâshânî, *Dar maktab-i jum'a* Vol.4 13/9/60 p. 131.

110. Rafsanjânî, *Dar maktab-i jum'a* Vol.4 31/2/61 p. 438.

111. Rafsanjânî, *Dar maktab-i jum'a* Vol.4 27/1/61 p. 360.

112. Khumaynî, *Ṣaḥîfa-yi nûr* 5/7/59, p. 549.

113. Khumaynî, *Jang wa jihâd* 23/4/61 p. 221.

114. Khumaynî, *Jang wa jihâd* 23/11/61 p. 274.

115. *Iṭṭilâ'ât*: Khumaynî, 18/11/65; Banî Ṣadr, 1/7/59; Mahdawî Kanî, 1/7/60, mentioned the Islamic fatherland four times in his speech.

116. Khumaynî, *Jang wa jihâd* 3/3/61 p. 307.

117. Khâmini'î, *Dar maktab-i jum'a* Vol.2 18/7/59 p. 340.

118. Khâmini'î, *Dar maktab-i jum'a* Vol.2/8/59 p. 364.

119. Khâmini'î, *Dar maktab-i jum'a* Vol.3 26/10/59 p. 63.

120. Khâmini'î, *Dar maktab-i jum'a* Vol.3 10/11/59 p. 83.

121. Yazdî, *Dar maktab-i jum'a* Vol.5 25/4/61 p. 102.

122. Ayalon, *Language and Change* p. 28.

123. Khâmini'î, BBC *SWB*, 19 April 1988.

124. Statement by War Information Headquarters, FBIS *Daily Report*, 18 April 1987.

125. Âyatullâh Ṣâni'î, *Iṭṭilâ'ât*, 25/6/65.

126. Farhang Rajaee, 'Iranian Ideology and World View', pp. 66-69.

127. Muntaẓirî, BBC *SWB* 23 July 1988.

128. Menashri, *Iran* p. 237.

129. Rafsanjânî, *Dar maktab-i jum'a* Vol.7 22/7/62 p. 168.

130. *Iṭṭilâ'ât-i jabha*, 20/10/66.

131. *Iṭṭilâ'ât-i jabha*, 20/10/66.

132. Chubin and Tripp, *Iran and Iraq at War* pp. 143-144, citing from a press conference held by Ṣaddâm Ḥusayn on 10 November 1980.

133. For the military and strategic reasons for the attack on Khûzistân, see Chapter 2.

134. *Jang bâ inqilâb* p. 28.

135. Imâmî Kâshânî, *Dar maktab-i jum'a* Vol. 4 13/9/60 p. 128; and Rafsanjânî, Vol.5 18/4/61 p. 92.

136. Rafsanjânî, *Dar maktab-i jum'a* Vol.5 18/4/61 p. 92.

137. Khumaynî, *Iṭṭilâ'ât*, 23/11/59.

138. Khumaynî, *Jang wa jihâd* 25/4/61 p. 143-144, 8/9/60 p. 279.

139. Khumaynî, *Iṭṭilâ'ât*, 10/9/64.

6 JUSTIFYING PEACE: THE ACCEPTANCE OF RESOLUTION 598

The attitude of the Islamic Republic to peace

During the first year of the war the Iraqi regime made several attempts to negotiate a peace agreement and put an end to the war, but these, and later attempts by the international community, were denounced by the Iranian leaders.[1] In their eyes all peace proposals would lead to an 'imposed peace' (*ṣulḥ-i taḥmîlî*) on Iran because the conditions the enemies presented were all to their own benefit and without any consideration for Iran.[2] Khumaynî emphasized that peace or reconciliation with the Iraqi regime was against the principles of Islam, since it would be peace with immoral people, which was out of the question. Peace was impossible with someone who did not know mercy, someone who did not believe in Islam or human values.[3] In one of his first sermons after the war had started, Khâmini'î gave several reasons for turning down the Iraqi peace proposals. He told his audience that Iran made no compromises but had real conditions for a cease-fire which it had formulated unilaterally. These conditions were: an unconditional Iraqi retreat from Iranian soil, acceptance of war guilt by the Iraqis, compensation for war damage to the Iranian and Iraqi nations and trial of the aggressors.[4] In his sermon of the following week a peace settlement was regarded not so much as unacceptable but as an absurdity, since God had promised victory to the Muslims anyway.[5] A new condition laid down by the Iranian leadership in 1982 was the demand that Iran would talk about peace only after the removal of Ṣaddâm Ḥusayn and the Ba'th regime.[6] Until then the demand had been the trial of Ṣaddâm Ḥusayn and others (Iraqi) who were responsible for the war. At the same time it was another justification for the continuation of the war. In 1982, when it had recaptured much of its territory, Iran could have accepted the proposals for a settlement but it refused to do so. In the sermons it was stressed that it was the Iranian population itself which wanted to continue the war until Ṣaddâm was removed the contribution of the Iranian leaders was played down.[7]

In another sermon, Khâmini'î said that a settlement was also out of the question because soldiers at the front were against it and were prepared to sacrifice themselves to preserve the borders of their land and revolution. He told his audience that he had assured a few *mujâhidîn* (those who fight on God's path) who were worried that Iran would agree to a settlement, that Iran was not planning a reconciliation.[8] Ṣaddâm knew that he could not win the war and a peace agreement could save him from an enormous defeat.[9] It was also clear that Ṣaddâm did not really want a peace settlement. He worked in the same way as Israel, by attacking and invading other countries and then using his conquests as a basis for negotiations to attain privileges.[10] Ṣaddâm's peace proposals were dealt with as un-Islamic, and he was depicted as someone who was unfamiliar with the principles of Islam. His proposal to stop the fighting in the month of ramaḍân because this was a sacred month, was greeted with jeers from Rafsanjânî.[11] Rafsanjânî told his attendants that ramaḍân is not a sacred (*ḥarâm*) month but a blessed (*mubârak*) one, which gives Muslims extra inspiration and incentive to fight. The leaders constantly emphasized that a settlement with Ṣaddâm Ḥusayn and the Iraqi regime was out of the question because he was a criminal and the regime's record was much too bad.[12]

Throughout the entire war, the leaders made it clear that the first and foremost reason not to negotiate a peace settlement was that, in the case of this war, peace would not be in conformity with Islam.[13] *Sûrat al-Kâfirûn* (unbelievers) was used to emphasize this.[14] The usual interpretation of *al-Kâfirûn* is that it emphasizes the distinction between monotheistic Islam and the pre-Islamic polytheistic religion.[15] As interpreted by al-Hijâzî, however, *al-Kâfirûn* imposed a ban on reconciliation with unbelievers. He said that, on the basis of this *sûra*, the Prophet, 'Alî and Ḥusayn had never considered a reconciliation (*sâzish*) with unbelievers and therefore the Islamic *umma* of Iran would never conclude a *bay'a* (pledge) with unbelievers either.[16]

For the justification of their decision not to negotiate a peace settlement, the Iranian leaders used the great figures of the Shî'î Islamic past as their examples. Moreover, the Islamic Republic was presented as following the line of the prophets and of Muḥammad: 'To compromise with oppressors is to oppress; those who tell us to compromise are either *jâhil* (ignorant) or agents. To compromise with a *ẓâlim* (oppressor) is *ẓulm* (oppression) of the *maẓlûmîn* (oppressed). That is contrary to the views of all the prophets'.[17] Muḥammad Riẓâ Mahdawî Kanî, at that time Prime Minister, cited *al-Ḥujurât* XLIX:9 to make clear that Iran could not compromise on the basis of this Qur'ânic verse.[18]

Khâmini'î cited one of the sayings of 'Alî to make clear that Iran was not opposed to peace in general, since peace was not incompatible with the principles of Islam. 'Alî, however, had also said that every peace settlement had to be in accordance with God's decree.[19] This meant that a settlement with Iraq was out of the question since it would mean submission to unbelief *kufr*, *ilḥâd* (atheism), *tajâwuz* (aggression), *zûr-khû'î* (violence) and *quldurî* (rapacity).[20] Khumaynî said that peace with Ṣaddâm would be as absurd as a peace treaty between the prophet Muḥammad and Abû Jahl, one of his fiercest opponents.[21]

Throughout the war, the Iranian leaders continued rejecting a peace option. Even in 1987, when the Islamic Republic had become more and more alienated from the rest of the world as a result of its uncompromising attitude in the Gulf, it must have been obvious to the leaders that a military victory on land as well as in the Gulf had become unattainable.[22] There was, however, no indication that the regime was prepared to change its policies, and there was a renewed and intensified campaign for mobilization at the end of 1987. Military weakness was not a reason to agree to a cease-fire, it was said in the sermons. The Iranian population should take the Prophet as an example because he also fought when his military position was weak.[23]

Towards a cease-fire

In a speech in November 1987, Ḥujjatulislâm Zanjânî referred to the treaty of Ḥudaybiya concluded between Muḥammad and the Meccans in 6/628. The story of Ḥudaybiya is that Muḥammad had set out on an expedition against Mecca after a dream in which he saw himself performing the *'umra* (lesser pilgrimage) in Mecca. When at Ḥudaybiya he met the Meccan forces who had set out to block Muḥammad's way, he did not fight but decided to conclude a treaty.[24] Zanjânî told his audience that, although the Prophet had deemed it necessary during the first years of the *hijra* to wage war against the unbelievers in order to destroy their organization, after the treaty of Ḥudaybiya the Prophet had regarded peace with the enemy as an opportunity for progress. A year later when he had become very powerful, it became clear that Muḥammad had taken the right decision. The Qur'ân exhorts Muslims to make peace as a strategy to nullify the military and political power of the enemy. Zanjânî continued by saying that the Islamic Republic had the same options as the Prophet: war or peace. However, considering the present position of Iran it was in the phase of 'Khandaq'.[25] This was a reference to the battle of *Khandaq* (battle of the Trench) in 5/627 when the Islamic community in Medina was besieged by the Meccans. An obvious, but implicit, conclusion to be drawn from Zanjânî's words was that the next phase would be that of peace. Basing their arguments on different Qur'ânic verses and Islamic traditions, until now the Iranian leaders had never mentioned peace with the enemy as a real option, and had always stated that any peace should be considered as 'imposed'. Zanjânî's sermon was the first hint that something had changed.

In 1988, there were more remarks in the sermons which indicated that, despite their seemingly uncompromising attitude, Iranian leaders were changing their policy. Khâmini'î said that all conspiracies had made the nation more determined and resolute to obtain the final victory. Referring to a tradition of the Prophet, Khâmini'î said that God had given the nation an important mission (*risâla*) and had taken care that it could endure until the fulfilment of this mission. Furthermore, the nation was more prepared than ever to raise the flag of 'There is no God but God'.[26]

Khâmini'î also said that military victories (he referred to the recent Iraqi victories) did not decide the outcome of war. The enemy had already achieved several victories, but that had not decided the war in their favour. Historical experience had shown that a nation with a will to resist and with trust in God would determine the outcome of war, he added.[27] These remarks must be seen in the light of a gradually changing rhetoric in the sermons from the end of 1987, the purpose of which seems to have been to prepare the Iranian population for a cease-fire in the near future. By emphasizing that military successes were not essential, a disappointing military outcome of the war for Iran was dismissed beforehand as unimportant. Furthermore, the fact that the task of diffusing the message of Islam (which, said Khâmini'î, God had assigned to the people of Iran) was given priority over a military victory over Iraq, seemed to be pointing to a deliberate diversion of the population's attention from the military situation to the much more abstract issue of a future mission of the Islamic revolution. But these remarks were sporadic, even until the announcement of the acceptance of Resolution 598 on 18 July 1988, and were overshadowed by the usual uncompromising and hostile language against Iran's enemies.[28]

Other remarks were made in which it was hinted that the regime was taking diplomatic steps to negotiate a settlement.[29] Khâmini'î admitted that Iran, besides military action, was also taking political action. It would be wrong, he said, not to use political language for this 'holy defence' and he described people who refused to consider political pressure as '*kâtûlîktar az pâp*' (more Catholic than the Pope). In reaction to rumours about the willingness to end the war, he said that a good leader is someone who does not decide in a hurry but brings the war to an end in the most appropriate way.[30] Leaders frequently said that the war would be continued until final victory: 'prolonging the imposed war'. Khâmini'î: 'our fighters will continue their just and holy battle until final victory'.[31] On June 13th, 1988 however, Khâmini'î did not speak about the final victory for Iran in the war. Instead, he said: 'unity and resistance are vital factors which help the Islamic revolution to achieve final victory', thereby shifting the attention from the war itself to the more indefinite goal of spreading the Islamic revolution.[32]

All peace negotiations and calls for a settlement of the war were worthless in the eyes of the Iranian leaders unless these were accompanied by justice (*'adâla*). Fighting had to continue until *'adâla* had been achieved.[33] Peace with justice meant, in practice, peace on Iranian terms, that is, including a trial of Ṣaddâm Ḥusayn as war criminal and aggressor.[34] A real peace settlement was not an imposed peace but a just peace (*ṣulḥ-i 'âdilâna*).[35]

The reaction in the speeches to the shooting down of an Iranian airbus by the American navy on 3 July 1988, killing all on board, can be compared to the reaction to the events in Mecca during the *ḥajj* of 1987 in which several hundreds of Iranians were killed. Both disasters were presented in the sermons as part of the conspiracy by worldwide arrogance to destroy the Islamic revolution and Islam and save the Iraqi regime.[36] Despite these hostile remarks, Iranian reaction in July 1988 was halfhearted: the leaders did not speak about retaliation for the American attack, probably because the regime already decided to accept UN Resolution 598, which called for a cease-fire. Vengeful statements which aroused public indignation would have endangered their plans for acceptance. Furthermore, the incident with the plane could be used as a basis for Iranian demands during peace negotiations. This was demonstrated when Ḥujjatulislâm Muwaḥḥidî Kirmânî said that despite the fact that the martyrs in the airbus were all *maẓlûm* (oppressed) and real martyrs, those who were martyred in Mecca and Medina at the hands of the usurpers (referring to the Saudi regime and the turmoil during the pilgrimage of 1987) were oppressed even more *(maẓlûm-tar)*.[37] Khumaynî did not use any harsh language either. He told his audience that the shooting down was very serious indeed and that for all air passengers care had to be taken that this would never happen again.[38]

The acceptance of Resolution 598

Throughout the war Iran accused the UN Security Council of having a strong pro-Iraqi bias. According to Bardehle, this idea was not totally unfounded.[39] The Security Council's bias against Iran was for instance clear in Resolutions 479 and 514. The first was accepted after the Iraqi invasion of Iran in 1980, the second in 1982, after the Iranian invasion of Iraq. Resolution 479 only called for a termination of the fighting, whereas in Resolution 514 both parties were summoned to withdraw behind internationally accepted borders. Resolution 579, accepted in 1986 by the Security Council, again failed to bring the war to an end. Iran saw positive elements in this last resolution but rejected it all the same because it did not condemn Iraq as the aggressor.[40] But in the sermons there was no reflection of the fact that Iranian leaders saw positive elements in the resolution. Khâmini'î said that Iran rejected it and definitely opposed the Security Council because from the beginning of the war the Council had protected the aggressor and this resolution was also for the protection of Ṣaddâm.[41]

Whereas Iranian leaders in sermons presented Resolution 598, after it had been submitted to Iran in 1987, as unacceptable because of the presence of the United States and other countries in the Gulf,[42] a few months later they said that they were ready to accept the resolution on condition that the article about responsibility for the war became the first and primary article of the resolution.[43] On 17 July 1988, however, Khâmini'î accepted (the unchanged) Resolution 598 in a letter to the Secretary-general of the United Nations. The letter was made public by Rafsanjânî the next day.[44]

The speeches and sermons after the acceptance were mainly used to explain, and elaborate on, Khumaynî's message to the Iranian population on the eve of the first anniversary of the Mecca disaster during the *ḥajj* of 1987. He said he had agreed with the acceptance of the resolution and the cease-fire because of some incidents and factors he did not want to elaborate on, and added, 'I consider it to be in the interest of the revolution and of the system [referring to the Islamic Republic]. God knows that, were it not true that all of us and our honour and credibility should be sacrificed for the sake of the interests of Islam and the Muslims, I would have never agreed to this issue, and death and martyrdom would have been more bearable to me'.[45]

The justification of the acceptance in the sermons can be divided into three elements. In the first place there was repetition and confirmation of Khumaynî's words that the acceptance was in the interest of the system and the revolution. The leaders did not say openly that the revolution was in danger but said that the goals of the revolution had to be realized and the message spread. The war had become not a burden for the Iranian population, but a burden for the realization of the goals of the revolution, the spreading of the message to the oppressed in the rest of the world and the struggle against worldwide arrogance. Because this struggle had not ended, prayer leaders asked the population to remain ready for mobilization.[46] By shifting attention from the ending of the war to the 'real' struggle against worldwide arrogance, which was still continuing, and by continuing their harsh language against their enemies, leaders in fact tried to belittle the importance of the war for Iran. Rafsanjânî even said that the war had become an obstacle to the solution of fundamental problems and the establishment of Islam in society. This was a complete reversal in the rhetoric of the sermons. Not only had the war always been presented as a most fundamental question for Iran, but it was emphasized continuously how much the war had been responsible for national unity and support for the Islamic system. In its early years the war was probably used as a distraction from internal problems and as an instrument for the ending of internal opposition to the regime. When he spoke about the war as an obstacle to the solution of the real problems, Rafsanjânî publicly acknowledged that these problems had not been resolved by the war.[47]

For the second element of the justification a parallel with Ḥudaybiya was drawn.[48] The presentation of the acceptance of Resolution 598 as a victory was completely in accordance with the way the treaty of Ḥudaybiya was presented in the sermons.[49] The aim of presenting the acceptance as a victory for the Islamic Republic was not only to justify the leadership's changed attitude to a settlement, but to justify Iran's redefinition of its world view as well. Until the acceptance the world view of the Iranian leaders was mainly based on the idea that peace with their enemies was out of the question. In order to justify this complete reversal in their thinking, Khumaynî's decision to accept a cease-fire was compared with Muḥammad's decision at Ḥudaybiya to conclude a treaty with the Meccan unbelievers, once more presenting the policies of the regime as completely in line with the policies of the Prophet. We have seen that 'Alî's instructions and advice during the battle of Ṣiffîn (37/657) served as an example for the Iranian leaders for their own conduct in the war with Iraq, but although Ṣiffîn ended in arbitration, it did not play a role in the rhetoric during the peace negotiations.

One of the most important factors in the justification of the war was the fact that Khumaynî in his function as leader (*rahbar*) of the Islamic Republic and *imâm-i umma* had endorsed the war: 'Concerning peace, negotiation, and cease-fire, we continue to be guided by the *imam*'s directives, which say that peace and compromise with oppressors and enemies are impossible'.[50]

Khumaynî's decision to accept Resolution 598 was crucial. It is immaterial whether he took the final decision himself or was he had been brought to do so by political pressure from 'pragmatists' such as Rafsanjânî, as Menashri has claimed.[51] The fact is that the decision was presented in the rhetoric as Khumaynî's personal decision and that it was the consequence of his unique leadership,[52] his intelligence, his sagacity and also of divine inspiration and support.[53] By comparing Khumaynî's decision with the Prophet's decision to conclude a treaty with unbelievers, the leadership tried to counter criticism of the acceptance by stressing the people's support for Khumaynî. Khâmini'î and Rafsanjânî said repeatedly that the whole nation unanimously accepted Khumaynî's decision, as was clear from the massive demonstrations of loyalty to the imâm (*râhpiymâ'î-yi bay'at-i imâm*). Muntaẓirî was also very clear on this point:

> I call on the dear Iranian nation to honour the position of the imamate and velayat, to reaffirm their allegiance to the imam of the ummah, faithful to him, to declare once again that they are present in all areas of the revolution and are ready to defend and protect Islam, the revolution, and the leadership.[54]

It cannot be a coincidence that the prayer leaders spoke about Ḥudaybiya and *bay'a* at the same time. It was clearly meant as a reference to the *bay'at al-riḍwân* (the Pledge under the Tree), the oath which Muḥammad asked the Muslims to take during the negotiations at Ḥudaybiya.[55] It is usually understood as an oath not to flee but 'it is more likely that it was an oath to follow Muḥammad in whatever he decided. If the latter, the oath marked an increase in Muḥammad's constitutional powers'.[56] By glorifying Khumaynî's attitude and leadership more than ever before, and by presenting his acceptance as something beyond the understanding of ordinary Iranians, Khâmini'î and Rafsanjânî in fact elevated the acceptance to a point at which criticism of the decision was criticism of the leader of the Islamic Revolution and the Islamic republic, and this was a very serious offence.

The acceptance of Resolution 598 was justified as a victory, in the same way as the treaty of Ḥudaybiya was presented in the sermons.[57] The Iranian leaders had several reasons for doing this, the most important being to challenge the critics of the acceptance. Rafsanjânî said that at the time of the Prophet there had also been people who saw the treaty as submission to unbelief. But then *sûrat al-Fatḥ* was revealed in which God announced a great victory for the Muslims.[58] These victories were the performance of the lesser pilgrimage and the beginning of the submission of the Arab peninsula to Islam. The solution of several problems which the Muslims at that time were faced with and the neutralization of criticism of the '*munâfiqûn*' (hypocrites) were results of the treaty.[59] He added that the circumstances the Islamic Republic was in at that moment were the same as the circumstances of the Muslims at the time of Ḥudaybiya. The second reason for presenting the acceptance as a victory was that the leaders wanted to disarm criticism of the fact that so many 'martyrs' had given their lives in vain. The sacrifice of all these martyrs had not been useless at all because they were the blessing of the Islamic society, they had brought about fame for the nation and they had been successful in guarding the greatest achievement (*dast-âward*) in history: the Islamic revolution.[60] The leaders presented the acceptance as a great victory because world opinion was no longer against the Islamic Republic,[61] because Ṣaddâm was shown to be criminal,[62] and a warmonger, and because acceptance showed that the Islamic Republic was full of compassion.[63] Moreover, the whole war was presented as a great victory for Iran, Rafsanjânî even presenting it as belonging to the list of historical victories of Islam.[64] Last but not least, as a result of 95 months of *difâ'-i muqaddas* (holy defence), the combined forces of East and West and reactionary Arabs had not succeeded in their plan to bring down the Islamic revolution. In fact, they were now busy establishing relations with the Islamic Republic.[65] According to Muḥammad Khâtimî, Minister of Islamic Guidance, the eight years of holy defence had been the most important event the revolution had brought about.[66]

There is a striking similarity between the arguments used to reject the peace proposals, the arguments to accept Resolution 598 and the manner in which the war had been justified earlier. As in the war rhetoric, so, too, in the acceptance of peace, sacralization took place; firstly, the distinction between Islam, the Islamic revolution and Islamic Republic on the one hand, and the *kufr* and the *ṭâghûtî* powers on the other, was spelt out. Secondly, the example Muḥammad and 'Alî had given in their attitude to peace negotiations was as fundamental in the peace rhetoric as it had been in the war rhetoric. Finally, the leaders presented peace as being in the interest of the survival of the republic and the spreading of the revolution, just as, during the eight preceding years, the war had been presented as a major instrument in the consolidation of the revolution and the republic. Thus, the distinctive types of discourse which had been important during the war, theological, historical-exemplary, universalist and nationalist, were again pressed into service, this time to legitimize the cessation of hostilities.

Notes

1. B. Gorawantschy, *Der Golfkrieg zwischen Iran und Irak, 1980-88. Eine konflikttheoretische Analyse* (Berlin: Lang, 1993) p. 139.

2. Khumaynî, *Jang wa jihâd* 12/8/61 p. 148; Muntaẓirî, Friday sermon in *Jang-i taḥmîlî* 9/8/59 p. 77.

3. Khumaynî, *Jang wa jihâd* 8/7/59 p. 128, *Ṣaḥîfa-yi nûr. Majmû'a-yi rahnamûdhâ-yi ḥaḍrat-i imâm Khumaynî* (Tehran: Ministry of Culture and Islamic Guidance, 1370/1991) p. 555.

4. Khâmini'î, *Dar maktab-i jum'a* Vol.2 2/8/59 p. 360. See also Khumaynî, *Jang wa jihâd* 8/12/59 p. 133; 13/4/60, 18/12/60 p. 134, 24/12/60 p. 135-7.

5. Khâmini'î, *Dar maktab-i jum'a* Vol.2 9/8/59 p. 369. He recited the first part of *Muḥammad* XIXVII:35: 'So do not grow faint and call not for peace, seeing ye have the upper hand, and Allah is with you, and will not defraud you of your works'.

6. For the implicit demand for removal, see for instance Imâmî Kâshânî, *Dar maktab-i jum'a* Vol.5 23/7/61 p. 283; Ardabîlî, 14/8/61 p. 337; Khâmini'î 12/9/61 p. 394; Rafsanjânî, Vol.7 21/5/83 p. 28.

7. Imâmî Kâshânî in sermon, *Iṭṭilâ'ât*, 23/4/63.

8. Khâmini'î, *Dar maktab-i jum'a* Vol.3 21/1/60 pp. 166-167.

9. Khâmini'î, *Dar maktab-i jum'a* Vol.3 17/11/59 p. 93.

10. Khâmini'î, *Dar maktab-i jum'a* Vol.3 p. 94.

11. Rafsanjânî, *Dar maktab-i jum'a* Vol.3 12/4/60 p. 274.

12. Khumaynî, *Jang wa jihâd* 3/5/61 pp. 118-119; Khâmini'î, *Dar maktab-i jum'a* Vol.2 2/8/59 p. 360; Rafsanjânî in introduction to *Jang-i taḥmîlî* p. 13, in sermons, *Iṭṭilâ'ât* 2/7/64, 13/7/65.

13. Rafsanjânî in sermons *Iṭṭilâ'ât* 2/7/64, 13/7/65.

14. Speech before sermon by parliamentary representative for Tehran, Fakhruddîn al-Ḥijâzî, *Iṭṭilâ'ât*, 11/3/64. *al-Kâfirûn* CIX: 'Say: "O ye unbelievers, I serve not what ye serve, And ye are not servers of what I serve; I am not a server of what ye have served, Nor are ye servers of what I serve; Ye have your religion, and I have mine"'.

15. Ṭabâṭabâ'î, Muḥammad Ḥusayn, *Tafsîr al-mîzân* (Tehran: Muḥammadî, 1363/1984) Vol.20 p. 373; Muḥammad b. Jarîr al-Ṭabarî, *Jâmi' al-bayân 'an ta'wîl 'ây al-qur'ân* (al-Qâhira: Dâr al-Ma'ârif, 1955-1969); Bell, *The Qur'ân* Vol.2 p. 682; Rudi Paret, 'Sure 109', in: *Der Islam* 39 (1964) pp. 197-200. W. Montgomery Watt, *Muhammad at Mecca* (Oxford: Clarendon Press, 1952), p. 107 'Sûrat al-Kâfirûn (109) is traditionally what Muḥammad was told to give by way of answer to the suggestion that he should compromise. This is a complete break with polytheism, and makes compromise impossible for the future'.

16. al-Ḥijâzî, *Iṭṭilâ'ât*, 11/3/64.

17. Khumaynî, *Ittilâ'ât*, 11/4/63.

18. Mahdawî Kanî on the occasion of War Week, *Ittilâ'ât*, 1/7/60.

19. Khâmini'î, *Dar maktab-i jum'a* Vol.3 21/1/60 p. 167, cited a letter by 'Alî to Malik al-Ashtar, the Governor of Egypt.

20. Khâmini'î, *Dar maktab-i jum'a* Vol.3, p. 167.

21. Khumaynî, *Jang wa jihâd* 6/8/59 p. 130.

22. Shahram Chubin and Charles Tripp, *Iran and Iraq at War* (London: I.B. Tauris, 1988) pp. 219-220.

23. Hujjatulislâm Zanjânî in sermon, *Ittilâ'ât*, 23/8/66. See for similar remarks: Khâmini'î, *Ittilâ'ât*, 11/4/67.

24. See for details of the treaty: W. Montgomery Watt, *Muhammad at Medina* (Oxford: Clarendon Press, 1956) pp. 46-52; and Watt, 'al-Hudaybiya' in: *The Encyclopaedia of Islam*[2] Vol.3 p. 539.

25. Zanjânî in sermon, *Ittilâ'ât*, 23/8/66.

26. Khâmini'î in sermon, *Ittilâ'ât*, 6/1/67. The paper did not publish this tradition.

27. Khâmini'î in sermon, *Ittilâ'ât*, 7/3/67.

28. Mûsawî Ardabîlî in sermon, *Ittilâ'ât*, 15/11/66: 'Iran will never accept an imposed peace. There is no other solution for this war than a military victory'; Khâmini'î 6/1/67: 'the nation will continue the way whereby the aggressor and the Ba'th regime will be brought down'; Lârîjânî, in speech before sermon, 24/2/67: 'Until *fitna* is removed we will continue the war'. See for similar remarks also Rafsanjânî, 28/3/67; and Mûsawî Ardabîlî, 4/4/67.

29. Khâmini'î in sermon, *Ittilâ'ât*, 24/1/67. See also Ardabîlî, 4/4/67. He asked for a solution (*hall*) for the war.

30. Khâmini'î in sermon, *Ittilâ'ât*, 21/3/67.

31. Khâmini'î, *Ittilâ'ât*, 31/1/67.

32. Khâmini'î, *Ittilâ'ât*, 24/3/67.

33. Mahdawî Kanî, *Dar maktab-i jum'a* Vol.6 p. 384; Khâmini'î in sermon, *Ittilâ'ât* 19/11/64-8/2/86.

34. Mûsawî Ardabîlî in sermon, *Ittilâ'ât*, 25/11/65.

35. Khâmini'î, *Dar maktab-i jum'a* Vol.4 60/12/28, p. 309; Mûsawî Ardabîlî, Vol.4 20/1/61 p. 350, Vol.5 9/7/61 p. 257.

36. Rafsanjânî in sermons, *Ittilâ'ât*, 31/5/66; 18/4/67.

37. Kirmânî, in speech before sermon, *Iṭṭilâ'ât*, 25/4/67.

38. Khumaynî, *Iṭṭilâ'ât*, 14/4/67.

39. Peter Bardehle, 'Die Resolution 598 des Sicherheitsrats - Grundlage für die Waffenruhe im Konflikt zwischen Iran und dem Irak' in: *Orient* 31 (1990) pp. 261-272, p. 263.

40. Bardehle, 'Die Resolution 598', p. 264.

41. Khâmini'î in sermon, *Iṭṭilâ'ât*, 19/7/65.

42. Rafsanjânî in sermon, *Iṭṭilâ'ât*, 14/6/66.

43. Khâmini'î in sermon, *Iṭṭilâ'ât*, 25/7/66; Rafsanjânî, *Iṭṭilâ'ât* 23/8/66.

44. See for instance *Iṭṭilâ'ât*, 28/4/67, 30/4/67; FBIS *Daily Report* 20 July 1988 and BBC *Summary of World Broadcasts* 22 July 1988.

45. BBC *Summary of World Broadcasts* 20 July 1988.

46. Khâmini'î in sermon, *Iṭṭilâ'ât*, 1/5/67; Rafsanjânî, 8/5/67.

47. Rafsanjânî, *Iṭṭilâ'ât*, 8/5/67.

48. Earlier, the parallel with Ḥudaybiya had been one of the arguments of the official Egyptian *'ulamâ'* to endorse the Camp David Agreement of March 1979.

49. Rafsanjânî, *Iṭṭilâ'ât*, 8/5/67.

50. Shîrâzî, in speech before sermon, *Iṭṭilâ'ât*, 13/6/63.

51. David Menashri, 'Khomeini's Vision: Nationalism or World Order?', in: *The Iranian Revolution and the Muslim World* (Boulder: Westview Press, 1990) p. 390-391.

52. Khâmini'î, *Iṭṭilâ'ât*, 1/5/67.

53. Rafsanjânî, *Iṭṭilâ'ât*, 8/5/67.

54. BBC *Summary of World Broadcasts* 23 July 1988.

55. Watt, 'al-Ḥudaybiya', p. 539.

56. Watt, 'al-Ḥudaybiya', p. 539. Cf. *al-Fatḥ* XLVIII:18 'Allah was satisfied with the believers, when they were swearing allegiance to thee under the tree, and knew what was in their hearts, so He hath sent down the Assurance upon them and hath recompensed them with a clearing-up (or 'conquest') near at hand'.

57. Rafsanjânî, *Iṭṭilâ'ât*, 8/5/67.

58. Rafsanjânî, *Iṭṭilâ'ât*, 8/5/67.

59. Rafsanjânî, *Iṭṭilâ'ât*, 8/5/67.

60. *Shuhadâ' muwaffaq shudand buzurgtarîn dast-âward-i ta'rîkh-i islâm ya'nî jumhûri-yi islâmî bâ khûn wa fidâ-kârî-yi khûd-i-shân ḥifẓ kunand*. Khâmini'î, in sermon *Iṭṭilâ'ât*, 1/5/67; 22/5/67.

61. Rafsanjânî, *Iṭṭilâ'ât*, 8/5/67.

62. Mûsawî Ardabîlî in sermon, *Iṭṭilâ'ât*, 15/5/67; Khâmini'î, 22/5/67.

63. Rafsanjânî, *Iṭṭilâ'ât*, 28/4/67.

64. Rafsanjânî, *Iṭṭilâ'ât*, 19/5/67.

65. Khâmini'î, *Iṭṭilâ'ât*, 22/5/67; Rafsanjânî, 29/5/67.

66. Muḥammad Khâtimî, *Iṭṭilâ'ât* 28/6/67.

CONCLUSION

When Iraqi troops invaded Iranian territory in September 1980, the Iranian leaders seemed less than surprised. For them the war was merely new evidence of the conflict between the Islamic revolution and worldwide imperialism. Even before the outbreak of the war, Khumaynî had spoken implicitly and explicitly about a state of war between Muslims and the superpowers. Nor did other leaders hesitate to stress that the Islamic Republic was already at war with its enemies. In Iranian eyes, Iraq's motive for waging a war was not a regional conflict between Arabs and Iranians or a territorial dispute, but the fact that the Islamic Republic was a threat to the strategic and economic interests of the superpowers.

The premise of this study is that from the onset of the war, the Iranian leaders sacralized the whole conflict in their speeches. This could be expected, given the fact that the majority of the leaders were clerics and that the legitimacy of their rule and their authority was based on religious principles. But the sacralization was all-pervasive. Islam even played a major role in speeches whose context was not religious. Furthermore, other arguments such as economic, military, or territorial arguments were either not used or else combined with religious arguments. For the leaders, Islam was the instrument to express themselves about every subject connected with the war.

The sacralization of the war was not limited either to Islamic beliefs and doctrine or to Islamic symbols and imagery, as had sometimes been the case in previous Iranian wars. In the war with Iraq, beliefs and doctrine, symbols and imagery, were equally important both for the justification of the war and for the mobilization of the population. These beliefs and symbols were sometimes mixed together and sometimes used separately. The leaders were consistent and uniform in their remarks about the war and differences in their policies were not reflected in the war rhetoric. They all gave the same picture of the war and referred to the same symbols and beliefs. This means that the war rhetoric of Khumaynî, Khâmini'î, Rafsanjânî and other leaders mirrors their uniformly religious background.

We have seen that the Islamic beliefs used in the rhetoric could be divided into theological notions concerning war, such as *jihâd* and *fitna*; theological notions which emphasized the dichotomous world view of the Iranian leaders, such as *îmân* and *kufr*, *ḥaqq* and *bâṭil*; the belief in an all-powerful God who had preordained the war; and the belief in the reappearance of the Lord of the Time. The role of Islamic symbols and imagery was as significant in the rhetoric as that of Islamic doctrine. The two main elements were the image of the golden age of Islam, and the martyrdom of Ḥusayn.

The *jihâd* doctrine played a major role in the sacralization of the war, since throughout the war the Iranian leaders laid much emphasis on the fact that the war was a defensive *jihâd* in which everybody had a legal obligation to participate. This argument was sustained with Islamic rules of war, not with references to international rules considering warfare. Furthermore, the Iranian leadership reserved a central place for the glorification of martyrdom in this *jihâd* and stressed that dying for the cause of God in a *jihâd* was the most certain way of receiving God's reward and obtaining a place in Paradise. Hence, it can be concluded that the role of the credenda, the Islamic beliefs, was as important in the justification of the war and the mobilization of the population as that of emotive symbols such as Ḥusayn's martyrdom.

The Iranian leaders used various parts of the Shî'î *jihâd* doctrine in order to solve the problem of a war with another Muslim country. They made use not only of the *jihâd* rules regarding non-Muslims, but also of those which are applicable to Muslim dissenters. They broadened the conditions for the defensive *jihâd*, from the defence of Islam and the Muslim community to the defence of the Islamic revolution and the national, economic and political interests. This was made clear in the stress laid upon the honour of martyrdom for the sake of national aims. It is remarkable that the Iranian leaders still thought it necessary to stress constantly that Khumaynî, as guide of the revolution and leading jurist, had endorsed this war and ordered people to fight, when one considers the fact that the Iranian leaders had also stated that Iran was engaged in a defensive *jihâd*. According to Shî'î law, the *imâm* does not have to play a leading role in such a *jihâd*. However, for the purpose of mobilization, the leaders made use of the enormous charisma Khumaynî possessed for large parts of the population, expressed in the popular slogan '*labbayka yâ imâm*'.

The war was presented as a struggle between Islam and *kufr* (unbelief). This last notion was used to denote the enemies of the Islamic Republic, in particular Iraq and the United States. Islam in this sense signified the Islamic political system and interpretation of Islam as practised and acknowledged in the Islamic Republic. Iran was the vanguard of this revolutionary Islam which was contrary to the reactionary Islam of the Arab Islamic countries in the region. This revolutionary Islam aimed at spreading the divine message of Islam and liberating oppressed people everywhere, although the liberation of Muslims who were oppressed by Israel had priority. The leaders fitted the war into this world view by arguing that the war, while it had been imposed on Iran, was at the same time an instrument to realize the aims of the revolution. In July 1982, after the occupation of Iraqi territory by the Iranian army, the leaders justified their new role as an attacking force in the war by arguing that the occupation was the first step towards the liberation of the oppressed people of Palestine and Lebanon.

The Iranian leaders used several theological notions and doctrines in order to make clear that they were justified in continuing the war. They emphasized that the Islamic Republic was unique and outstanding and that nothing could be compared with it, be it on the level of ethics, doctrines, beliefs or history. Its uniqueness was emphasized by way of polarizing the difference between the two parties, Iran and Iraq, with theological notions. Iran's special status was due to the amount of *îmân* (belief) which separated Iranian Muslims from other Muslims. The Iranian leaders tried to distinguish the Islamic Republic even more from other Islamic states by saying that, in this period, the Iranians were chosen by God to represent *ḥaqq* (truth). The argument that God had selected the Islamic Republic to defend *ḥaqq* and fight against *bâṭil* was the ultimate sacralization of the war and again showed the correctness of the leaders' decision to continue the war until the very end.

In the speeches, the period of Muḥammad and 'Alî's governments was presented as the 'golden age of Islam'. This is not remarkable in itself, since most Shî'î Muslims consider this time as the period of Islam par excellence. The references to a golden age fit into the quest for authenticity which is typical of the present Islamic world. However, the Iranian leaders are very distinctive in that they see the past not just as a model to emulate but as a frame of reference for their own excellence: to show that with the Islamic Republic a 'second golden age of Islam' has been created. The association between the Islamic Republic and the community of Muḥammad was made as much to legitimize the rule of the clerics as to stress the difference between the superior Islamic character of Iran and that of other 'Islamic' states. The Iranian leaders argued that the governments of Muḥammad and 'Alî were examples of effective and correct government, and they did not hesitate to emphasize the similarities between those governments and that of the Islamic Republic. The evocative episodes of the battles of Badr (624), Khaybar (628) and Ṣiffîn (657) were used to emphasize the fact that the Islamic Republic had to face the same problems as the Prophet and 'Alî during their reigns. But these battles were used mainly for sacralization - to make clear that the new Republic had been assigned the same task as the Prophet Muḥammad and his descendants, that is, fighting for the preservation of Islam. The whole association with this historical period makes clear that the Iranian leaders, just like Sunnî Islamists, conceive of Islam as something ahistorical and timeless.

Although the governments of Muḥammad and 'Alî played major roles in the political rhetoric of the leaders, for the sacralization of the war their symbols were overshadowed by the emotive symbol of the martyrdom of the third *imâm*, Ḥusayn. References to Ḥusayn were common in all speeches. Ḥusayn was presented as a revolutionary and a war hero who had fought against tyranny and striven for the preservation and revival of Islam. His sacrifice in the cause of Islam was both a justification of the regime's engagement in this war, since the Islamic Republic fought for the same goals, and an example for Muslims to follow. With the picture of the war as a re-enactment of the martyrdom of Ḥusayn at Karbalâ', the leaders did not follow the traditional interpretation of Ḥusayn's martyrdom, which held that Ḥusayn's sacrifice was a unique and inimitable event in history, beyond the capacity of human beings to follow. According to this traditional interpretation, it was through lamenting Ḥusayn's martyrdom, especially during *'âshûrâ'*, that one could receive a place in Paradise. But this interpretation did not play a role in the war. On the contrary, at the beginning of the war the battlefields became the Karbalâ' and *'âshûrâ'* of the Iranian soldiers but when the war had its devastating effect on Iranian cities, every day and every place became the *'âshûrâ'* of the Iranian population. Moreover, not only those who had died on the battlefield but also those who had been killed by Iraqi attacks came to be regarded as martyrs.

Other parts of Islamic history and Iranian history were on the whole disregarded. In the speeches of the Iranian leaders, the dispute with Iraq over the Shaṭṭ al-'Arab was treated as if it was unprecedented, whereas in fact the Shaṭṭ al-'Arab had been a bone of contention between the Ottoman Empire and the Ṣafawid and Qajar dynasties. The two wars with Russia at the beginning of the nineteenth century, which were supported by the Iranian clergy, were never mentioned in the rhetoric during the war with Iraq. Even the fact that these wars had been declared to be *jihâd* did not receive any attention.

After the establishment of the Islamic Republic, the leaders tried very hard to discourage any millenarian expectations of the population by stressing that the reign of the *mahdî*, the hidden twelfth *imâm*, had not yet arrived but that the government of the Islamic Republic was preparing the way for him. His appearance would not occur as long as the earth was filled with injustice and oppression as was the traditional belief; he would come once the Islamic Republic had installed justice. At the same time, this link between the appearance of the *mahdî* and the installation of justice by the Islamic Republic served to strengthen the legitimacy of the Iranian government. In their war rhetoric, the leaders gave a revolutionary interpretation to the expectation of the *mahdî*, as they had done during the revolution. The war was justified on the basis that millenarian expectations did not mean quietistic waiting and enduring oppression. In the war with Iraq Muslims were again legally obliged to fight oppression as they had been in the time of the Shah. It is true that sometimes, in times of hardship, there was a certain amount of exploitation of millenarian beliefs in the war rhetoric, but on the whole, the references to the hidden presence of the Lord of the Time on the battlefield as an intercessor between God and man outnumbered the references to the Hidden *imâm* in his messianic role of *mahdî*.

In his speeches before the war, Khumaynî had vehemently attacked nationalism, regarding it as an obstacle to Muslim solidarity and unity. But during the war, his speeches and those of other leaders showed that they themselves were not free from national sentiment. They stressed the differences between the Iranian population and the Arabs, at the same time reproaching Ṣaddâm Ḥusayn for exploiting these differences. Occasionally, Iran's pre-Islamic imperial past was stressed in the rhetoric. This is striking because Khumaynî had always contested the Shah's veneration for pre-Islamic Iran, declaring it irreconcilable with Iran's religious identity. However, expressions of nationalism were in general combined with references to the Islamic character of Iran. This religious nationalism was mainly expressed through the image of the Islamic Republic as a special nation. The population was presented as a people favoured not only by God, but also by the Prophet Muḥammad, who had after all preferred Salmân Fârisî, a companion of Persian origin. Moreover, the Iranians were portrayed as better Muslims than Arabs, because of their ties with the prophets, Muḥammad, 'Alî and the Shî'î *imâms*, because of their obedience to Islamic law but also because of their fighting spirit, which was unparalleled even in the history of Islam. Whereas Iran's outstanding position was stressed through the comparison of the government with the governments of the 'golden age' of Islam, in the field of society, the uniqueness of Iran lay in the creation by the Iranian population of a new 'golden age'. The leaders kept emphasizing that the attitude of the Iranian population was without parallel, even in Islamic history, in its religious conviction, its willingness to sacrifice itself and its obedience to Islamic law.

The rhetoric of the Iranian leaders during the war showed continuity with the revolutionary rhetoric in 1977-79. The importance of the liberation of the oppressed was part of this continuity, albeit that before the revolution liberation had been limited to the oppressed in Iran. This continuity became especially clear in the way the leaders perceived their enemies. The Shah, their main enemy before the revolution, had been replaced by Ṣaddâm Ḥusayn, but the leaders in general referred to the same historical bogeys, Yazîd and Mu'âwiya, and used the same language and theological descriptions, such as *ṭâghût*, for Ṣaddâm Ḥusayn and his regime, as they had used for the Shah. The United States and Israel remained the main foreign enemies of Khumaynî and his followers. The United States was again presented as the arch-enemy of Islam and the interests of Muslims, responsible for the destruction of Iran as it had been responsible for the moral decay of Iran before the revolution. This time it had got Ṣaddâm Ḥusayn to do its dirty work. Another aspect of the continuity with the revolution was that the war was presented as an instrument to realize revolutionary goals. Until after the acceptance of Resolution 598, the war was presented as an obstacle to the realization of these goals.

The use of symbolic tags quite often bore little relationship to the underlying realities. This is visible in the naming after evocative places such as Jerusalem or Karbalâ' of military operations which in reality had quite limited objectives (such as the capture of the Iranian town of Mihrân). The war was presented as a cosmic struggle against 'the great Satan', but when the war escalated to the Gulf, and the international community became involved, leaders kept saying that the war could not be decided in the Gulf but had to be decided on the battlefield. Only there could the decisive blow be dealt to Iraq. This shows again that, despite the continued presentation in the sermons of the war as a struggle between Islam and unbelief and between truth and falsehood, and of the United States, in its role as 'great Satan' and vanguard of 'worldwide arrogance', as the main enemy of the Islamic Republic, in reality the Iranian leaders regarded the war as one with Iraq only. If the issue really had been a direct conflict with the United States, a confrontation in the Gulf would have been a more obvious course to take. Iran's peace conditions, which concentrated on the recovery of Iranian territory and on the person of Ṣaddâm Ḥusayn, showed even more clearly that the war with Iraq was the real issue.

There were many contradictions in the statements of the leaders, for instance with regard to the continuation of the war. Depending on the occasion, Iranian leaders said sometimes that Iran wanted to end the war, and sometimes that it wanted to continue it and accused the enemy of wanting to do the opposite. Another contradiction was the way the Iranian leaders spoke about Ṣaddâm Ḥusayn. They employed theological terminology to describe their enemy but they were not very consistent in this, which is remarkable, considering that they were all highly educated theologians. In particular, they seem to have been unable to decide whether he was a Muslim, an unbeliever, a heretic or merely a sinner. They indiscriminately used concepts like *kâfir* (unbeliever), *mushrik* (polytheist), *mulḥid* (deviator), *bâghî* (dissenter), and *fâsiq* (sinner), which are used in Islamic theology to denote different categories of people. However, one has to keep in mind that these descriptions were made in the course of the war in order to downplay the 'good' of the enemy. They were not made in a theological college or during a debate among clerics. All these descriptions served one purpose: to polarize the conflict between Iran and Iraq and to make clear that Iran was justified in waging war against Iraq, because Ṣaddâm Ḥusayn in all his guises only had one purpose in mind and that was the destruction of Islam and the Islamic Republic. The descriptions were instrumental in sacralizing the struggle between Iran and Iraq and defining it as one between good and evil.

The leaders agreed that the war in itself was a terrible thing, that it was an imposed one (*Jang-i taḥmîlî*) and that Ṣaddâm Ḥusayn was a war criminal. He, together with the United States, was held responsible for the outbreak of the war. However, at the same time they stressed the positive side of the war and argued that the United States and Ṣaddâm Ḥusayn were instruments of God, the real instigator of the war, who wanted to test the Muslims and separate the believers from the non-believers. The leaders furthermore emphasized that the war was a blessing, and that it was beneficial and constructive for the Iranian people. As a result of the war, Iranian society had become united, harmonious, and sincere. It was even said that the revolution had not achieved this much unity. For the sake of mobilization and justification, the war was placed above the revolution. This emphasis on the way the revolution had taken root in Iranian society must be seen in the light of 'coming to terms with reality', namely the realization of the failure to export the revolution. But highlighting the blessings of war was also an instrument to make Iran's disappointing military results more palatable. In 1986, when it had become clear that revolutionary and Islamic slogans could neither relieve the burden of the war on the Iranian population nor mask the economic problems of the Republic, the leaders avoided calling the war a blessing. As before, prayer leaders connected a victory with unity and firmness of the population and with willingness to sacrifice. But there were also signs that the leaders tried to come to terms with the growing resentment of the war. The growing number of remarks made in the sermons to rebuke criticism was proof of this. Utterances such as 'We must not doubt the final victory' and 'We will gain the final victory when God thinks it right' replaced remarks that victory was certain and to be expected in the near future.

After the acceptance of Resolution 598 in July 1988, the leaders sacralized their decision to accept a cease-fire by making use of the same religious line of reasoning which they had employed during the war. Again, the theological notions of *islâm* and *kufr*, and Islamic symbols were used. The distinctions between Islam, the Islamic Republic and the revolution, and *kufr* and its proponents were highlighted. Historical analogies regarding peace decisions of the Prophet were as fundamental for the rhetoric after the acceptance of the cease-fire as his decisions to fight had been during the war.

With the acceptance of Resolution 598, it became much clearer that in the first years of its existence, the Islamic Republic was a mobilization regime, where consent was expressed through mass mobilization. Indeed, the main reason for the acceptance was that the leaders had become afraid that the very existence of the Islamic Republic was endangered because the Iranian population had become war-weary and did not support the war any more. From 1986 onwards the regime had great difficulty in mobilizing volunteers who were willing to fight on the battlefield, and more and more people were joining those who opposed Iran's participation in the war. After the acceptance of the armistice, the leaders emphasized that the population's support for Khumaynî's decision to stop the war was expressed in massive rallies throughout the country.

In the course of this study, I have confronted the reader with many conclusions based on the statements of the Iranian leaders. However, we should not forget that we have been dealing with representations of reality, not with the reality of the war itself. We have not learnt much about the role the war played in the lives of ordinary Iranian people and the way they coped with the tremendous loss of life, health and wealth. Whether the sacralization was perceived by them as inspiration or solace in their daily struggle remains an open question, but during an impressive visit to

Bihisht-i zahrâ, Tehran's main cemetery, where tens of thousands of soldiers are buried, those who visited the graves of soldiers pointed out to me that they were much comforted by the idea that their loved ones had died for the sake of God and Khumaynî.

BIBLIOGRAPHY

Primary sources: Persian

Khâmini'î, *Chahâr sâl bâ mardum* (Tehran: Ḥizb-i jumhûrî-yi islâmî, 1364/1985).

Khumaynî, *Dar justujû-yi râh az kalâm-i imâm: Milla, umma. Az bayânât wa i'lâmiya-hâ-yi imâm Khumaynî az sâl 1341 tâ 1361* Vol.9 (Tehran: Amîr Kabîr, 1362/1983).

Khumaynî, *Dar justujû-yi râh az kalâm-i imâm: Mustaḍ'afîn, mustakbarîn. Az bayânât wa i'lâmiya-hâ-yi imâm Khumaynî az sâl 1341 tâ 1361* Vol.1 (Tehran, Amîr Kabîr: 1363²/1984).

Khumaynî, *Dar justujû-yi râh az kalâm-i imâm: Jang wa jihâd. Az bayânât wa i'lâmiya-hâ-yi imâm Khumaynî az sâl 1341 tâ 1361* Vol.2 (Tehran: Amîr Kabîr, 1363²/1984).

Khumaynî, *Dar justujû-yi râh az kalâm-i imâm: Shahîd wa shahâda. Az bayânât wa i'lâmiya-hâ-yi imâm Khumaynî az sâl 1341 tâ 1361* Vol.4 (Tehran: Amîr Kabîr, 1370/1991).

Khumaynî, *Ḥukûmat-i islâmî. Majmû'a-yi darshâ-yi rahbar-i shî'îyân-i jihân taḥta 'unwân: 'wilâyat-i faqîh'* (n.p., 1391/1971).

Khumaynî, *Ṣaḥîfa-yi nûr. Majmû'a-yi rahnamûdhâ-yi ḥaḍrat-i imâm Khumaynî* (Tehran: Ministry of Culture and Islamic Guidance, 1370/1991).

Muntaẓirî, *Jang-i taḥmîlî dar bayânât-i âyatullâh al-'uẓmâ Muntaẓirî* (Tehran: Ministry of Islamic Guidance, 1367/1988).

Hâshimî Rafsanjânî, *Nuṭuq-hâ-yi qabl az dastûr-i ḥujjatulislâm wa-l-muslimîn Ḥâshimî Rafsanjânî riyâsat-i majlis-i shûrâ-yi islâmî* (Tehran: Majlis-i shûrâ-yi islâmî, 1362/1983).

Dah sâl bâ ṭarrâḥân-i grafîk-i inqilâb-i islamî, 1357-1367, compiled by Dâwud Ṣâdiq 'Alî, (Tehran: Ḥawza-yi hunarî-yi sâzimân-i tablîghât-i islâmî, 1368/1989) Vols.2-3.

Dar maktab-i jum'a. Majmû'a-yi khuṭbahâ-yi namâz-i jum'a-yi Tehran Vol.2 (Tehran: Ministry of Islamic Guidance, 1364/1986).

Dar maktab-i jum'a. Majmû'a-yi khuṭbahâ-yi namâz-i jum'a-yi Tehran Vol.3 (Tehran: Ministry of Islamic Guidance, 1365/1987).

Dar maktab-i jum'a. Majmû'a-yi khuṭbahâ-yi namâz-i jum'a-yi Tehran Vol.4 (Tehran: Ministry of Islamic Guidance, 1367/1989).

Dar maktab-i jum'a. Majmû'a-yi khuṭbahâ-yi namâz-i jum'a-yi Tehran Vol.5 (Tehran: Ministry of Islamic Guidance, 1368/1989).

Dar maktab-i jum'a. Majmû'a-yi khuṭbahâ-yi namâz-i jum'a-yi Tehran Vol.6 (Tehran: Ministry of Islamic Guidance, 1369/1990).

Dar maktab-i jum'a. Majmû'a-yi khuṭbahâ-yi namâz-i jum'a-yi Tehran Vol.7 (Tehran: Ministry of Islamic Guidance, 1369/1991).

Farhang-i jabha (tablû-yi niwishtihâ, ed. by Sayyid Mihdî Fahîmî (Tehran: Intishârât-i ḥawza-yi hunarî-yi sâzimân-i tablîghât-i islâmî, 1369/1990).

Gudharî bar du sâl-i jang (n.p., Daftar-i siyâsî-yi sipâh-i pâsdârân-i inqilâb-i islâmî, n.d.).

Jang bâ inqilâb, barrasî zamînahâ-yi tajâwuz-i rizjîm-i 'Irâq 'alâ Îrân (Tehran: 1360/1981).

Jang-i taḥmîlî, armaghân-i shûm-i qadrathâ-yi shayṭânî (Tehran: Sitâd-i buzurkhdâsht-i panjumîn sâlgard-i pîrûz-i inqilâb-i islâmî, 1362/1983).

Jang-i taḥmîlî. Difâ' dar barâbar-i tajâwuz. The Imposed War. Defence versus Aggression. Al-Ḥarb al-mafrûda. Al-Difâ' amâma l-'udwân (Tehran: Supreme Defence Council, 1365/1986). Vol.4.

Kârnâma-yi 'amalîyât-i sipâhiyân-i islâm dar hasht sâl-i difâ'-i muqaddas (Tehran: Markaz-i farhangî-yi sipâh-i pâsdârân-i inqilâb-i islâmî, 1373/1994[3]).

Khaṭṭ-i tawṭi'a (Tehran: Sipâh-i pâsdârân-i inqilâb-i islâmî, 1366/1987).

Khurramshahr az âsâra tâ âzâdî (n.p., Daftar-i nashr-i farhang-i islâmî, 1363/1984).

Nigarish bar jang-i taḥmîlî-yi rizhîm-i ba'th-i 'Irâq 'alâ jumhûrî-yi islâmî (Tehran: Ministry of Foreign Affairs, 1360).

Nihâdhâ-yi dawlatî wa jang-i taḥmîlî. Bakhsh-i awwal az âghâz-i jang tâ 'amalîyât-i fatḥ al-mubîn (n.p., Dabîr khâna-yi shûrâ-yi hamangî-yi tablîghâtî-yi dawlatî, 1361/1982).

Tahlîlî bar jang-i taḥmîlî-yi rizjîm-i 'irâq 'ala jumhûrî-yi islâmî-yi irân Vol.2 (Tehran: Ministry of Foreign Affairs, 1367/1988).

Periodicals

Iṭṭilâ'ât
Iṭṭilâ'ât-i jabha
Jumhûrî-yi islâmî
Kayhân

Primary sources: English

Faith versus Aggression. al-Îmân yuqâwimu al-i'tidâ' (Tehran: Ministry of Islamic Guidance, 1982).

The Imam and the Ommat. The Selected Messages of Imam Khomeini concerning Iraq and the War Iraq Imposed upon Iran (Tehran: Ministry of Islamic Guidance, 1981).

Periodicals

BBC *Summary of World Broadcasts: Middle East*

FBIS *Daily Report*

Secondary sources: Arabic and Persian

Âzarî Qumî, *Khaṭṭ-i îmâm wa wîzhgîhâ-yi ân* (Qum: Dâr al-'Ilm, n.d.).

Dihkhudâ, 'Alî Akbar, *Lughat-namâ* (Tehran: Dânishgâh-i Tehrân, 1328).

Difâ' wa-al-amr bi-l-ma'rûf wa-l-nahy 'an al-munkar (Tehran: Mu'âwanîya al-'alâqât al-dawlîya fî munaẓẓama al-'âlam al-islâmîya, 1407/1987).

Al-Ḥillî, Najm al-Dîn, *al-Mukhtaṣar al-nafî' fî fiqh al-imâmîya* (Tehran: Maktabat al-Asad, 1387/1967).

Ibn Mâja, *Sunan* (n.p., Dâr iḥyâ' al-kutub al-'arabîya, 1373/1953).

Khumaynî, Rûḥullâḥ, *Kashf al-asrâr* (Tehran, n.p., n.d.).

Khumaynî, *al-Jihâd al-akbar. Qâ'id al-thawra al-islâmiyya fî îrân âyatullâh al-'uẓmâ al-mujtahid ul-imâm al-Khumaynî* (Cairo: Manshûrât al-maktabat al-islâmiyya, n.d.).

Al-Kulaynî, *al-Uṣûl min al-kâfî*, Vol.2 (Beirut: Dâr al-ta'arruf, 1401).

Al-Mudarrisî, Muḥammad Taqî, *al-Fikr al-islâmî. Muwâjaha ḥaḍârîya* (Beirut: Dâr al-Jubayl, 1395/1975).

Al-Mufîd, Shaykh Muḥammad ibn al-Nu'mân, *Awâ'il al-maqâlât fî l-madhâhib al-mukhtârât* (Tabriz, n.p., 1371/1952).

Al-Ṭabarî, Abû Ja'far Muḥammad b. Jarîr, *Jâmi' al-bayân 'an tâ'wîl ây al-qur'ân* (Cairo: Dâr al-Ma'ârif, 1955-1969).

Al-Ṭabarsî, Abû 'Alî al-Faḍl ibn al-Ḥasan, *Majma' al-bayân fî tafsîr al-qur'ân* (Beirut: Dâr iḥyâ' al-turâth al-'arabî, 1412/1992).

Ṭabâṭabâ'î, Muḥammad Ḥusayn, *Tafsîr al-mîzân* (Tehran: Muḥammadî, 1363/1984).

Al-Ṭûsî, Abû Ja'far, *al-Nihâya fî mujarrad al-faqîh wa-l-fatâwî* Vol.1 (Tehran: Maktabat al-Asad, 1387-1967).

Secondary sources: Other languages

Abedi, M., and G. Legenhausen (ed.), *Jihâd and Shahâdat. Struggle and Martyrdom in Islam* (Houston: IRIS, 1986).

Abrahamian, Ervand, *Khomeinism* (London: I.B. Tauris, 1993).

Abrahamian, Ervand, *Radical Islam. The Iranian Mojahedin* (London: I.B. Tauris, 1989).

Abdulghani, J.M., *The Years of Crisis* (Baltimore: Johns Hopkins University Press, 1984).

Akhavi, Shahrough, 'Elite Factionalism in the Islamic Republic of Iran', in: *The Middle East Journal* 41 (1987) pp. 181-201.

Algar, Hamid, *Religion and State in Iran 1785-1906. The Role of the Ulama in the Qajar Period* (Berkeley: University of California Press, 1969).

Ali, S.V. Mir Ahmed, *Husain.The Saviour of Islam* (Qom: Shafagh Publications, 1987).

Antoun, Richard T., *Muslim Preacher in the Modern World. A Jordanian Case Study in Comparative Perspective* (Princeton: Princeton University Press, 1989).

Arjomand, Said Amir, 'The Ulama's Traditionalist Opposition to Parliamentarianism: 1907-1909', in: *Middle Eastern Studies* 17 (1981) pp. 174-190.

Arjomand, Said Amir (ed.), *From Nationalism to Revolutionary Islam* (London: Macmillan, 1984).

Arjomand, Said Amir, *The Shadow of God and the Hidden Imam. Religion, Political Order, and Societal Change in Shi'ite Iran from the Beginning to 1890* (Chicago: University of Chicago Press, 1984).

Arjomand, Said Amir, *The Turban for the Crown. The Islamic Revolution in Iran* (Oxford: Oxford University Press, 1988).

Arjomand, Said Amir, 'A Victory for the Pragmatists: The Islamic Fundamentalist Reaction in Iran', in: *Islamic Fundamentalisms and the Gulf Crisis*, ed. by J. Piscatori (n.p.,The American Academy of Arts and Sciences, 1991) pp. 52-69.

Arjomand, Said Amir (ed.), *The Political Dimensions of Religion* (Albany: SUNY Press, 1993).

Ayalon, Ami, 'From Fitna to Thawra', in: *Studia Islamica* 66 (1987) pp. 145-174.

Ayalon, Ami, *Language and Change in the Arab Middle East. The Evolution of Modern Political Discourse* (New York: Oxford University Press, 1987).

Ayoub, Mahmoud, *Redemptive Suffering in Islam. A Study of the Devotional Aspects of 'Âshûrâ in Twelver Shi'ism* (The Hague: Mouton, 1978).

Ayoub, Mahmoud, 'The Speaking Qur'ân and the Silent Qur'ân: A Study of the Principles and Development of Imâmî Shî'î *tafsîr*', in: *Approaches to the History of the Interpretation of the Qur'ân*, ed. by Andrew Rippin (Oxford: Clarendon Press, 1988) pp. 177-198.

el-Azhary, M.S., *The Iran-Iraq War. An Historical, Economic and Political Analysis* (London: Croom Helm, 1984).

Azodanloo, Heidar Ghajar, *Discourses of Mobilization in Post-revolutionary Iran* (Unpublished Ph D thesis, University of Minnesota, 1992).

Azodanloo, Heidar Ghajar, 'Characteristics of Ayatullah Khomeini's Discourse and the Iraq-Iran War', in: *Orient* 34(1993) 3,p. 414-415.

Bakan, David, 'Some Philosophical Propadeutics toward a Psychology of War', in: *The Psychology of War and Peace. The Image of the Enemy*, ed. by Robert W. Rieber (New York: Plenum Press, 1991) pp. 41-58.

Bakhash, Shaul, *The Reign of the Ayatollahs. Iran and the Revolution* (New York: Basic Books, 1984).

Balta, Paul, *Iran-Irak. Une Guerre de 5000 ans* (Paris: Éditions Anthropos, 1987).

Bardehle, Peter, 'Die Resolution 598 des Sicherheitsrats - Grundlage für die Waffenruhe im Konflikt zwischen Iran und dem Irak', in: *Orient* 31 (1990) pp. 261-272.

Batatu, Hanna, 'Shi'i Organizations in Iraq: al-Da'wah al-Islamiyah and al-Mujahidin', in: *Shi'ism and Social Protest*, ed. by Juan R.I. Cole and N.K. Keddie (New Haven: Yale University Press, 1986) pp. 179-200.

Beetham, David, *The Legitimation of Power* (London: Macmillan, 1991).

Björkman, W., 'Kâfir', in: *Encyclopaedia of Islam*[2] Vol.4 pp. 407-9.

Brockett, A., 'Munâfiqûn', in: *Encyclopaedia of Islam*[2] Vol.7 pp. 561-562.

Brunschvig, R., 'barâ'a' in: *Encyclopaedia of Islam*[2] Vol.1 p. 1026-1027.

Buhl, F., 'Munâfiqûn', in: *Encyclopaedia of Islam*[1] Vol.6 p. 722.

Buhl, F. (C.E. Bosworth), 'Millat', in: *The Encyclopaedia of Islam*[2], Vol.7, pp. 60-61.

Busse, Heribert, 'Herrschertypen im Koran', in: *Die islamische Welt zwischen Mittelalter und Neuzeit*, ed. by U. Haarmann und P. Bachmann (Beirut: Orient Institut, 1979) pp. 56-80.

Chehabi, H.E. 'Religion and Politics in Iran: How Theocratic is the Islamic Republic?', in: *Daedalus* 120 (1991) pp. 69-91.

Chelkowski, Peter, 'From Maqâtîl Literature to Drama', in: *Al-Ṣerâṭ* 12 (1986) pp. 227-264.

Chelkowski, Peter, 'Popular Shi'î Mourning Rituals', in: *Al-Serât* 12 (1986) pp.209-226.

Chelkowski, Peter, 'Khomeini's Iran as Seen through Bank Notes', in: *The Iranian Revolution and the Muslim World*, ed. by David Menashri (Boulder: Westview Press, 1990) pp. 85-101.

Chubin, Shahram, 'Iran and the War: From Stalemate to Ceasefire', in: *The Iran-Iraq War: Impact and Implications*, ed. by E. Karsh (London: Macmillan, 1989) pp. 13-25.

Chubin, Shahram and Charles Tripp, *Iran and Iraq at War* (London: I.B. Tauris, 1988).

Connolly, William, 'Introduction: Legitimacy and Modernity', in: *Legitimacy and the State*, ed. by William Connolly (Oxford: Blackwell, 1984).

Constitution of the Islamic Republic of Iran (transl. by Hamid Algar) (Berkeley: Mizan Press, 1980).

Cordesman, Anthony H. and A.R. Wagner, *The Lessons of Modern War* Vol.2 The Iran-Iraq War (Boulder: Westview Press, 1991).

Cordesman, Anthony H., 'Lessons of the Iran-Iraq War: Part One', in: *Armed Forces Journal International* 119 (1982) pp. 32-46.

Cottam, Richard, *Nationalism in Iran* (Pittsburgh: University of Pittsburgh Press, 1964).

Dekker, I.F. and H. Post, 'The Gulf War from the Point of View of International Law', in: *Netherlands Yearbook of International Law* 17 (1986) pp. 75-105.

Dessouki, Ali E. Hillal, 'The Iraq-Iran War: An Overview', in: *The Iraq-Iran War. Issues of Conflict and Prospects for Settlement*, ed. by Ali E. Hillal Dessouki (Princeton: Center of International Studies, 1981) pp. 1-5.

Dorraj, Manochehr, *From Zarathustra to Khomeini. Populism and Dissent in Iran* (Boulder: Lynne Rienner, 1990).

Eickelman, Dale F. and J. Piscatori, *Muslim Politics* (Princeton: Princeton University Press, 1996).

Enayat, Hamid, *Modern Islamic Political Thought* (London: Macmillan, 1982).

Ende, Werner, *Arabische Nation und islamische Geschichte. Die Umayyaden im Urteil arabischer Autoren des 20. Jahrhunderts* (Beirut: Orient Institut, 1977).

Entessar, Nader, 'The Military and Politics in the Islamic Republic of Iran', in: *Post-Revolutionary Iran*, ed. by Hooshang Amirahmadi and M. Parvin (Boulder: Westview, 1988) pp. 56-73.

Faridzahdeh, Abdolali, *Die Umwandlung des shiitischen Islams in die politische Ideologie des Chiliasmus und Nativismus* (Unpublished Ph D thesis, 1987).

Fathi, Asghar, 'The Islamic Pulpit as a Medium of Political Communication', in: *Journal for the Scientific Study of Religion* 2 (1981) p. 164.Ferdows, Adele, 'Shariati and Khomeini on Women', in: *The Iranian Revolution and the Islamic Republic*, ed. by N.R. Keddie (n.p., Middle East Institute, 1982).

Firzli, Nicola and Nassim Khoury (ed.), *The Iraq-Iran Conflict* (Paris: Éditions du Monde Arabe, 1981).

Fischer, Michael M.J., *Iran. From Religious Dispute to Revolution* (Harvard: Harvard University Press, 1980).

Fyzee, Asaf A.A., *A Shi'ite Creed. A Translation of Risâlatu'l-I'tiqâdât of Muḥammad b. 'Alî Ibn Babawayhi al-Qummi known as Shaykh Ṣadûq* (London: Oxford University Press, 1942).

Gardet, Louis, 'Fâsiḳ', in: *Encyclopaedia of Islam*[2] Vol.2 pp. 833-834.

Gardet, Louis, 'Fitna', in: *Encyclopaedia of Islam*[2] Vol.2 p. 931.

Gardet, Louis, 'Îmân', in: *The Encyclopaedia of Islam*[2] Vol.3 p. 1171.

Gellner, Ernest, *Nations and Nationalism* (Oxford: Blackwell, 1983).

Gellner, Ernest, *Postmodernism, Reason and Religion* (London: Routledge, 1992).

Ghods, M. Reza, *Iran in the Twentieth Century. A Political History* (Boulder: Lynne Rienner, 1989).

Gholamasad, Dawud, 'Heiliger Krieg und Martyrium bei den iranischen Schiiten im Golfkrieg, 1980-1988', in: *Kriegsbegeisterung und mentale Kriegsvorbereitung*, ed. by M. van der Linden and G. Mergner (Berlin: Duncker & Humblot, 1991) pp. 219-230.

Gholamasad, Dawud, 'Weltanschauliche und sozialpsychologische Aspekte der iranischen Kriegsführung. Einige sozialpsychologische Aspekte des Martyriums der iranischen Kriegsfreiwilliger - eine Auswertung ihrer Testamente', in: *Orient* 30 (1989) pp. 557-569.

Gieling, Saskia, 'The Institution of Marja'iya in Iran and the Nomination of Khamanei in December 1994', in: *Middle Eastern Studies* 33 (1997) pp. 777-787.

Göbel, Karl-Heinz, *Moderne Shiitische Politik und Staatsidee* (Berlin: Leske & Budrich, 1984).

Gorawantschy, Béatrice, *Der Golfkrieg zwischen Iran und Irak, 1980-88. Eine konflikttheoretische Analyse* (Berlin: Lang, 1993).

Grummon, Stephen R., *The Iran-Iraq War. Islam Embattled* (New York: Praeger, 1982).

Haar, J. ter, *Volgelingen van de imam. Een kennismaking met de shi'itische islam* (Amsterdam: Bulaaq, 1995).

Haddad, Yvonne, *Contemporary Islam and the Challenge of History* (Albany: SUNY Press, 1982).

Haeri, Abdul-Hadi, 'Shaykh Faẓl Allâh Nûrî's Refutation of the Idea of Constitutionalism', in: *Middle Eastern Studies* 13 (1977) pp. 327-339.

Haeri, Safa, *Law of Desire. Temporary Marriage in Shi'i Iran* (Syracuse: Syracuse University Press, 1989).

Haeri, Safa, 'The Missing Prisoners', in: *Middle East International* 388 (1990) p. 13.

Haghayeghi, Mehrdad, 'Politics and Ideology in the Islamic Republic of Iran', in: *Middle Eastern Studies* 29 (1993) pp. 36-52.

Halliday, Fred, 'Year IV of the Islamic Republic', in: *Middle East Report* 13 (1983) pp. 3-8, p. 4.

Ḥamîdullâh, Muḥammad, *The Muslim Conduct of State* (Lahore: Muhammad Ashraf, 1953^3).

Hegeman, J.H., *Justifying Policy. A Heuristic* (Amsterdam: Free University Press, 1989).

Hegland, Mary, 'Two Images of Husain: Accommodation and Revolution in an Iranian Village', in: *Religion and Politics in Iran. Shi'ism from Quietism to Revolution*, ed. by Nikki R. Keddie (New Haven: Yale University Press, 1983) pp. 218-235.

al-Ḥillî Ibn Muṭahhar, *al-Bâb al-ḥâdî 'ashar*, trans. by W.M. Miller (London: Royal Asiatic Society, 1928).

Hiro, Dilip, 'Chronicle of the Gulf War', in: *Middle East Report* 126 (1984) pp. 3-14.

Hiro, Dilip, *The Longest War: The Iran-Iraq Military Conflict* (London: Grafton, 1989).

Hobsbawm, E.J., *Nations and Nationalism since 1780* (Cambridge: Cambridge University Press, 1990).

Hossein Razi, G., 'An Alternative Paradigm to State Rationality in Foreign Policy: The Iran-Iraq War', in: *Western Political Quarterly* 41 (1988) pp. 689-723.

Hossein Razi, G., 'Legitimacy, Religion, and Nationalism in the Middle East', in: *American Political Science Review* 84 (1990) 1, pp. 69-91.

Hünseler, Peter, 'The Historical Antecedents of the Shatt al-'Arab Dispute', in: *The Iran-Iraq War. An Historical, Economic and Political Analysis*, ed. by M.S. el-Azhary (London: Croom Helm, 1984) pp. 8-19.

Hunter, Shireen T., *Iran and the World. Continuity in a Revolutionary Decade* (Bloomington: Indiana University Press, 1990).

IISS, *The Military Balance, 1980/81* (London: International Institute for Strategic Studies).

Islam and Revolution. Writings and Declarations of Imam Khomeini, Trans. and annotated by Hamid Algar (Berkeley: Mizan Press, 1981).

Ismael, Tareq Y., *Iraq and Iran. Roots of Conflict* (New York: Syracuse University Press, 1982).

Izutsu, Toshihiko, *God and Man in the Koran. Semantics of the Koranic Weltanschauung* (Tokyo: Keio Institute of Cultural and Linguistic Studies, 1964).

Izutsu, Toshihiko, *Ethico-Religious Concepts in the Qur'ân* (Montreal: McGill University Press, 1966).

Jannatî, Ahmad, 'Defense and Jihâd in the Qur'ân', in: *Tawḥîd* 1 (1404) pp. 39-58.

Jafri, S.H.M., *The Origins and Early Development of Shi'a Islam* (Qum: Ansariyan, n.d.)

Johannes J.G. Jansen, 'Mu'min', in: *Encyclopaedia of Islam*^{2} Vol.3, p. 555).

Jansen, Johannes J.G., *The Neglected Duty. The Creed of Sadat's Assassins and Islamic Resurgence in the Middle East* (New York: Macmillan, 1986).

Jeffery, Arthur, *The Foreign Vocabulary of the Qur'ân* (Baroda: The Oriental Institute, 1938).

Juergensmeyer, Mark, *The New Cold War? Religious Nationalism Confronts the Secular State* (Berkeley: University of California Press, 1993).

Juynboll, Th. W. *Handleiding tot de kennis van de Mohammedaansche wet volgens de leer der Sjâfi'itische school* (Leiden: Brill, 1930^4).

Kanovsky, Eliyahu, 'Economic Implications for the Region and World Oil Market', in: *The Iran-Iraq War. Impact and Implications*, ed. by E. Karsh (London: Macmillan, 1989) pp. 231-251.

Karsh, Efraim (ed.), *The Iran-Iraq War: Impact and Implications* (London: Macmillan, 1989).

Karsh, Efraim, *The Iran-Iraq War: A Military Analysis* (London: International Institute for Strategic Studies, 1987).

Katzman, Kenneth, *The Warriors of Islam. Iran's Revolutionary Guard* (Boulder: Westview: 1993).

Kepel, Gilles, *Le Prophète et pharaon: Les mouvements islamistes dans l'egypte contemporaine* (Paris: La Découverte, 1984).

Khadduri, Majid, *The Gulf War. The Origins and Implications of the Iraq-Iran Conflict* (New York and Oxford: Oxford University Press, 1988).

Khadduri, Majid, 'Harb - The Legal Aspect', in: *Encyclopaedia of Islam*[2] Vol.3 p. 180.

Khadduri, Majid, *War and Peace in the Law of Islam* (Baltimore: Johns Hopkins University Press, 1955).

Khosrokhavar, Farhad, *L'Islamisme et la mort. Le martyre révolutionnaire en Iran* (Paris: L'Harmattan, 1995).

King, Ralph, *The Iran-Iraq War. The Political Implications* (London: International Institute for Strategic Studies, 1987).

Knysh, Alexander, '*Irfan* Revisited: Khomeini and the Legacy of Islamic Mystical Philosophy', in: *Middle East Journal* 46 (1992) pp. 631-653.

Kohlberg, Etan, 'The Development of the Imâmî Shî'i Doctrine of *Jihâd*', in: *Zeitschrift der Deutschen Morgenländischen Gesellschaft* 126 (1976) pp. 64-86.

Kohlberg, Etan, 'Some Shî'î Views of the Antediluvian World' in: *Studia Islamica* 51 (1980). pp. 41-66.

Kohlberg, Etan, 'Barâ'a in Shî'î Doctrine', in: *Jerusalem Studies in Arabic and Islam* 7 (1986) pp. 139-175.

Kohlberg, Etan, 'Shahîd', in: *Encyclopaedia of Islam*[2] Vol.9 pp. 203-207.

Kraemer, Joel L., 'Apostates, Rebels and Brigands', in: *Israel Oriental Studies* 10 (1980) pp. 34-73.

Krüger, Hilmar, *Fetwa und Siyar* (Wiesbaden: Harrassowitz, 1978).

Kruse, Hans, *Islamische Völkerrechtslehre* (Bochum: Brockmeyer, 1979[2]).

Kruse, Hans, '*Takfir* und *jihâd* bei den Zaiditen des Jemen', in: *Welt des Islams* 24 (1984) pp. 424-457.

Lambton, A.K.S. 'A Nineteenth-Century View of Jihâd', in: *Studia Islamica* 32 (1970) pp. 181-192.

Landau, Jacob, *The Politics of Pan-Islam. Ideology and Organization* (Oxford: Clarendon Press, 1990).

Lapidus, Ira M., 'The Golden Age: The Political Concepts of Islam', in: *Annals of the American Academy of Political and Social Science* 523 (1992) pp. 13-25.

Lewis, Bernard, *The Political Language of Islam* (Chicago: University of Chicago Press, 1988).

Lewis, Bernard, 'Some Observations on the Significance of Heresy in the History of Islam', in: *Studia Islamica* 1 (1953) pp. 43-63.

Linant de Bellefonds, Y., 'fâsid wa- bâṭil' in *Encyclopaedia of Islam²* Vol.2 pp. 829-832.

McDermott, Martin J., *The Theology of al-Shaikh al-Mufid* (Beirut: Dar el-Machreq Éditeurs, 1978).

McLachlan, Keith, 'Territoriality and the Iran-Iraq War', in: *The Boundaries of Modern Iran*, ed. by K. McLachlan (London: UCL Press, 1994) pp. 57-71.

MacDonald, D.B., (E.E. Calverley), in 'Ḥaqq' in *Encyclopaedia of Islam²* Vol.3 pp. 82-83.

Maddy-Weitzmann, Bruce, 'Islam and Arabism: The Iran-Iraq War', in: *Washington Quarterly* 5 (1982) pp. 181-185.

Madelung, W., 'Mulḥid' in: *Encyclopaedia of Islam²* Vol.7 p. 546.

Mahrad, Ahmad, *Der Iran-Irak Konflikt* (Frankfurt am Main: Peter Lang, 1985).

Mallat, Chibli, 'Religious Militancy in Contemporary Iraq: Muhammad Baqer as-Sadr and the Sunni-Shia Paradigm', in: *Third World Quarterly* 10 (1988) pp. 699-729.

Martin, Vanessa, *Islam and Modernism. The Iranian Revolution of 1906* (London: I.B. Tauris, 1989).

Mashayekhi, Mehrdad, 'The Politics of Nationalism and Political Culture', in: *Iran. Political Culture in the Islamic Republic*, ed. by S.K. Farsoun and M. Mashayekhi (London: Routledge, 1992).

Massarat, Mohsen, 'Der Gottesstaat auf dem Kriegsschauplatz', in: *Peripherie* 29 (1988) pp. 45-84.

Menashri, David, *Iran. A Decade of War and Revolution* (New York: Holmes and Meier, 1990).

Menashri, David, 'Khomeini's Vision: Nationalism or World Order?', in: *The Iranian Revolution and the Muslim World* (Boulder: Westview Press, 1990) pp. 40-57.

Mofid, Kamran, *The Economic Consequences of the Gulf War* (London: Routledge, 1990).

Moghadam, Val, 'Women, Work, and Ideology in the Islamic Republic', in: *International Journal of Middle East Studies* 20 (1988) pp. 245-263.

Momen, Moojan, *An Introduction to Shi'i Islam* (New Haven: Yale University Press, 1985).

Morabia, Alfred, *Le Ğihad dans l'Islam médiéval. Le 'combat sacré' des origines au XIIe siècle* (Paris: Albin Michel, 1993).

Morony, M.,'Kisrâ' in: *Encyclopaedia of Islam²* Vol.5 p. 185.

Mossavar-Rahmani, Bijan, 'Economic Implications for Iran and Iraq', in: *The Iran-Iraq War. New Weapons, Old Conflicts*, ed. by S. Tahir-Kheli and S. Ayubi (New York: Praeger, 1983) pp. 51-64.

Mühlmann, Wilhelm E., 'Chiliasmus' in: *Wörterbuch der Soziologie*, ed. by W. Bernsdorf (Stuttgart: Enke Verlag, 1969) p. 156.

Naff, Thomas, 'Towards a Muslim Theory of History', in: *Islam and Power*, ed. by A.S. Cudsi and A. Dessouki (London: Croom Helm, 1981).

al-Najjar, Mustafa and Najdat Fathi Safwat, 'Arab Sovereignty over the Shatt al-Arab during the Ka'bide Period', in: *The Iran-Iraq War. An Historical, Economic and Political Analysis*, ed. by M.S. el-Azhary (London: Croom Helm, 1984) pp. 20-37.

Nasr, S.H. (ed.) et.al. *Expectation of the Millennium. Shi'ism in History* (Albany: SUNY Press, 1989).

Noth, Albrecht, *Heiliger Krieg und heiliger Kampf in Islam und Christentum* (Bonn: Röhrscheid, 1966).

O'Ballance, Edgar, 'The Iraqi-Iranian War: The First Round', in: *Parameters* 11 (1981) pp. 54-59.

O'Ballance, Edgar, *The Gulf War* (London: Brassey's Defence Publishers, 1988).

Paret, Rudi, *Die legendäre Maghazi-Literatur. Arabische Dichtungen über die muslimischen Kriegszüge zu Mohammeds Zeit* (Tübingen: Mohr, 1930).

Paret, Rudi, 'al-Burâḳ', in: *Encyclopaedia of Islam*[2] Vol.1 p. 1310.

Paret, Rudi, 'Ibrâhîm', in: *Encyclopaedia of Islam*[2] Vol.3 pp. 980-981.

Paret, Rudi, 'Sure 109', in: *Der Islam* 39 (1964) pp. 197-200.

Peters, Rudolph, *Islam and Colonialism. The Doctrine of Jihad in Modern History* (The Hague: Mouton, 1979).

Peters, Rudolph, 'The Political Relevance of the Doctrine of Jihad in Sadat's Egypt', in: *National and International Politics in the Middle East. Essays in Honour of Elie Kedourie*, ed. by L. Lugram (London: Frank Cass, 1986) pp. 252-271.

Peters, R., 'Shahîd', in: *Encyclopaedia of Islam*[2] Vol.9 p. 207.

Pipes, Daniel, 'A Border Adrift: Origin of the Conflict', in: *The Iran-Iraq War. New Weapons, Old Conflicts*, ed. by Shirin Tahir-Kheli and Shaheen Ayubi (New York: Praeger, 1983) pp. 3-25.

The Qur'ân: Translated, with a Critical Re-arrangement of the Surahs by Richard Bell (Edinburgh: Clark, 1953).

Rajaee, Farhang, *Islamic Values and World View. Khomeyni on Man, the State and International Politics* (Lanham, MD: University Press of America, 1983).

Rajaee, Farhang, 'Iranian Ideology and Worldview: The Cultural Export of Revolution', in: *The Iranian Revolution and its Global Impact*, ed. by John L. Esposito (Miami: Florida International University Press, 1990) pp. 63-80.

Rajaee, Farhang (ed.), *The Iran-Iraq War. The Politics of Aggression* (Gainesville: University Press of Florida, 1993).

Ram, Haggay, '"Islamic Newspeak": Language and Change in Revolutionary Iran', in: *Middle Eastern Studies* 29 (1993) pp. 198-219.

Ram, Haggay, *Myth and Mobilization in Revolutionary Iran. The Use of the Friday Congregational Sermon* (Washington: American University Press, 1994).

Ramazani, R.K. 'The Iran-Iraq War and the Persian Gulf Crisis', in: *Current History* 87 (1988) pp. 61-64, and p. 86.

Ramazani, R.K. *Revolutionary Iran. Challenge and Response in the Middle East* (Baltimore: Johns Hopkins University Press, 1986).

Rank, Hugh, *The Pep Talk. How to Analyze Political Language* (Park Forest, Ill.: Counter-propaganda Press, 1984).

Reissner, Johannes, *Iran - Irak: Kriegsziele und Kriegsideologien. Zum Problem der Vermittlung* (Ebenhausen: Stiftung Wissenschaft und Politik, 1987).

Richard, Yann, 'La Fonction parénétique du 'âlem: La Prière du vendredi en Iran depuis la révolution', in: *Die Welt des Islams* 29 (1989) pp. 61-82.

Richard, Yann, 'The Relevance of "Nationalism" in Contemporary Iran', in: *Middle East Review* (1989) pp. 27-36.

Ringgren, H., 'The Conception of Faith in the Koran', *Oriens* 4 (1951), pp. 1-20.

Rosenau, James N., *National Leadership and Foreign Policy. A Case Study in the Mobilization of Public Support* (Princeton: Princeton University Press, 1963).

Roy, Olivier, *L'Échec de l'Islam politique* (Paris: Éditions du Seuil, 1992).

Sachedina, A.A., *Islamic Messianism. The Idea of Mahdi in Twelver Shi'ism* (Albany: SUNY Press, 1981).

Sargent Lyman, Tower, *Contemporary Political Ideologies. A Comparative Analysis* (Belmont: Wadsworth, 1993[9]).

Schimmel, Annemarie, 'Muḥammad' in: *Encyclopaedia of Islam*[2] Vol.7 p. 376.

Schmidtke, Sabine, 'Modern Modifications in the Shi'i Doctrine of the Expectation of the Mahdi (Intiẓar al-Mahdi): The Case of Khomeini', in: *Orient* 3 (1987) pp. 389-406.

Schmucker, Werner, 'Iranische Märtyrertestamente', in: *Die Welt des Islams* 27 (1987) pp. 185-249.

Sick, Gary, 'Trial by Error: Reflections on the Iran-Iraq War', in: *Middle East Journal* 43 (1989) pp. 230-245.

as-Sirri, Ahmed, *Religiös-politische Argumentation im frühen Islam (610-685). Der Begriff Fitna: Bedeutung und Funktion* (Frankfurt: Lang, 1990).

Sivan, Emmanuel, *Radical Islam. Medieval Theology and Modern Politics* (New Haven: Yale University Press, 1985).

Smith, Jane I., *An Historical and Semantic Study of the Term Islam as seen in a Sequence of Quran Commentaries* (Missoula: Scholars Press, 1975).

Smith, J.I. and Y.Y. Haddad, *The Islamic Understanding of Death and Resurrection* (Albany: SUNY Press, 1981).

Sourdel, Dominique, 'L'Imamisme vu par Cheikh al-Mufid', in: *Revue des Études Islamiques* 40 (1972).

Staudenmaier, William O., 'Military Policy and Strategy in the Gulf War', in: *Parameters* 12 (1982) pp. 25-35.

Staudenmaier, William O., 'A Strategic Analysis', in: *The Iran-Iraq War. New Weapons, Old Conflicts*, ed. by S. Tahir-Kheli and S. Ayubi (New York: Praeger, 1983) pp. 27-50.

Stork, Joe, 'Reagan Re-flags the Gulf', in: *Middle East Report* 17 (1987) pp. 2-50.

Ṭabarsî, *Majma' al-bayân* Vol.6

Ṭabâṭabâ'î, 'Allâmah Sayyid Muḥammad Ḥusayn, *Shi'ite Islam*, trans. and ed. by Seyyed Hossein Nasr (Albany: SUNY Press, 1975).

Tahir-Kheli, S. and S. Ayubi (ed.), *The Iran-Iraq War. New Weapons, Old Conflicts* (New York: Praeger, 1983).

Tavakoli-Targhi, Mohamad, 'Refashioning Iran: Language and Culture during the Constitutional Revolution', in: *Iranian Studies* 23 (1990) pp. 77-101.

Thaiss, Gustav, 'Religious Symbolism and Social Change: The Drama of Husain' in: *Scholars, Saints, and Sufis*, ed. by N.R. Keddie (Berkeley: University of California Press, 1972) pp. 349-366.

Vadet, J.C. 'Quelques remarques sur la racine FTN dans le Coran et la plus ancienne littérature musulmane', in: *Revue des Études Islamiques* 37 (1969) pp. 87-96, pp. 98-101.

Vajda, Georges, 'Le Problème de la vision de Dieu (ru'ya) d'après quelques auteurs šî'ites duodécimains', in: *Le Shî'isme imâmite* (Paris: Presses Universitaires de France, 1970) pp. 31-54.

Vaziri, Mostafa, *Iran as Imagined Nation. The Construction of National Identity* (New York: Paragon House, 1993).

Veccia Vaglieri, L., '(al)-Ḥusayn b. 'Alî b. Abî Ṭâlib' in: *Encyclopaedia of Islam*[2], Vol.3 pp. 606-615.
Veer, Peter van der, *Religious Nationalism. Hindus and Muslims in India* (Berkeley: University of California Press, 1994).

Waldmanparet, M.R., 'The Development of the Concept of *kufr* in the *qur'ân*', in: *Journal of the American Oriental Society* 88 (1968) pp. 442-455.

Watt, W. Montgomery, 'al-Ḥudaybiya', in: *The Encyclopaedia of Islam*[2] Vol.3 p. 539.

Watt, W. Montgomery, *Muhammad at Mecca* (Oxford: Clarendon Press, 1952).

Watt, W. Montgomery, *Muhammad at Medina* (Oxford: Clarendon Press, 1956).

Watt, W. Montgomery, 'Shi'ism under the Umayyads', in: *Journal of the Royal Asiatic Society* (1960) pp. 158-172.

Watt, W. Montgomery, 'The Conception of *îmân* in Islamic Theology', in: *Der Islam* 43 (1967) pp. 1-10.

Wellhausen, J., *Reste arabischen Heidentums* (Berlin: Walter de Gruyter, 1927).

Wensinck, A.J., *The Muslim Creed. Its Genesis and Historical Development* (London: Frank Cass, 1965).

Wensinck, A.J., 'Shawwâl', in: *The Encyclopaedia of Islam*[1], Vol.7 p. 343.

A.J. Wensinck, 'Talbiya', in: *Encyclopaedia of Islam*[1] Vol.8 p. 640.

Wright, Claudia, 'Religion and Strategy in the Iraq-Iran War', in: *Third World Quarterly* 7 (1985) pp. 839-852.

Zabih, Sepehr, *The Iranian Military in Revolution and War* (London: Routledge, 1988).

INDEX